THE TRAFALGAR CHRONICLE
Dedicated to Naval History in the Nelson Era

New Series 9

Journal of THE 1805 CLUB

Edited by
JUDITH E PEARSON AND JOHN A RODGAARD

In association with The 1805 Club

Seaforth
PUBLISHING

Text copyright © individual authors 2024

First published in Great Britain in 2024 by
Seaforth Publishing,
A division of Pen & Sword Books Ltd,
George House, Unit 12 & 13, Beevor Street, Off Pontefract Road,
Barnsley, South Yorkshire S71 1HN

www.seaforthpublishing.com

British Library Cataloguing in Publication Data
A catalogue record for this book is available from the British Library

ISBN 978 1 3990 7808 5 (paperback)
ISBN 978 1 3990 7809 2 (epub)

All rights reserved. No part of this publication may be reproduced or transmitted in any form or by any means, electronic or mechanical, including photocopying, recording, or any information storage and retrieval system, without prior permission in writing of both the copyright owner and the above publisher.

The right of the individual contributors to be identified as the authors of this work has been asserted by them in accordance with the Copyright, Designs and Patents Act 1988.

Pen & Sword Books Limited incorporates the imprints of Atlas, Archaeology, Aviation, Discovery, Family History, Fiction, History, Maritime, Military, Military Classics, Politics, Select, Transport, True Crime, Air World, Frontline Publishing, Leo Cooper, Remember When, Seaforth Publishing, The Praetorian Press, Wharncliffe Local History, Wharncliffe Transport, Wharncliffe True Crime and White Owl.

Designed and typeset in Times New Roman by Mousemat Design
Printed and bound in the UK by CPI Group (UK) Ltd, Croydon, CR0 4YY

Contents

President's Foreword – Admiral Sir Jonathon Band   5

Editors' Foreword – Judith E Pearson and John A Rodgaard   7

Articles on the 2024 Theme: Naval Intelligence in the Georgian Era

Secret Intelligence in the Age of Nelson – Steven E Maffeo   10

A Grand Tour on a Budget: Naval Officers and Intelligence Gathering in the Age of Sail – Evan Wilson   25

Cat and Mouse, Misinformation, Thwarted Plans and Victory that Never was: Nelson and Villeneuve's Atlantic Chase, 1805 – Andrew Venn   34

'A Great and Signal Service': Admiral Vernon at Porto Bello, November 1739 – Anthony Bruce   44

The Unwanted Coup: James Callander, Spiridon Forestri, and British Espionage in the Ionian Islands during the War of the Second Coalition – Nicholas James Kaizer   55

Admiral Arthur Phillip, 1738–1814: Naval Officer, Explorer, Spy, Mercenary, Administrator – Tom Fremantle   68

Featured Monograph on Naval Intelligence

The Fortunes and Misfortunes of Baron d'Imbert, 1763–1844: French Naval Officer and Royalist Agent – Natacha Abriat   81

Biographical Portraits

The Evolution of British Naval Leadership and Decision-Making in the Face of Sickness – David Rothwell   107

The Seafaring Saga of Joshua Penny, 1788–1815 – William S Dudley	120
Trafalgar's Last Survivors – Hilary L Rubinstein	135

Articles of General Interest

The War of 1812 in Parliament: Britain's Naval Operations and the Political Discourse, 1812–15 – Kevin D McCranie	146
Facts and Firsts for the United States Navy: Remembering the Cruise of the USS *Essex*, 1812–14 – Brenden L Bliss	159
The Cost of Wartime Innovation: Copper Bottoms and British Naval Operations During the American War, 1779–83 – S A Cavell	174
The Historical Significance Behind the Name of Villeneuve's *Bucentaure* – John Easton Law	182
Who Will Rule? The Struggle for Power in Rio de la Plata, 1808–10 – Ricardo Caetano de Moraes	192
Contributors' Biographies	201
Notes	203
The 1805 Club	224

Colour Plate section between pages 80 and 81

President's Foreword

This year's edition of the *Trafalgar Chronicle*, in every respect, fulfils The 1805 Club's mission to 'inspire greater understanding of the maritime world of the eighteenth and nineteenth centuries...in recognizing the role of the sailing navies of the Georgian Period (1714–1837) and promoting their legacy into the modern seafaring age.' The journal is impressive in the quality and variety of its content and illustrations, and in the expertise of its writers, editors, and publisher, Seaforth Publishing.

For this year's theme of *Naval Intelligence in the Georgian Era*, the editors invited 'well-researched tales of intelligence gathering, espionage, secret plots, assumed identities, deception and denial, clandestine operations and intrigues'. Seven contributors did just that, much to the satisfaction of the editors and, I predict, the delight of our readers. Captain Steven E Maffeo, USN (Ret) graciously provided the lead article, an excerpt from his book, *Most Secret and Confidential: Intelligence in the Age of Nelson*.

As someone who had years in the naval service, as both a consumer of intelligence and one who gathered and reported time-sensitive information, I can state that Captain Maffeo's piece reminded me how little has changed in the methods and sources that produce intelligence; how little has changed except for the enabling technology that gathers and transports information and 'finished' intelligence at the speed of electrons.

Additional articles provide examples of intelligence gathering methods, espionage, and how naval commanders relied on intelligence in carrying out their missions. Of particular interest is the monograph by Natacha Abriat: a biographical depiction of Chevalier d'Imbert, a French naval officer and royalist agent during the wars of French Revolution and the Napoleonic wars who, at one point, worked for the Admiralty, establishing a network of spies in France: a tale of daring covert intelligence and counter-intelligence operations.

Other articles cover a variety of topics and take place in at least a dozen locales across the globe. How did Royal Navy commanders fulfill their missions when their men became ill from tropical diseases in the Caribbean? Who was Joshua Penny and why did he live in a cave in South Africa for eighteen months? Who were the last survivors of the Battle of Trafalgar? During the War of 1812, how did Parliament react when the Royal Navy lost single ship battles to the fledgling US Navy? How did Admiral David Porter of the USS *Essex* meet defeat in Valparaiso? What changed when England coppered her ships during the War for American Independence? What is the historical significance of the name *Bucentaur*, Villeneuve's flagship at Trafalgar? What female member of the Portuguese royal family conspired with a British admiral to rule Rio de la Plata in South America?

Our esteemed contributors hale from seven countries and four continents; all possessing remarkable credentials in their fields of endeavour. They have given our readers quality in their writing styles, creative approaches to content and through research that, no doubt, absorbed countless hours. The Georgian Era brought the world a wealth of maritime art – and in the *Trafalgar Chronicle* the carefully selected period illustrations add a meaningful and memorable visual dimension to their words. I commend the director of Seaforth Publishing, Julian Mannering and his staff for the well-managed layout of text and pictures and another stunning cover.

I look forward to finding out what the editors garner for next year's theme: *Naval Leadership in the Georgian Era.* More edifying reading awaits.

ADMIRAL SIR JONATHON BAND GCB DL
Former First Sea Lord
President of the 1805 Club

Editors' Foreword

'Reasonably sophisticated, national-level and naval intelligence' existed during the 'Age of Fighting Sail' and 'aside from its crude technology and primitive communications, it lacked only the formal, institutionalised, and bureaucratic organizations that began to emerge in the *late* nineteenth century—which in turn evolved into the modern, extremely technical intelligence communities of today.' Thus, international naval intelligence expert, Captain Steven E. Maffeo, USN (Ret) opens this 2024 edition of the *Trafalgar Chronicle*, which focuses on the theme 'Naval Intelligence in the Georgian Era'. The article is excerpted from his book: *Most Secret and Confidential: Intelligence in the Age of Nelson*. Following his paper on 'Secret Intelligence in the Age of Nelson' are five more well-researched articles on how Britain's 'reasonably sophisticated', but thoroughly informal intelligence capability, gathered and applied the obtained intelligence to further the strategic and operational objectives of the Royal Navy.

Dr Evan Wilson of the US Naval War College explains how young naval officers made 'grand tours' of the Continent, ostensibly to expand their cultural knowledge so that they could be viewed as gentlemen; they also observed and sometimes reported on the naval strength of England's enemies and competitors. Through historian Andrew Venn we learn about Nelson's use of intelligence in chasing Villeneuve across the Caribbean. Likewise, Dr Anthony Bruce describes how Admiral Edward Vernon relied on intelligence in his taking of Porto Bello, Panama.

Next topic: spies. Nicholas James Kaizer, a Canadian scholar and teacher gives us a tale of British espionage in the Ionian Islands, while Tom Fremantle elucidates on how Admiral Arthur Phillip (1739–1814) was not only a Royal Navy office, explorer, and administrator of the penal colony that marked the founding of New South Wales; Phillip had also served as a mercenary with the Portuguese, reporting his observations to England.

In this edition of the *Trafalgar Chronicle* we have a first – a featured monograph by Natacha Abriat, director and curator of the Cultural Heritage Research Department of the Occitanie region of France. When we issued our Call for Papers last year, and we stated that proposers should send us papers of 3000 to 5000 words in length, we were surprised when Ms Abriat sent us a paper of over 13,000 words! However, the paper proved such an exciting tale of secrecy, subterfuge, and danger that we had to publish it. It is a biography of Chevalier d'Imbert – a French naval officer and a royalist intelligence agent during the turmoil of the French Revolution and through Napoleon's rise and fall. D'imbert's loyalty to the French monarchy led to his exile in Italy, espionage on the behalf of Britain and eventual imprisonment in France. This article offers a unique perspective on the role of intelligence during the French Revolutionary and Napoleonic wars.

In our biographical offerings, Dr David Rothwell analyses the complexities of naval leadership when a commanding officer must balance three priorities: the mission, the possibility of glory and riches and the health of his men. Rothwell's example is Admiral Sir John Thomas Duckworth 1st Baronet, GCB, who, while faithfully fulfilling his mission in the West Indies, also had to countenance the loss of thousands of men due to malaria and yellow fever. He faced a difficult choice between duty and caring for the health of his men. Would you consider his actions typical for the period?

Joshua Penny (1788–1815) was an American merchant sailor who was pressed into the Royal Navy and was transferred from ship to ship. He deserted in South Africa, where he encountered additional misfortune. Eventually, he took refuge in a cave. How he returned to the US after a nine-year absence is a saga of luck, risk-taking, and hardship. The story comes from award-winning author and historian Dr William S Dudley, former director of the US Navy Historical Center, now Naval History and Heritage Command, Washington, DC.

Who was the last survivor of the Battle of Trafalgar? Several people claimed that distinction. Another award-winning author and historian, Dr Hilary Rubinstein from Melbourne, Australia examines the question through her analysis of late nineteenth-century news articles on the subject.

Turning to General Interest, this year's *Trafalgar Chronicle* garnered five gems. Dr Kevin D McCranie, of the US Naval War College, documents the debates in Parliament concerning the Royal Navy's humiliating losses in single ship actions against the fledgling US Navy during the War of 1812. Dr Branden L Bliss of Hawaii Pacific University offers the cruise of the US Frigate *Essex*, 1812–1814, and her defeat at Valparaiso, Chile. Dr Samantha Cavell, of Southeastern Louisiana University, examines the controversy surrounding the coppering of Britain's ships during the American War of Independence. Dr John Law, an expert on Italian medieval and renaissance studies, brings us an intriguing tale about how Villeneuve's flagship at Trafalgar, *Bucentaure,* acquired her name. Professor Ricardo Caetano de Moraes, of Rio de Janeiro, Brazil, gives us a glimpse into the political wranglings of the Portuguese royalty and a British admiral concerning who would rule the coastal territories of South America, centering on the Rio de la Plata, 1808–1810.

EDITORS' FOREWORD

What always amazes us, as editors, is the geographic reach of each edition's offerings, as well as the overlap, in terms of personages and places, that figure into these rich tales of naval history. In this issue we have articles taking place on the Atlantic, the Mediterranean and the Pacific as well as on four continents. Vernon appears in two articles, as do Nelson and Villeneuve. Four articles mention Napoleon. Three articles center on Central America and South America, while the Caribbean can be found in another three. All of the articles in this edition are stories of conquest, courage, and achievement, often, poignantly, at the cost of human lives, suffering and sacrifice.

We are grateful to our contributors who have brought their talents and expertise to bear in these pages. We look forward to bringing you next year's issue, which will carry the theme: *Naval Leadership in the Georgian Era*.

We welcome ideas, comments, inquiries, and feedback from our readers. If you have an opportunity, please review this edition of the *Trafalgar Chronicle* in your favourite naval history magazine or newsletter. Some university and college libraries now receive this journal, and if your institution has an interest in doing so, please let us know: contact us at tc.editor@1805Club.org.

So now we recommend that you pour a glass of your favorite beverage, pull up a comfy chair, relax, and take your mind on a voyage through the Georgian Era of naval history.

JUDITH E PEARSON, PHD
BURKE, VIRGINIA

JOHN A RODGAARD, CAPTAIN USN, RET
MELBOURNE, FLORIDA

Secret Intelligence in the Age of Nelson

Steven E Maffeo

Editors' note: This article is extracted from, and informed by, Captain Maffeo's book Most Secret and Confidential: Intelligence in the Age of Nelson *(Annapolis, Maryland: Naval Institute Press, 2000 and 2012; London: Chatham Publishing, 2000).*

Slightly more narrow in scope than the overall maritime Georgian era (roughly 1714 to 1820), the great 'Age of Fighting Sail' – often associated with Britain's Vice-Admiral Horatio Lord Nelson – essentially ran from 1754 to 1815. Present within this context of the French and Indian War, the American Revolutionary War, the French Revolutionary War, the Napoleonic War and the War of 1812 were fundamental characteristics common to modern, multi-source intelligence. Reasonably sophisticated, national-level naval intelligence existed during this time and, aside from its crude technology and primitive communications, it lacked only the formal, institutionalised, and bureaucratic organisations that began to emerge in the *late* nineteenth century – which in turn evolved into the modern, extremely technical intelligence communities of today.

At the end of the eighteenth century many countries had created diplomatic information systems, developed cryptography and cryptanalysis, established networks of spies, arranged for clandestine mail interception and opening, and built infrastructures to record, distribute and file the resulting information. This mass of information contained degrees of sensitive material – or *secret* intelligence. That said, no government differentiated secret intelligence from other information; moreover, most governments essentially regarded *all* information as their property – secret or not. No distinction existed between *public domain* and *classified* information.

It is illustrative to focus upon the British and the Royal Navy to describe and analyse national and naval intelligence during this period. Eighteenth-century British intelligence was organisationally centred in the diplomatic establishment, with an extensive consular network of overseas correspondents. This network was supplemented by a well-funded programme of espionage – along with considerable foreign trade analysis and ship movement information supplied by Lloyd's insurance marketing association. And, perhaps surprisingly, if the British government had an intelligence 'agency' in this period, it was His Majesty's Post Office; its information collection activities, communications systems, legal sanctions to open mail, and cryptanalytic assets all delivered an extraordinary amount of general information and 'secret' intelligence. The key consumers of national-level intelligence were the King, the Prime Minister, the several Secretaries of State (Foreign Office, Home Office, and War and the Colonies) – as well as the First Lord and First Secretary of the Admiralty.

The Admiralty had an intelligence collection ability. And, because the First Lord was at the Cabinet level, the Royal Navy was also continuously privy to national-level intelligence. This information was passed to the fleet as individual First Lords and First Secretaries saw fit. Moreover, this was a two-way channel – information from deployed fleet units moved back to the Admiralty and from there to the other Cabinet-level ministers.

Signals and information transmission, because of the essentially low technology, were problematic regarding accurate and timely dissemination. Writing was done with pencils or quill pens – quite often with poor penmanship. Signals were sent by crude semaphore and flag systems, requiring good visibility and basic line of sight. Documents were often lost or captured. Surface mail, land or sea, was excruciatingly slow.

Naval commanders were continuously hamstrung by their constant shortage of small vessels for communications and reconnaissance. Although the numeric count of such ships, for the British, appears high, there were never enough available to address the requirements adequately. During several campaigns Nelson himself lost a number of opportunities for decisive battle through his inability to properly scout the movements of French forces.

So, this period of naval history – vital for its cataclysmic struggles in what were virtual world wars – is rightly called the Age of Fighting Sail. Many people also term this period the 'Age of Nelson', so-called for its most prominent figure. This was a time when Great Britain sought to command and control the sea against all comers in order to survive, let alone win.[1] It was a period of enormous fleets and enormous naval establishments. In fact, in the eighteenth century the Royal Navy 'was by far the largest and most complex of all government services and indeed, by a large margin, the largest industrial organisation in the western world. It faced problems of management and control then quite unknown in even the greatest private firms.'[2] This period saw the pinnacle of sailing warship strategic deployment and fighting tactics as well as the zenith of the Royal Navy's historical effectiveness and glory.

To emphasise – though often ignored by military and particularly naval historians – multi-source naval intelligence *was* available to operational commanders. Indeed, military and naval intelligence activity was considerable.

However – again to emphasise – the military and naval establishments were technologically primitive and thus significantly hampered, particularly in analysis and communications. This situation severely limited the rapid exploitation and dissemination of intelligence information that may otherwise have decisively influenced the outcome of many more significant battles and campaigns than it did.[3] Nevertheless, though far too few records were kept, and though there really were no true permanently established intelligence organisations, British strategic and operational intelligence proved to be reasonably effective.

The close of the eighteenth century saw operational and tactical naval intelligence almost exclusively in the hands of the senior officer present at any given locale, for often he was the only one in place experienced enough, and fundamentally competent, to evaluate it. Moreover, he was the only one who was going to use it. In any event, he had no staff – competent or otherwise – to handle it on his behalf. In stark contrast, today's naval commanders have large staffs of highly trained and experienced experts in all fields, including intelligence.

In the late eighteenth and early nineteenth centuries, in political and military thinking, intelligence was a very informal and a very loosely applied term. It is interesting to note, however, that only twenty-three years after the fall of Napoleon the great Swiss military thinker (and Napoleonic Wars veteran) Lieutenant General Antoine-Henri, Baron Jomini, published a relevant and comprehensive analysis of what intelligence should be. He wrote that intelligence should encompass a well-arranged system of espionage, reconnaissance by skilful officers, the questioning of prisoners of war, the forming of hypotheses of probabilities and the observation (and perhaps interpretation of) signals.[4]

Nevertheless, the reality of intelligence in the period from 1754 to 1815 was fairly simple – essentially, any information that stimulated orders or changed plans was 'intelligence'.[5] Perhaps, in the last analysis, this is a valid, though very broad and informal definition even two hundred years later.

Two hundred-plus years ago intelligence was not really established as any sort of separate bureaucratic function. It essentially went without saying that political intelligence was really the primary business of the state. It was partially collected, and definitely analysed, at the top of government, 'by Napoleon, by Fouché for Napoleon, by their British adversary Pitt, by Lord Liverpool to a slightly lesser extent, by Canning to a greater extent, and certainly by Metternich'. In the eighteenth century diplomacy had become bureaucratised and professionalised, 'supplemented by the use of secret agents at the highest level of government. Kings resorted to what in France was called *secrets du roi*, the use of their own private, secret diplomatic agents.'[6]

The origin of a secret intelligence system (*espionage civile*) in England dates from around 1330, when King Edward III developed a great interest in foreign commerce and shipping.[7] The prominence and very existence of such systems varied radically, however, from era to era, king to king, and ministry to ministry. In fact, this aspect of history has not received a great deal of attention. Historians of diplomacy do not generally focus upon 'what second secretaries are doing in lobbies and on the back-stairs. There are situations, however, in which such secret manoeuvres are the real heart of the diplomatic game, and to attempt to unearth them is the only way of discovering not only what happened but also why it happened.'[8]

Sources of intelligence – the Post Office and Lloyd's

So, at this time, the British government fundamentally had no centralised intelligence agency. Instead, various offices in the bureaucracy participated in, and contributed to, what intelligence activity there was. It may be surprising to read that the eighteenth-century British Post Office was the most important of these in regard to collection, processing, 'finishing' and transmitting intelligence information. This is a huge subject in and of itself, and historians have written much on it.

Very briefly, we can consider this. Post Office staff maintained a wide scope of collection activities. In Scotland, Ireland, and the colonies, deputy postmaster generals reported on civil and military affairs. Postal agents gathered shipping news and information about suspicious persons or activities. The captains of packet vessels collected shipping news and lists of passengers on board merchant ships; in addition they were sometimes employed in the observation of foreign naval dispositions.

The Post Office was also very much in the business of processing, or creating, 'finished' intelligence. This was primarily accomplished in the arena of intercepting mail, carefully opening it, analysing it, copying it, resealing it and sending it on to the intended recipient. The Post Office would then send either unedited, full-text copies, or synthesised 'interceptions', to the several secretaries of state. All these practices, dating back to the Tudor period, were legally validated several times by legislative acts. Indeed, the Post Office Act of 1711 gave the activity unassailable legality.[9]

In London, postal employees opened foreign correspondence in a special office generally known as the 'Secret Office'. This office's products – called 'The Secrets' were sent to a small number of authorised officials. The Secrets were routinely marked 'Private and Most Secret' or 'Most Secret and Confidential'.

Interceptions that were encoded went to the 'Decyphering Branch'. In fact, the one British government office that really came the closest to being a fulltime, unadulterated, focused, and professional intelligence service was this small Decyphering Branch, which had been created in 1703.[10]

In addition to the Post Office, another remarkable institution was heavily involved in the British national intelligence business. The huge international insurance and reinsurance marketing association that today does business as Lloyd's of London existed in the eighteenth century. Called then Lloyd's Coffee House (for that is how it informally began, as early as 1688), its membership of merchants, bankers, seafarers, ship owners, international traders and insurance underwriters was extraordinarily knowledgeable about all aspects of British and worldwide maritime shipping and naval affairs. In fact, in late 1805, the news of the Battle of Trafalgar was posted at Lloyd's even before the London newspapers broke the story.

While clearly not an arm of the government, Lloyd's often readily shared the immense, detailed and timely information in its possession (obtained via its own highly developed communications network) with Whitehall, sending it either directly to the Admiralty or to other top-level ministries, depending upon the exact nature and relevance of the information. Indeed, Lloyd's had developed a unique system of maritime intelligence. On a worldwide basis, intelligence of arrivals and departures, 'together with other news of naval and military importance, from Lloyd's' agents, was sent on immediately to the Admiralty; and the Admiralty in turn forwarded convoy and other useful information to Lloyd's.'[11]

Intelligence at the Admiralty
At this point we should refocus upon the Admiralty. In May 1805, as he took the position of First Lord, Admiral Sir Charles Middleton – First Baron Barham – wrote that he found 'there is no method whatever observed in arranging or collecting information ... which is of the utmost consequence on judging of the

Admiral Charles Middleton, later Lord Barham (1726–1813) by Isaac Pocock (1782–1835), 1850. (© National Maritime Museum, Greenwich, London)

Board Room of the Admiralty, by Augustus Pugin (1762–1832) and Thomas Rowlandson (1756–1827). Plate III in Rudolph Ackermann's (1764–1834) *Microcosm of London*, 1808. (Wikimedia Commons)

enemy's intentions. No time ought to be lost in adopting some plan for this purpose.'[12]

Barham had legitimate concerns, but he somewhat overstated the case. As already mentioned, the Admiralty was a primary recipient of intelligence information from national level resources, and this information was then integrated into the navy's own intelligence, communications and command process. The further evaluation, transmission and dissemination of this intelligence was at the discretion of the First Lord or First Secretary, both of whom corresponded directly and frequently with government ministers, diplomats posted abroad, fleet commanders-in-chief, squadron commanders and, not infrequently, individual ship commanding officers.

The navy was always hugely interested in timely operational and tactical intelligence. Thus, even during times of peace 'the Admiralty sent fast ships … to "look" into … ports to count the ships and to evaluate their likely ability to sortie'.[13] They conducted their own reconnaissance missions, principally against

Spanish and French naval bases. In addition, they hoped for early warning of enemy and potential enemy mobilisation and movement, which could come from several other sources – including, of course, London-controlled agents, embassy and consular networks, and the debriefing of merchant ship captains returning from overseas.

But there was no real structure to naval intelligence or, for that matter, military intelligence. In fact, the first British War Office and the first Admiralty directors of intelligence were only appointed much later – in 1887.

Yet, at the end of the eighteenth century the Admiralty First Lord and First Secretary were the main brokers for intelligence analysis and distribution to the operating forces. That said, some first lords and secretaries were not particularly interested in intelligence, nor did they take much initiative in collecting and relaying it. Thus, the system underwent significant ups and downs.

Perhaps the key official in the Admiralty was the First – or Principal – Secretary to the Lords Commissioners. Included among the enormous scope of his duties was the control of almost all correspondence between the Admiralty and commanders around the world. As a result, this individual was critical in the passing of information in and out of the 'nerve centre' of the Admiralty on all subjects, which certainly included intelligence. The men who held this position during the period of this study were Sir Philip Stephens, Sir Evan Nepean, William Marsden, William Wellesley-Pole and John Croker.

Leaving this post in 1795, Stephens had held it for a little over thirty years, during which time he frequently handled secret intelligence and secret service money. Indeed, over 150 years later one French scholar, Francis P Renaut, concluded that Stephens (apparently truly maximising his position) was so much involved in this business that Renaut actually named him 'the head of the British intelligence service'.

> In [a modest Admiralty room] on tables covered with a constant flow of papers and documents, is decided the actual fate of England ….
>
> From there come the orders which move simple pawns on the chessboard of seas of the flotillas of the Antilles, of America, of the Indies, or of the North Sea. That is where are stored the hurried [writings] of the English admirals from all the seas, the reports of even the lowest commander of a [warship], the coded information transmitted by blockade runners ….
>
> Inside these four walls is found the man who holds in his hands the responsibility of the Navy and, therefore, that of the kingdom. This man is not the minister responsible before the King and before Parliament …. This is not the First Lord of the Admiralty …. No, the man who gladly carries

the crushing weight of the enormous Naval machinery of England is none other than Mr. Philippe Stephens, Secretary of the Admiralty....

The Secretary of the Admiralty is not ... the automaton that [merely records] the decisions of the lords of the Admiralty and transmits them for execution; it is not the passive role of secretary of a naval committee, controller of orders issued, simple organ of transmission or of signature or of receiving [copies of orders].

In fact, the activity of [this civil servant] is immense, covering all the domains of British naval power since the head of the naval administration is none other than he. He centralizes all correspondence and countersigns all the essential acts [laws] of the ministry. Nothing is hidden from him and nothing ... escapes [his notice].[14]

Perhaps 'Head of the British intelligence service' is an exaggeration in discussing the Admiralty secretary or even the Admiralty First Lord; however, more than one expert agrees that the Admiralty's intelligence 'network' – such as it was – specifically functioned as their project.

How admirals and captains worked with intelligence

Admirals commanding squadrons or fleets, and captains commanding ships, had to analyse the information in their hands either for their own operational use or for transmission to their superiors. Otherwise they would be in a pitiable condition, as described by Professor Michael Handel, for a commander 'unable to estimate his capabilities ... will advance in a stumbling and hesitant manner, looking anxiously first to his right and then to his left, and be unable to produce a plan. Credulous, he will place confidence in unreliable reports, believing at one moment this and at another that.'[15]

Sir John Jervis, the famous Admiral Lord St Vincent, was always a sharp analyst, never credulous, and always careful. Note this early 1803 letter to First Secretary Sir Evan Nepean at Whitehall:

> The paper of intelligence you have sent me carries strong marks of having been fabricated in London, although it may have come from Paris last. Those who have been accustomed to the Channel can alone judge of the importance to be given to it. Before the ships now preparing for the Mediterranean are dispatched, it may be wise to probe this paper of intelligence to the quick.[16]

Although he never served in a Whitehall office, it nevertheless must be noted that Lord Nelson's analytical abilities ranged from the broadest strategic issues to the smallest tactical details. A remarkable example of his focus upon detail follows.

In July 1805, Nelson's fleet was returning from the West Indies, where he had chased French Vice-Admiral Pierre-Charles Villeneuve and from where he was now pursuing him back to Europe. A British frigate encountered an American merchant ship; the American had earlier discovered a dismasted, abandoned British privateer, which had apparently been attacked by another ship and partially burned. The frigate had confiscated a log book and other items and ultimately passed them on to the flagship. Lord Nelson was immediately approached and he shortly worked to explain the mystery to his officers – as well as derive any useful intelligence that he could. After an attentive examination he said:

> I can unravel the whole: this Privateer had been chased and taken by the two Ships that were seen in the WNW. The Prize master, who had been put on board in a hurry, omitted to take with him his reckoning; there is none in the Log-book: and this dirty scrap of paper, which none of you could make anything of, contains his work for the number of days since the Privateer last set Corvo [island in the Azores], with an unaccounted-for run, which I take to have been the Chase, in his endeavour to find out his situation by back-reckonings.
>
> The [seamen's] jackets I find to be the manufacture of France, which prove the Enemy was in possession of the Privateer; and I conclude, by some mismanagement, she was run on board of afterwards by one of them, and dismasted. Not liking delay (for I am satisfied those two Ships [remarked in the log book] were the advanced ones of the French Squadron), and fancying we were close at their heels, they set fire to the Vessel, and abandoned her in a hurry.
>
> If my explanation, gentlemen, be correct, I infer from it they are gone more to the Northward, and more to the Northward I will look for them.[17]

Upon occasion, deployed admirals carried with them advisers to help them understand the complexities of their mission or the geographic area in which they were operating. The Reverend Alexander John Scott remains perhaps the most interesting of such admirals' advisers or 'secretary intelligencers'. He was a master linguist (modestly claiming only eight languages; admitting that elementary Danish had taken him three days, and Russian several weeks). He proved himself invaluable to Lord Nelson during the Trafalgar campaign, serving as chaplain and private secretary. 'The examination of all papers and letters found on board [captured prizes], as well as of the captains of the vessels,

Nelson Meditating in the Cabin of the *Victory* Previous to the Battle of Trafalgar, by Charles Lucy (1814–73), engraved by Charles W Sharpe (1818–99), c1854. (Wikimedia Commons)

was one of Scott's occupations.' The handling of correspondence with foreign [officers and courts] in their respective languages occupied much of his attention.

Dr. Scott was in the habit of reading to his chief French, Italian, Spanish and other foreign newspapers. Dr. Scott had also to wade through numberless ephemeral foreign pamphlets, which a mind less investigating than Lord Nelson's would have discarded as totally unworthy of notice ....

Day after day might be seen the admiral in his cabin, closely employed with his secretary over their interminable papers. They occupied two black leathern armchairs, into the roomy pockets of which Scott, weary of translating, would occasionally stuff away a score or two of unopened private letters found in prize ships, although the untiring activity of Nelson grudged leaving even one such document unexamined ....

[Scott's] abilities as an agent on shore was even greater than ... his employment as a foreign secretary.... He was exactly the man required – full of observation, agreeable wherever he went – able to understand all he heard and saw .... Often, therefore, as he was sent into Spain, to Naples, &c. &c., apparently for his pleasure or for the benefit of his health, it was never without some special purpose .... There can be no doubt that the risks he ran were considerable and ... when Dr. Scott was absent on these services, Lord Nelson was in a state of the most restless uneasiness and anxiety on his account; and when the few days' absence was over, 'was always more pleased to see Dr. Scott safe back than at the success of his missions'.[18]

One can only imagine how much more effective intelligence work at this level would have been had there been more admirals and captains blessed with such remarkable assistants. By the way, readers of Patrick O'Brian's novels might well see a parallel here between Admiral Nelson/Dr Scott and Captain Aubrey/Dr Maturin.

Moreover, this is all well before any great specialisation among officers or any established specialised career patterns. Of course, what we now refer to as 'staff' officers existed – including physicians, surgeons, chaplains, pursers – holding their various appointments from the Admiralty or the Navy Board. 'Sea' officers were homogeneous, however. To use more modern US Navy parlance, all 'line' officers were 'unrestricted' in the broadest sense. Holding commissions from the Admiralty, their career training ran mostly to navigation, seamanship, gunnery and command. Furthermore, every sea officer was just that; with the exception of port admirals, dockyard commanders, a handful of flag officers and captains serving on specific boards, and a few lieutenants in shore impressment and signal station billets, no naval officers served ashore. 'In particular,' Captain Geoffrey Bennett wrote, 'all commanders-in-chief flew their flags afloat.'[19]

Indeed, every admiral (and every captain, *en petit*) concurrently had to wear many hats. Depending upon the proximity of his next superior, by default he was, to one degree or another, his own strategist, diplomat, interpreter, tactician, administrator, disciplinarian, recruiter, personnel manager, communications officer, meteorologist, hydrographer, maintenance officer, engineer, logistician, provisioner, paymaster and intelligence officer. And not 'intelligence officer' by name, of course; once again the point is that there were no naval intelligence officers in those days. Of a British captain's forty-eight duties, specified by regulation, the closest reference is the one that required him to 'keep secret the private signals'.[20] Intelligence, even as of 1815, had 'not yet really extended to intelligence for wars, and it was not a staff specialty. It was still the case, as with Napoleon, that the chiefs of armies [and fleets] tended to be their own intelligence officers.'[21]

Truly, the captain (and admiral) had to be jack of all trades and, in reality, master of all as well.

Other intelligence managers: Bonaparte, Wellington, Washington and more

Speaking of Napoleon, as we wind up this particular discussion of national and military intelligence in this time period, we must take a look at Napoleon Bonaparte – both as a general and as head of state.

> Napoleon relied a good deal on intelligence in his campaigns, which he insisted on analysing personally rather than getting it through staff officers so he could decide for himself how much credence to attach to each piece. Methods of gaining intelligence included interrogating deserters and prisoners, sending out cavalry patrols, and even dressing soldiers as farm labourers after having taken the real labourers' wives hostage. Napoleon was conscious of the way that spies and officers on scouting missions could mistake corps for detachments and vice versa and often repeated what they had heard from 'panic-stricken or surprised people' rather than what they had witnessed. His orders for his [spies] and officers were 'To reconnoiter accurately defiles and fords of every description. To provide guides that may be depended upon. To interrogate the priest and the postmaster. To establish rapidly a good understanding with the inhabitants. To send out spies. To intercept public and private letters. In short, to be able to answer every question of the general in-chief when he arrives at the head of the army.'[22]

To move hundreds of thousands of men hundreds of miles into enemy territory, 'Napoleon would need accurate intelligence of its terrain, especially its rivers, resources, ovens, mills, and magazines.' The topographical engineers who made his maps were ordered to include every piece of information imaginable, especially:

> ... the length, width, and nature of the roads ... streams must be traced and measured carefully with bridges, fords, and the depth and width of the water. The number of houses and inhabitants of towns and villages should be indicated and the heights of hills and mountains should be given.[23]

Serving him when he was head of state as well as his own chief general, Napoleon's three principal secretaries, 'Bourrienne, who held the post from 1797 to 1802, de Méneval (1802–13), and Fain (1813–15) all developed their own shorthand to keep up with his torrent of words at their desks', while he typically sat on a sofa.[24]

> At home as on campaign, he slept only when he needed to, regardless of the time of day. 'If he slept', his finance minister Comte Molé recalled, 'it was only because he recognized the need for sleep and because it renewed the energies he would require later.' He needed seven hours' sleep in twenty-four, but he slept, as one secretary recalled, 'in several short naps, broken at will during the night as in the day'.[25]

Napoleon hated wasting a minute of the day, habitually multitasking. Uncommon for the time period, he did like taking long hot baths almost daily, 'but during those hours he would have newspapers [certainly including British papers] or political writings read to him, as he also did when his valet shaved him, and sometimes during breakfast.'[26] Indeed:

> ... in his eagerness to get things done he sometimes rose at 3 a.m. .... He expected almost as much from his administrative aides. They were always ready to give him precise up-to-the-hour information on any matter ... and he judged them by the accuracy, order, readiness, and adequacy of their reports. He did not consider his day finished until he had read the [many daily] memoranda and documents ... from the various departments of his government. He was probably the best-informed ruler in history.[27]

If he were the best-informed head of state, it came from an intense desire to be so, combined with extraordinary effort – neither of which were common.

In fact, rulers, ministers, generals and admirals were sometimes not picky

Napoleon Dictating to His Secretaries, 1896 by Paul L N Grolleron (1848–1901).
In *The Life of Napoleon Bonaparte*, Vol. III, by William Milligan Sloane, Ph.D. (1850–1928),
(New York: The Century Company)

as to the quantity or quality of intelligence they had to work with. As late as 1808, with an expedition preparing to go to Sweden, the British Secretary of State for War and the Colonies (Robert Stewart, Viscount Castlereagh) admitted 'an almost complete ignorance of the region in which [the expedition] was to operate ... His lack of knowledge including fundamental questions relating to the strength, positions, and morale of the Swedish, Norwegian, and Russian armies.'[28] (As an aside, Admiral Nelson had not been very impressed with Castlereagh upon meeting him in 1805).[29]

Bureaucratic disorganisation contributed to potential intelligence failures as much as unprepared or disinterested politicians and military officers. The absence of organisation, particularly in the British Foreign Office, often involved simple neglect of routine business. For example, Sir James Bland Burges, when parliamentary undersecretary, wrote to his wife that the enormous 'numbers of dispatches which come from and go to Foreign Courts are piled up in large [cupboards], but no note of them is taken, nor is there even an index to them; so that, if anything is wanted, the whole year's accumulation must be rummaged over before it can be found …. As to the past, it would be an Herculean task to attempt to put things right, but it is my intention to take better care in future, and to enter the purport of every dispatch in a volume properly prepared for that purpose.'[30]

The British had nothing on the Austrian chancellor, Baron Franz M Thugut. Nelson had been singularly impressed by the ruthless Austrian espionage and counterintelligence system, headed by Thugut.[31] Nevertheless, when the chancellor left his position in 1801 it was reported that there were 170 unopened reports and 2,000 unread letters found in his office.[32]

Intelligence officer and academic historian Michael Herman, Litt D, once wrote that 'until the mid-nineteenth century … controlling [intelligence] collection and evaluating the results were integral parts of … military command.' Historian and biographer Christopher Hibbert, MC, also stated that, 'George Washington [was] his own intelligence clearinghouse, consolidating information from his regimental commanders and passing along intelligence to them in return.' Military historian and theorist Dr Martin Van Creveld observed that, 'Napoleon, like Wellington, interpreted intelligence data himself.'[33] So it was with national, military and naval intelligence in this important period.

In summary, it is clear that considerable, good intelligence work took place in the period under discussion at all levels – national, military and naval. This, of course, is despite institutional informality, practically nonexistent staffing, the interest *or lack of interest* of key officials, the low technology, and the almost primitive communications available at that time.

It is also clear that there is an undeniable constant whether we consider operations in 1801 or 2001. Aside from the quality and quantity of forces, and irrespective of the fundamental talent and leadership of commanders, what often matters – very profoundly – is how that commander uses or ignores available intelligence.

Lloyd's Coffee House, London 1789, by William Holland, see colour plate 1

A Grand Tour on a Budget: Naval Officers and Intelligence Gathering in the Age of Sail[1]

Evan Wilson

Editors' note: This article is a modified version of a paper Dr Wilson presented at the biannual McMullen Naval History Symposium, in September 2023 at the US Naval Academy, Annapolis, Maryland. He presented this paper as part of a panel titled 'Learning About Navies' sponsored by The 1805 Club.

Let us construct two logic chains, which at first glance appear to have little in common. Here is the first:

Eighteenth-century Europe was a highly competitive inter-state environment. Hardly a year went by in the eighteenth century without a war somewhere. These small states, on the edge of Eurasia, fought each other on the continent and they fought each other abroad for empires. That competition bred technological, financial and administrative innovation because it put stress on polities, militaries and societies.

Navies were at the forefront of this competition. Especially for western European states, navies provided the means by which they expanded their empires, protected their exploitation of imperial resources and attacked other empires' resources. Navies guarded the slave trade, the sugar trade and the spice trade.

Navies therefore could not afford to fall behind their competitors. A common misperception (shared by none of the readers of this journal, of course) is that the age of the ship of the line from about 1650 to 1815 did not see major technological advancements. In fact, there were important innovations in ship design, hull sheathing and metallurgy, as well as in tactics and signalling, not to mention medicine and logistics, which meant that the navies of 1650 and the navies of 1815 were different in fundamental ways – even if, to an untrained eye, the ships look similar. Navies had to keep up with these developments or else they were liable to suffer at the beginning of the next war, which always seemed to be right around the corner (and certainly in the British case it was, after 1739).[2]

In peacetime, naval competition took the form of intelligence gathering. It is more common to read about intelligence gathering in wartime, both because we have good evidence of tactical intelligence gathering and its impact, and because of the phenomenon of the captured enemy ship. Studying a prize was a ready way to learn how the enemy built its ships. The most famous example of this is the British capture of the French 74-gun *Invincible* in 1747. She proved to be 50 per cent larger than the standard British 70-gun third-rate and fired a broadside 75 per cent heavier.[3] Those differences sent shockwaves through the British naval establishment. But it would be foolish for a navy to learn ship design only by capturing enemy ships – it might never get the chance. Navies needed a method of collecting intelligence in peacetime.

Navies did not have formal intelligence services. No state in eighteenth-century Europe had what we would recognise as a well-organised security service, but all states collected intelligence and ran agents in enemy territory. In Britain, intelligence collection was the responsibility of every department, although the Foreign Office tended to take the lead. But the Admiralty ran its own agents and gathered its own intelligence. Aside from these loosely organised efforts, however, navies also relied on officers keeping up with the latest developments and reporting back what they saw. Intelligence gathering could take the form of port visits, hiring shipbuilders from other countries, and translations of shipbuilding publications from around Europe.

And now for something completely different: a second logic chain.

In eighteenth-century Britain, every middle-class adult male wanted to be perceived as a gentleman. Being perceived as a gentleman entitled a man to respect. It carried with it certain expectations about how he would be treated. It improved his social standing, and it allowed him to move in the social circles to which he aspired.

To convince others that he was a gentleman, there was no one thing he could do. There was no agreed upon definition of a gentleman, but it was connected to money, to honour and to behaviour. That meant that the most common way to go about being perceived as a gentleman was to act like one – fake it 'til he made it. Acting like a gentleman meant, at its simplest, dressing well and wearing a sword. There was more to it than that, but that was the minimum standard.

British naval officers were precisely the kind of middle-class adult males who wanted to be perceived as gentlemen, but who had to try hard to earn that perception. To be fair, meeting the minimum requirements of gentility was easy: a naval officer's uniform, after the 1740s, counted (barely) as 'dressing well', and of course naval officers carried swords as part of that uniform. Officers complained that blue was an unfashionable colour – they were very jealous of red-coated army officers – but the point is that they had a uniform and a sword, and those got them over the key first hurdle.

But other aspects of being a naval officer made it more difficult to be perceived as a gentleman. Three aspects of naval officers' careers in particular mattered on this front: pay, education and sociability. First, they were not paid much. A naval officer's base pay on active duty was at the bottom end of the respectable spectrum, and when he was not on active duty, half-pay was, well, half of respectable. Prize money helped, but not everybody made a fortune at sea. Second, naval officers usually went to sea as teenagers so they could get six years of sea time in advance of sitting for the lieutenants' exam when they turned twenty. From that requirement flowed two problems. Getting a gentleman's education while at sea, when the only books on board were there because the midshipman or the captain brought them, was an unreliable proposition. Also, naval officers were creatures of the sea, of the wardroom, and of the all-male, exposed-to-the-elements environment in which they performed their duty. They were not creatures of the drawing room or the salon. To reiterate: some aspects of being a naval officer made it difficult to be perceived as a gentleman.[4]

Every young man who embarked on a Grand Tour was perceived to be a gentleman. Eighteenth-century British elites often undertook Grand Tours of continental Europe as a capstone of their education. Accompanied by a tutor, the young gentleman visited the sites of classical antiquity, often in Italy, and purchased works of art for display back in Britain. Grand Tours were expensive, but that was partly the point. A Grand Tour lent an air of exclusivity. It was also how British elites kept themselves abreast of fashions in Paris, art in Italy and music in Austria. Britain, remember, was a European cultural backwater. The British elite had to work at moving among the circles of the European nobility in ways that those on the Continent did not.

Going on a tour of Europe could help a naval officer appear to be a gentleman, because again, all Grand Tourists were gentlemen. Just the appearance of going on a Grand Tour, or at least for a man to be able to say that he had visited Paris or Rome, was worth some social capital.

The confluence of these two logic chains, this essay argues, was what we might call 'Grand Tours on a Budget'. Naval officers had incentives to embark on European tours, but they did not usually have the means to hire a tutor and collect art. Nevertheless, they could improve their educational credentials through language and cultural study, and in turn that would help them improve their social standing. Being able to tell some socialite that they learned French in France, or heard Mozart in Vienna, mattered.

Simultaneously, officers were interested in, and were expert observers of, the naval capabilities of their potential enemies. They gravitated toward what they knew, and what they knew were dockyards and ships, not artefacts and art. They used their connections in the maritime world to move freely around Europe, and they wrote down what they saw. They did this because they knew that their professional success depended to some degree on their knowledge of their enemies' capabilities. They also did this because they thought they might learn something from their enemies.

Two examples of Grand Tours
The remainder of this essay discusses two Grand Tours on a Budget to illustrate the ways in which intelligence gathering and social aspirations intersected to generate these strange trips. The first is John Jervis's 'Grand Tour'. He became Admiral of the Fleet and Earl of St Vincent in his later years, but before he was famous, from 1772 to 1775, Captain Jervis undertook several expeditions on his own initiative. He studied French in France and then travelled with his friend Captain Samuel Barrington through the Baltic to St Petersburg. In 1775, the two men surveyed the coast of France in a yacht, paying particular attention to Brest, Lorient, Rochefort and Bordeaux. Jervis's journal with his notes from these trips survives in the National Archives at Kew.

The second Grand Tour on a Budget happened a decade later. In the 1780s, Midshipman Francis Venables Vernon travelled via merchant ships to Smyrna, took another ship to Alexandria and back, and then a caravan inland from Smyrna. On his return leg, he sneaked into the French arsenal at Toulon, and then made his way overland from Marseilles to Paris before travelling to Dublin and then back home to Wales. He published an account of his journey in 1792.

Examining these journeys suggests several conclusions about

Portrait of John Jervis, c1769, later Earl of St Vincent, as a young man. Oil on canvas after Francis Cotes (1726–70). (National Portrait Gallery, London)

View of Toulon Harbour, c1750, by Claude-Joseph Vernet (1714–89), (Musée de la Marine, Paris)

the intersection of social aspirations and intelligence gathering. First, these were Grand Tours *on a Budget*, which meant that they were not really Grand Tours. The Grand Tour was the aspiration; in practice, if the officer was not independently wealthy (and neither Jervis nor Vernon was), he had to make compromises.

For example, when Jervis arrived in Paris, he went straight to his bank, still dressed in his travelling clothes and muddy boots. But he was turned away by a rude clerk, and it took him ten days to get access to his money. Jervis put in his journal, 'N.B. Always go to your banker well dressed & in your carriage.'[5]

Vernon began his journey under orders – he volunteered to take dispatches to Gibraltar in 1783. But while he was there, the war ended, and he had no further responsibilities. The second mate on the merchant ship he had taken to Gibraltar got sick, so Vernon used his sailing expertise to volunteer to replace him. In other words, Vernon's was a working Grand Tour – a far cry from a tour undertaken by a nobleman and his tutor. At the same time, he brought with him

Gibraltar from the North-West, engraving from *Gibraltar and its Sieges* by Thomas Nelson (London: 1884). (Naval History and Heritage Command, Washington, DC)

letters of introduction from London to two English gentlemen in Smyrna, which is classic gentlemanly behaviour. He anticipated his destination and drew on his network at home to make his travels easier. Here again, though, he was not travelling like a nobleman would have travelled. To undertake his tour, Vernon relied on his ability to move easily in the maritime world. His seamanship and navigation skills transcended language barriers, and they allowed him to go from port to port and ship to ship in a way that a landsman would not have been able to do so easily. His return home from Smyrna, for example, was on board the Dutch third-rate *Alkmaar* (64). He befriended the captain 'on the social footing of brother officers' and hitched a ride.[6]

The second point to make about the journeys is that the officers cared more about social improvement than intelligence gathering. Vernon's book reads like a journal, recording descriptions of each city and of the journey, along with various stories that he picked up along the way. But he always had an eye out for the classical world. He made a point of detouring to Alexandria by taking passage on a French ship, and he was thrilled when the ship stopped at Rhodes on the way. He found Pompey's Pillar, Caesar's palace and Cleopatra's needles (in their original locations – the obelisks have since been moved to London and New York). He clearly had an interest in the classical world, and he sprinkled his book liberally with Latin and Greek phrases as a way of showing off his education.

Jervis was already a post-captain in 1772, and he was in a good professional position, but he also seemed to be aware of the gaps in his knowledge. In 1769, his patron Sir Charles Saunders had arranged for Jervis to dine with the Duke of Gloucester, the King's brother, and on the basis of that dinner and the recommendations of some friends, Jervis was appointed to command the ship tasked with taking the Duke to Italy from May 1771 to May 1772. Jervis was by all accounts well-mannered and therefore able to host the King's brother at his table, but he did not speak French. The trip to France in the fall of 1772 was clearly designed to remedy that – he worked so hard at learning the language that he got sick.[7]

The other gap in Jervis's knowledge was the most important theatre for the Royal Navy: north-western Europe. Jervis had begun his career in the West Indies and then made a name for himself in the operations around Quebec during the Seven Years' War. He had also served in the Mediterranean three times by 1772, so he knew North America and the Mediterranean fairly well. But aside from one brief stint in the North Sea, Jervis had not spent much time off the west coast of France or in the Channel, and he had not spent any time in the Baltic. For him, a trip to St Petersburg served a dual purpose: he could examine the naval facilities at Kronstadt, which he did, and he could familiarise himself with navigating the Baltic. His journal is full of commentary on which charts were reliable, and which were not, and how to handle a given wind direction in a given place.

Intelligence gathering
Finally, the third point: what kind of intelligence did Jervis and Vernon actually glean from these trips? We can sort what they learned into four bins, from least helpful to the Admiralty to most helpful.

The least helpful category of intelligence was classic eighteenth-century sweeping judgments about nationalities, races, or religions. Readers should beware of Vernon's book: it is *very* antisemitic. But he also made the usual comments about French shipbuilding: 'No ships have finer bottoms than the French, as they in general sail exceeding fast, but 'tis in the working them they are inferior to the English.'[8] Jervis was famously prejudicial, and his journal is full of comments about the appearance of Russian women – he was not impressed. Needless to say, he was just as biased about naval capabilities.

Slightly more helpful to the Admiralty were appraisals of the size and readiness of foreign fleets. The most obvious benefit of being able to access the dockyards was that both Jervis and Vernon were able to get right up next to Russian and French ships, respectively. They could assess the state of the ships using their practised naval eyes. Vernon pretended to be Dutch and followed a fellow Dutch officer whom he had met into the French arsenal at Toulon, and he noted how strange it was to be right next to 'about 14 two-deckers, and many of them were my antagonists on the coast of America'.[9] But this intelligence was ephemeral. It was helpful if war was imminent, but less so if war was (as in both of their cases) four years or more away. Nevertheless, it was somewhat useful to the Admiralty to know whether dockyards were well-equipped and whether a fleet was going through the usual maintenance cycles or was suffering from some particular difficulties.

A more useful third category of intelligence for the Admiralty was coastal defence assessments. Both Jervis and Vernon, everywhere they went, commented on the defences of all coastal settlements. It was the first thing they noticed, after navigational markers. Coastal defence assessments were more valuable than the readiness of a fleet at a given moment because such defence was constrained by geography. When the next war came, Toulon was still going to be in the same place with the same basic defence structure. Jervis's first stop in Calais prompted him to say that the fortifications of the town were not that impressive, but he thought they could be easily improved to be made formidable.[10] In his book, Vernon laid down the longitude and latitude of Toulon for his readers, described the defences, and then noted that Toulon's harbour was protected by two moles, each 700 paces long. It reads as if he paced them out himself, and he probably did.[11]

The most useful category of intelligence was what we might call 'tips and tricks'. Despite their heavy prejudices, both Jervis and Vernon opened themselves up to new methods of doing things. Just by observing how the Dutch ship *Alkmaar* worked, Vernon guessed that Dutch amphibious operations might be more potent than those of the British. Whenever the Dutch were moving large quantities of men or materiel from the ship to the shore, he noticed that they used paddles, not oars. Using paddles allowed the Dutch to pack more onto their boats but still row quickly, especially over short distances.[12] Jervis, similarly, made careful note of how the Russians had borrowed from the Dutch to deal with shallow water in the Baltic. Often large ships would be built in harbours that had difficult exits over sandbars or shoals, so they would construct wooden camels, or giant floating boxes, and use sweeps to lift large ships over the bars.[13]

Such was the state of naval intelligence in the eighteenth century. It was ad hoc and it relied in part on this kind of bottom-up initiative from officers looking to see the world, but it was also essential for all navies. It was surprisingly easy to be a spy – Vernon made a Dutch friend and that was all it took to enter the French dockyard, while Jervis was invited to enter the Russian dockyards. The ease of access partly reflects the limited value of the intelligence; it also partly reflects a different world, when people assumed that a gentleman and a man of honour would not behave in an underhanded way. The past really is a foreign country.

This small project has opened up several questions for further research. It is worth investigating how common these Grand Tours on a Budget were. The logic chain constructed at the beginning of the essay suggests that there were plenty of officers who embarked on similar tours. Note, as well, that Barrington and Jervis went together, and Vernon encountered other English, French, and Dutch travellers on his journey – those incidents are hints that, in peacetime, such tours were relatively common. Readers may have other ideas for additional avenues to approach this question.

Another question is about the dissemination of intelligence. Vernon self-published his findings, and it does not seem that anyone noticed his book at the time. It would be surprising if anyone who mattered at the Admiralty read it in 1792. Jervis kept his findings in a journal, and they certainly informed his future commands. There is some debate among his biographers about how much he actually learned about the approaches to Brest before he commanded the blockade in 1800, but it is clear that he was better off having sailed those waters before than not having done so.[14] Journalling, however, is not an effective way to communicate intelligence about the state of an enemy's dockyard.

If the Grand Tours on a Budget were as common as the logic chain suggests they might have been, perhaps the intelligence gathered on them informed conversations about enemy capabilities and those conversations sometimes informed policy. It seems the Admiralty made no attempts to collect the information the officers had gained, however, so the actual influence of the Grand Tours on a Budget would be difficult to measure. Nevertheless, this essay has attempted to show that officers had good reasons to undertake such tours, both from a social status perspective and from a naval competition perspective.

Destruction of the French fleet at Toulon, 18 December 1793, see colour plate 2

Cat and Mouse, Misinformation, Thwarted Plans and the Victory that Never was: Nelson and Villeneuve's Atlantic Chase, 1805

Andrew Venn

Having spent the best part of two years blockading the French in the Mediterranean, by early 1805 Nelson was more than ready for a battle. When word came that Villeneuve had finally set out from Toulon in early 1805, Nelson knew that this was his opportunity to bring about a decisive action. He and his fleet soon gave chase. What followed would prove to be a series of thwarted plans, escapes and near misses in a game of Cat and Mouse that spanned the Atlantic. It wouldn't be until that fateful day on 21 October 1805 that Nelson would finally get his chance to inflict a crushing blow to French naval power.

This article explores the significant events for both fleets during the chase as well as the near misses and misinformation along the way as Nelson put pressure on Villeneuve. The culmination of the chase and the Battle of Cape Finisterre, on 22 July 1805, will also be examined, looking at the impact of this battle for both sides. With all of this in mind, one of the overarching questions of this article is 'what if?'. What if Nelson's intelligence on Villeneuve's whereabouts had been accurate and the two fleets did encounter each other during the chase, and what if the Battle of Cape Finisterre had been a decisive battle one way or the other? How would this have affected the events that followed and Trafalgar?

1803: Renewed hostilities between France and England
The Peace of Amiens ended on 18 May 1803, bringing an end to just over a year of uneasy peace between France and Britain which, in the words of N A M Rodger, had satisfied no one for long.[1] The resumption of hostilities came with a renewed vigour by Napoleon to force Britain out of the war, this time permanently, by mounting an invasion. A huge force, dubbed the *Armée d'Angleterre* (Army of England) was assembled at Boulogne on France's northern coast. By early 1805, this army consisted of over 160,000 men and 24,000 horses.[2] However, despite such a large force, the English Channel, and with it the threat of the Royal Navy, would prove to be a persistent thorn in the now Emperor of France's side. It would be a huge undertaking to even put such

a force to sea, let alone slip through and land on Britain's southern coast without being harassed by the ships of the Royal Navy. It was estimated that to simply embark the army would take nearly a week, then a further two days to cross, and all in relatively calm weather.[3] In this respect, Napoleon's enemy was not only the British, but also the elements.

To negate the effect of the former, Napoleon devised a series of plans between September 1804 and September 1805 to lure the British away from the Channel. The crux of the plans, numbering eight in all, was for the French fleets to break their blockades, join together and lure the Royal Navy fleets away from the Channel by force or by deceit. With the enemy out of the picture, Napoleon's navy could then escort the barges carrying troops across the Channel. Following Spain's declaration of war on Britain in December 1804, Napoleon in theory had the numbers to overpower the Royal Navy. However, the problem was that his forces were spread among Brest, Rochefort, L'Orient, Toulon, Ferrol, Cartagena and Havana, and most of these ports were subject to British blockade.[4] Napoleon's plans focused on addressing this as the main priority, hoping to assemble as many ships as possible in one place.[5]

Although on paper, and in the mind of the emperor, the plans seemed simple enough, the reality was far different. It was a strategy that relied on deceiving the enemy and hoping they would react exactly as expected. It also relied on specific movements happening in strict timelines, with little respect to the realities of sea travel. It was perhaps a strategy that was better suited for land, but simply relied on too many factors to work at sea. The plans were also influenced by Napoleon's lack of trust in his admirals and took the form of increasingly complex and hard and fast instructions in the hope they would act exactly as he wanted them to.[6]

Nelson at Toulon
Vice-Admiral Lord Horatio Nelson was appointed Commander-in-Chief of the Royal Navy's Mediterranean Station and its fleet in 1803, arriving off Toulon in July. With Napoleon's continental ambitions threatening Sicily, a key cornerstone in Britain's hold of the Mediterranean, Nelson held a combined responsibility to both watch over the French fleet at Toulon and defend Sicily and Malta.[7] Instead of keeping a close blockade of Toulon, Nelson preferred to sit back and watch from a distance, knowing that should the fleet try to escape, he would be ready to intercept.[8] The French fleet was commanded by Admiral Louis-René Latouche-Tréville, an ageing and well-respected veteran of many of the mid-eighteenth century's wars. That was until August 1804, when the Admiral succumbed to a relapse of a previous medical condition and died. His replacement was a man Nelson had faced before at the Nile, Vice-Admiral

Pierre-Charles Villeneuve, who knew all too well of what his adversary was capable. Despite the two having met in battle, Villeneuve did not have the same reputation as Latouche-Tréville and Nelson would have perhaps taken the measure of his adversary mainly through what he had derived about Villeneuve's actions during the Battle of the Nile and from subsequent intelligence.

In December 1804, Napoleon sent orders to Villeneuve that he was to take his fleet to South America and the West Indies. There, he would meet with the Rochefort squadron under Rear-Admiral Édouard-Thomas Missiessy. The combined fleet would then sail back to the Channel to support the invasion effort and deal with any British forces had they not already given chase.[9] Missiessy made his move on 11 January 1805, departing Rochefort with four ships of the line and 3,500 men. Villeneuve seized the opportunity and followed suit on 14 January with his fleet of eleven ships of the line and six frigates. Unbeknownst to the two admirals at the time, Napoleon had cancelled the plans two days prior.[10] Two fifth-rate British frigates, *Seahorse* (38) and *Active* (38), followed in pursuit but were soon chased off. Apparently, the commanders of these two ships did not convey Villeneuve's location and direction to Nelson.[11]

Acting on a suspicion that Villeneuve could be heading east, Nelson led his forces further into the Mediterranean. Luckily for him, Villeneuve shortly ran into a storm and retreated to Toulon. Nelson eventually received word of what had happened and returned to station mid-February.[12] Following this debacle, Villeneuve wrote to the Minister of the Navy, Denis Decrès, to resign, citing a dislike for the confusion the emperor had created with his multiple plans and a desire not to be shamed when the plans went wrong. However, Villeneuve was ordered to remain.[13]

Napoleon issued another plan in February 1805, this time ordering Vice-

Amiral de Villeneuve, eighteenth-century engraving by unknown artist with initials E.T. (Musée de la Marine, Paris)

Admiral Honoré-Joseph-Antoine Ganteaume to sail his fleet of twenty-one ships of the line from Brest and rendezvous with Villeneuve and Missiessy at Martinique in the West Indies. Under Ganteaume's command, the fleet would then sail for the Channel to support the invasion attempt.[14] It was this plan that would set events into motion that eventually culminated in the Battle of Trafalgar.

Villeneuve exited Toulon on 30 March with a fleet comprising eleven ships of the line and six frigates. This time they were successful in leaving the Mediterranean and headed for Cadiz to collect Admiral Federico Gravina's Spanish fleet. There they encountered a small British squadron, led by Vice-Admiral Sir John Orde, comprising five ships of the line. Despite forming a line of battle, Orde's smaller force did not engage the French fleet and he soon withdrew to the Channel Fleet.[15] Villeneuve proceeded to collect six Spanish ships and one French, much to the chagrin of Gravina, who disliked the idea of being inferior to Villeneuve, and sailed for the West Indies on 10 April. However, some of the Spanish ships found their cables had tied together, which caused delays. Only one of the Spanish ships would catch up to Villeneuve's fleet en route to Martinique. The rest joined ten days after.[16]

It took until 4 April for Nelson, anchored at Agincourt Sound (situated in the Maddalena Islands of northern Sardinia), to be informed that Villeneuve had broken out of Toulon. Nelson had often commented that his lack of frigates in the Mediterranean, the so-called 'eyes of the fleet', was detrimental to his efforts, and the delay in word being passed to him highlights this.[17] Again acting on instinct, Nelson took his fleet south and east to Sicily, worried for its safety. It was there on 18 April that he received intelligence as to Villeneuve's true course, so quickly followed, arriving at Gibraltar on 6 May.[18] Shortly after this, on 11 May, acting on intelligence he had received

Amiral Edouard-Jacques, comte Burgues-Missiessy (1756–1837), by Alexandre-Charles Debacq, nineteenth century. (Palais du Luxembourg)

from Rear-Admiral Donald Campbell, Nelson made the decision to pursue Villeneuve across the Atlantic. He knew the importance of the West Indies to British maritime commerce and recognised his duty to prevent Villeneuve from disrupting it.[19] The chase was well and truly on.

Incidentally, around the same time as these events were occurring, back in Britain the Admiralty had concerns of their own. As part of Britain's new alliance with Russia, a small British army force was en route to the Mediterranean, to join with a much larger Russian army force, and together, support King Ferdinand in retaking his Kingdom of the Two Sicilies and securing his capital, Naples, from Napoleon. The force set sail on 19 April with an escort of two ships of the line commanded by Rear-Admiral John Knight.

Shortly after, news arrived of Villeneuve's escape. The Admiralty realised that neither Sir John Orde nor Nelson, the latter whom they hadn't heard from in some time, knew to expect the convoy. Vice-Admiral Cuthbert Collingwood was ordered to sail for Cadiz with fourteen ships at his disposal to ensure its safe passage. The Admiralty feared that Villeneuve could easily intercept the convoy and overpower its escorts. Fortunately, Knight had received intelligence from James Gambier, the British Consul General in Lisbon, who met him at sea, as to Villeneuve's exploits and took refuge in the Tagus.[20] As a matter of fact, Villeneuve knew nothing of the convoy and was well on his way to the West Indies by this point. The convoy arrived safely at Malta in July, unopposed by any French forces.[21]

Villeneuve in the Caribbean ... with Nelson close behind
Villeneuve arrived at Martinique on 13 May, under orders to wait forty days for Missiessy and Ganteaume's fleets to arrive. Little did he know that support would not be coming. Missiessy, having been at sea since early January, grew tired of waiting and sailed for home on 28 March.[22] Ganteaume never broke the blockade at Brest; Napoleon repeatedly denied his requests to attack the blockading force directly.[23] All that was left for Villeneuve to do in the meantime was to make himself a nuisance to British ambitions in the Caribbean. He started by attacking HMS *Diamond Rock*, a small rocky island jutting out of the sea just south of Martinique and the original 'Stone Frigate'. The 600ft high fortification was held by a small British force numbering just over 100, manning two 24pdr and two 18pdr guns. Villeneuve's force attacked at 0800 on 31 May, eventually capturing the rock at the cost of fifty men dead or wounded.[24] Although a success, the action was a mere folly when compared to what Napoleon had planned for Villeneuve's forces.

It was around this time that Villeneuve received new orders from Napoleon to capture a laundry list of British possessions while awaiting Ganteaume,

Prie du Rocher le Diamant. Galrie Histque de Versaill. An etching of the 'Stone Frigate', HMS *Diamond Rock* by Chavanne; M Gavard Meyer, and Charles Gavard, 25 June 1805.
(© National Maritime Museum, Greenwich, London)

before the combined force was to sail to Ferrol, collect the ships there and head for the Channel.[25] Sailing on 4 June, it was a stroke of luck that the French almost immediately ran into a British convoy, which they proceeded to capture.[26] It was from this convoy that Villeneuve heard the news he had been dreading: Nelson had arrived in the West Indies.

Nelson and his fleet of twelve ships of the line arrived at Barbados on 4 June and were informed of Villeneuve's presence. However, the Commander-in-Chief at St Lucia, General Thomas Brereton, having received incorrect intelligence, conveyed the same to Nelson: the enemy had been sighted in Gros Islet Bay and were inevitably heading to Trinidad.[27] As a result of this Nelson was led to falsely believe Villeneuve was landing troops there. Arriving on 7 June and realising he had been misled, Nelson then learned about Villeneuve's attack on *Diamond Rock*.[28] Acting on his own intuition, and perhaps tired of receiving incorrect intelligence, Nelson surmised the enemy was heading back to Europe. Now only two days behind Villeneuve and with a renewed vigour to bring his enemy to battle, Nelson set off again in pursuit across the Atlantic.

He dispatched HM brig-sloop *Curieux* (18) to inform the Admiralty of Villeneuve's whereabouts, a move that, unbeknownst to Nelson at the time, would be a factor in preventing Villeneuve from carrying out his orders.

Curieux sighted Villeneuve on 19 June but her commanding officer, Lieutenant Bettesworth, chose to press on to Britain rather than informing Nelson. Coincidentally, Nelson reached Gibraltar on the same day, having overtaken Villeneuve.[29] *Curieux* would make landfall at Plymouth on 7 July and Bettesworth arrived in London at the Admiralty the day after. Bettesworth choosing to sail for Britain rather than informing Nelson could be interpreted as a failure that prevented Nelson from bringing his adversary to action. However, it is arguable that Bettesworth pursued the more logical approach by informing the Admiralty and ensuring the security of the Channel. After all, it was not guaranteed that Nelson would have been able to catch the combined fleet even with Bettesworth's intelligence. First Lord of the Admiralty Lord Barham used the opportunity to reorganise his fleets to counteract the threat. Admiral William Cornwallis was ordered to lift the blockade of Rochefort and send those ships to reinforce Vice-Admiral Sir Robert Calder's force off Ferrol. Twenty-first-century historian Martin Robson wrote that with this move, 'Barham was the true architect of the successful outcome of the Trafalgar Campaign.'[30] The pieces were now all in place for what would be the final part of the preliminary Trafalgar campaign.

The Battle of Cape Finisterre – and the aftermath
On the morning of 22 July at 1100, Vice-Admiral Robert Calder, commanding a blockading squadron off Ferrol, spotted Villeneuve's fleet through the fog off Cape Finisterre. Although Calder's fleet of fifteen was outnumbered by the Franco-Spanish forces, the three three-deckers under his command gave him confidence.[31] The two fleets did not engage until early evening at 1700, and even then the action was sporadic and confused. The Spanish ships did most of the fighting for the combined fleet. As a result of the action, the British captured the Spanish third-rates *San Raphael* (70) and *Firme* (70).[32] With night falling and visibility poor, Calder signalled for his ships to cease action. In the confusion, it was a further hour before some ships stopped firing.[33] The total losses among the British fleet numbered 198 killed and wounded, whereas the combined fleet suffered 476.[34] After a couple of days in which the two battle-damaged fleets remained somewhat close, Calder called off any chance of renewing the action and the combined fleet sought refuge at Vigo on the coast of Spain.[35]

Admiral Sir Robert Calder's action off Cape Finisterre, 23 July 1805. Oil on canvas by William Anderson, c1805, showing that British frigates have captured Spanish ships *Firme* and *San Raphael*. (© National Maritime Museum, Greenwich, London)

The lead-up to the Battle of Trafalgar

When news of Calder's action reached Britain, the press, who were expecting a great victory, treated the battle as a missed opportunity. Calder defended his fleet in his dispatches and justified his reasoning for not renewing the action.[36] However, despite the general air of disappointment, it can be argued that Calder had achieved exactly what he had set out to do: prevent Villeneuve from heading north to the Channel. After all, Calder had to contend with a numerical disadvantage, poor conditions and limited light, and even in such conditions managed to take two prizes and deter Villeneuve. Robson calls Calder's action the most crucial part of the entire Trafalgar campaign.[37]

Villeneuve eventually headed south to Cadiz, arriving on 21 August. At the same time, Nelson was heading north for Britain, but strong winds pushed him out into the Atlantic so there was little chance of the two meeting at sea.[38] Nelson reached Britain on 18 August for some much-needed rest, having spent two years at sea. The news would soon reach him that Villeneuve had returned to Cadiz, setting into motion what would be the final fateful weeks of Nelson's life.

Overall, Villeneuve's fleet achieved very little of substance during the break out. Villeneuve had not acted on the majority of orders given to him and had ended up in the same situation as before, being blockaded in port. He had succeeded in one part of the plan, and that was uniting his fleet with that of Gravina in a formidable force that would number thirty-three ships of the line at Trafalgar. Although he had not joined Ganteaume or Missiessy, it could be argued that this was through no fault of his own. Yes, Villeneuve did abandon his station in the West Indies at the first mention of Nelson rather than wait for reinforcements, but there was no guarantee that those reinforcements would arrive.

One sure thing was that Napoleon's invasion plans were all but over. Although Napoleon blamed his admirals for this, it is arguable that at the strategic level the blame lies with the emperor himself for supplying them with such rigid and unrealistic orders. As historian Sam Willis stated, none of Napoleon's plans were particularly realistic in a maritime context.[39] Napoleon knew that he would need to put aside his goal of invading Britain in favour of other pursuits and marched his army south to Austria. Having grown tired of Villeneuve's failures, Napoleon ordered Vice-Admiral François Étienne de Rosily-Mesros to replace him.[40] Learning of Napoleon's order, Villeneuve took his fleet to sea so that the change of command did not take effect.

When looking at the events of early 1805, is it easy to ask, 'what if'? What if Nelson and Villeneuve had crossed paths during the chase across the Atlantic? Would their engagement have had the same outcome as Trafalgar, or would the outcome have been similar to that of Calder's action? It was certainly Nelson's intention to bring the enemy to action, if at all possible. The following is believed to be Nelson's attack plan that he had drawn up during his pursuit of Villeneuve across the Atlantic:

> ... If the two Fleets are both willing to fight, but little manoeuvring is necessary the less the better; – a day is soon lost in that business: therefore I will only suppose that the Enemy's Fleet being to leeward, standing close upon a wind on the starboard tack, and that I am nearly ahead of them, standing on the larboard tack, of course I should weather them. The weather must be supposed to be moderate; for if it be a gale of wind, the manoeuvring of both Fleets is but of little avail; and probably no decisive Action would take place with the whole Fleet. Two modes present themselves: one to stand on, just out of gun-shot, until the Van-Ship of my Line would be about the centre Ship of the Enemy, then make the signal to wear together, then bear up, engage with all our force the six or

five Van-Ships of the Enemy, passing, certainly, if opportunity offered, through their Line. This would prevent them from bearing up, and the Action, from the known bravery and conduct of the Admirals and Captains, would certainly be decisive: the second or third Rear-Ships of the Enemy would act as they please, and our Ships would give a good account of them, should they persist in mixing with our Ships. The other mode would be, to stand under an easy but commanding sail, directly for their headmost Ship, so as to prevent the Enemy from knowing whether I should pass to leeward or windward of him. In the situation, I would make the signal to engage the Enemy to leeward, and to cut through Their Fleet about the sixth Ship from the Van, passing very close; they being on a wind, and you going large, could cut their Line when you please. The Van-Ships of the Enemy would, by the time our Rear came abreast of the Van-Ships, be severely cut up, and our Van could not expect to escape damage. I would then have our Rear Ship, and every Ship in succession, wear, continue the Action with either the Van-Ship, or second Ship, as it might appear most eligible from her crippled state; and this mode pursued, I see nothing to prevent capture of the five or six Ships of the Enemy's Van. The two or three Ships of the Enemy's Rear must either bear up, or wear; and, in either case, although they would be in a better plight probably than our two Van-Ships (now the Rear) yet they would be separated, and at a distance to leeward, so as to give our Ships time to refit; and by that time, I believe, the Battle would, from the judgement of the Admirals and Captains, be over with the rest of them. Signals from these moments are useless, when every man is disposed to do his duty. The great object is for us to support each other, and to keep close to the Enemy, and to leeward of him.

If the Enemy are running away, then the only signals necessary will be, to engage the Enemy as arriving up with them; and the other Ships to pass on for the second, third, &c. giving, if possible, a close fire into the Enemy in passing, taking care to give our Ships engaged, notice of your intentions.[41]

If it was the latter, it is interesting to speculate whether public opinion of Nelson would have soured in the same manner as that of Calder. And what if Ganteaume or Missiessy did rendezvous with Villeneuve's force? Perhaps with such a large fleet the admirals would have had the confidence to mount an assault on the Channel Fleet and support Napoleon's invasion attempts. Of course, this is all just mere speculation, but it is interesting to examine how events could have been different.

'A Great and Signal Service': Admiral Vernon at Porto Bello, November 1739

Anthony Bruce

Edward Vernon, newly promoted Vice-Admiral of the Blue, left England for Jamaica in July 1739 to take up his appointment as Commander-in-Chief of the West Indies Station.[1] With nine ships of the line, three fireships and two bomb vessels under his command, he had orders to lead reprisal operations against Spanish shipping, causing as much damage as possible in response to continuing attacks on British merchant ships in the Caribbean.[2] His journey was delayed by bad weather and by orders to cruise off Cape Finisterre for fourteen days in search of Spanish *azogues* (quicksilver) ships, which carried quicksilver to the silver refineries in Mexico. With no sign of the ships, he detached four vessels to maintain a presence off the Spanish coast while he continued towards Jamaica with his five remaining ships.[3] In his first weeks at sea, Vernon issued several additional instructions, including the requirement that individual captains should act on their own initiative when necessary, during an engagement.[4]

Following his early naval career, which included service in the War of the Spanish Succession, 1701–14, Vernon was elected as a Member of Parliament in 1722 and became increasingly critical of the administration headed by Sir Robert Walpole. In 1729, he launched a notable attack on the government's orders to Admiral Francis Hosier to blockade the Spanish treasure fleet at Porto Bello (Portobelo), Panama, during the Anglo-Spanish War, 1727–29, which led to the deaths of the admiral and

Admiral Edward Vernon, 1684–1757, c1746. Mezzotint by James McArdell (c1729–65) Irish. (Yale Center for British Art, gift of Mr and Mrs J Richard Dilworth)

four thousand seamen from disease. He was convinced that the port could be taken by only three hundred men and six ships – a prediction that he would realise some ten years later. His well-founded views were informed by his previous service as Commander of the Jamaica Station, 1719–21.

During the 1730s, tensions increased as a result of the activities of Spanish coastguards (*guardacosta*), who stopped and searched every British merchant ship they encountered in the West Indies and often seized their merchandise. As the prospect of war increased, Vernon approached the Admiralty for a command and was appointed as the head of the West Indies Station and its squadron of ships, a role for which he was well qualified. England formally declared war on 22 October 1739, ten days after Vernon arrived in Jamaica. It was later named the War of Jenkins' Ear (1739–48) in reference to Captain Robert Jenkins, whose ear was allegedly severed by Spanish *guardacosta* while his merchantman was being searched in 1731. His preserved ear was displayed in Parliament in 1738, as the opposition used the incident to increase pressure on a reluctant Walpole administration to take action against Spain.

The government did not give Vernon any specific targets in the West Indies beyond the following instructions: 'In case you shall find that the Spanish men of war or galleons either at Cartagena, Columbia, or Porto Bello lie so much exposed as that you shall judge it practicable to burn or destroy them in port, you are to attempt to do it, provided it may not too much hazard the disabling of our squadron under your command.'[5] In addition, he was directed to gather intelligence on Spanish interests in the West Indies in preparation for future British attacks and offer protection to the colonies of Georgia and Carolina.

Vernon took early action to gather intelligence on Spanish shipping movements as he sailed towards Jamaica. He ordered Captain Richard Herbert of the fourth-rate HMS *Norwich* (50) to stop at Barbados, where he was to contact the South Sea Company's (a British joint public and private stock company partnership) agent in order to 'get the best information you can of all the particulars relating to the course of the Spanish trade'.[6] He used the intelligence Herbert gathered when he sent *Norwich* – together with *Stratford* and *Princess Louisa* – in search of Spanish ships in the Caracas area of South America.

During the voyage, Vernon developed a plan to attack the galleons in Havana harbour and expected to combine his forces with those of Commodore Charles Brown, commander of the Jamaica squadron, whom he ordered to have 'all his Majesty's ships at Jamaica put in condition to put to sea with me as soon as possible'.[7] But on his arrival at Port Royal in Jamaica on 12 October, Vernon received confirmation that not all the galleons expected at Havana had yet appeared. With Brown's small squadron still cruising off the Cuban coast, he abandoned the idea.

In developing an alternative plan, Vernon considered the feasibility of attacking the galleons at Cartagena or Porto Bello and sought up-to-date intelligence before making a decision. Although collecting intelligence in the Age of Sail was 'generally haphazard and hampered by ... slow communications', Vernon secured information quickly and systematically from a variety of sources as he decided on his first target.[8] He had access to intelligence reports from British agents operating in Europe and information provided by the Admiralty. Sir Charles Wager, First Lord of the Admiralty, wrote to Vernon on 7 October about the location of the Ferrol fleet while reminding him of 'how impatient people are here to have the Spaniards blown up'.[9]

Vernon also had access to information assembled by Commodore Brown's squadron on the strength and disposition of Spanish naval forces in the Caribbean.[10] Other sources of intelligence included British agents in the West Indies, intercepted Spanish merchantmen and South Sea Company factors at Caragena. The factors were a useful source of information about the defences of Spanish ports until they were arrested after news of the declaration of war reached the West Indies. Vernon also had access to dispatches taken from Spanish *avisos* (dispatch boats) and French merchant ships, which were contracted to carry them.

To supplement these sources, on 19 October, Vernon dispatched Francis Perceval, his first lieutenant, in the sloop *Fraternity* with orders to sail to Cartagena 'to discover what ships they have in that harbour and if any appear likely to come lately from Europe to make the best of your way back for this port, expedition and intelligence being the view in sending you over'.[11] He was also asked to gather information about the strength of Cartagena's fortifications and the size of Spanish forces in the area. Vernon also assessed intelligence provided by Edward Trelawney, Govenor of Jamaica since 1738, who supported attacks on the Spanish *guardacosta* that were damaging British trade in the West Indies. Trelawny

Commodore Charles Brown, 1678/9–1753, a painting, British School, eighteenth century. (© National Maritime Museum, Greenwich, London)

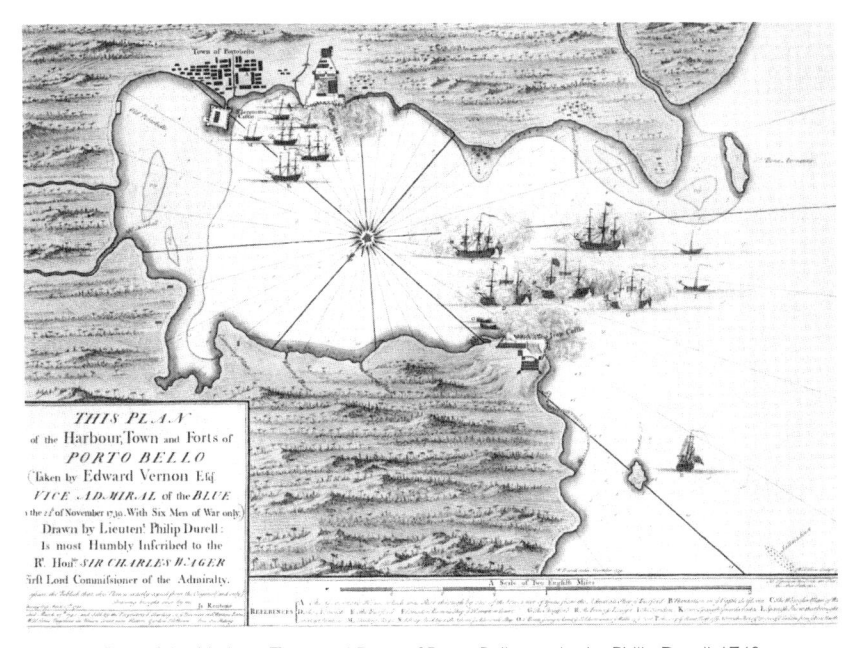

Plan of the Harbour, Town and Forts of Porto Bello, a print by Philip Durell, 1740.
(© National Maritime Museum, Greenwich, London)

suggested that Cartagena harbour should be Vernon's first priority for an attack, but, based on information received from other sources, Vernon decided that it was too well defended for the forces he had available.

He turned instead to Porto Bello on the north side of the Isthmus of Darien (now Isthmus of Panama), some 30 miles to the east of the modern city of Colón, where he might find Spanish galleons, but if they were not present he could destroy its fortifications. The small town held an annual commercial fair, where Spanish goods were exchanged for silver and other commodities from Peru. Spanish galleons (part of the *Flota de Indias*) shipped the goods to Porto Bello and returned to Spain loaded with silver and gold. The Porto Bello fair was the most important of several fairs held in the West Indies, which were 'the focal point around which the whole of Spain's trade with its South American dominions revolved'.[12] A successful operation could prevent the fair from being held there and effectively obstruct the return of the galleons to Spain.[13]

Porto Bello lies at the bottom of a large harbour, which was an important base for *guardacosta* and corsairs operating against British merchant ships in the Caribbean. Although it was defended by three strongly built castles, they had been badly neglected in recent years and were ill-prepared for an enemy attack.[14] The Iron Castle, which was built on a steep rock, was located on the north side of the harbour mouth; it was armed with 100 guns and manned by a garrison of 350 men. Gloria Castle, which was nearly two miles from the Iron Castle, was positioned to the west of Porto Bello on the south side of the bay. It was well-armed with eighty iron and forty brass cannon. The smaller St Jeronimo Castle was situated at the upper end of the harbour, a quarter of a mile from Gloria Castle; it would play no part in the defence of Porto Bello because its guns had not been mounted and were unable to fire a single shot.

The harbour entrance is about half a mile across and negotiating it could be difficult because of variable winds. Ships entering the harbour steer between the Salmadinas rocks and Drake Island (named after Sir Francis Drake, who died at Porto Bello in 1596). Vernon concluded that it would be a much easier target than Cartagena as he still believed that he could seize it with only six ships. He would 'endeavour to destroy all the defence of it so as to leave it an open defenceless bay in order to prevent their holding their fair at all or laying them open to our future attacks if they should attempt it'.[15] A successful operation would disrupt Spain's imperial trade significantly.

On 5 November, Vernon left Port Royal and steered directly for Porto Bello, with a squadron of seven ships, 2,495 seamen and 240 soldiers serving as marines. Trelawny ordered an embargo on the departure of shipping for three days in order to prevent intelligence about Vernon's movements from reaching the enemy. Apart from the five ships that had sailed with him from England, his squadron now included the third-rate HMS *Hampton Court* (70) (following Commodore Brown's return from Havana) and the sixth-rate HMS *Sheerness* (20). Shortly after his departure, he detached *Sheerness* to cruise off Cartagena, with orders to watch for the arrival of the Ferrol squadron from Spain and inform Vernon accordingly. She did not reach Porto Bello until early in December, having captured two Spanish ships carrying ammunition and supplies to Cartagena.

As they sailed towards Porto Bello, Vernon issued his plan of attack, which assumed that the prevailing wind in the harbour would be westerly. As they approached the harbour, Commodore Brown in *Hampton Court* would be in the lead, followed by *Worcester* (60), *Norwich* (50), and *Burford* (70), with *Strafford* (60) and *Princess Louisa* (60) at the end of the line.[16] Vernon left his captains in no doubt about the order of battle to be followed, regardless of the weather conditions they encountered. He emphasised that 'on what side soever the wind be for favouring our attempt to lead it into the harbour', he would 'make no alteration in my line of battle now strictly enjoined you to follow, which is for Commodore Brown to lead and all the ships to follow'.[17]

As the squadron entered the harbour, it would sail within a cable's length (about 600ft) of the Iron Castle, with each ship opening fire in turn. The first three ships would then sail into the inner harbour and attack the other two castles. Brown was to anchor as near as possible to the eastern end of Gloria Castle, with *Worcester* anchoring opposite the western bastion. Once *Norwich* had passed the Iron Castle, she was to anchor as near as possible to St Jeronimo Castle 'to batter it down'. Meanwhile, the three remaining ships would capture the Iron Castle. *Burford* would anchor close to it, while *Strafford* was 'to come to an anchor against the easternmost part of the castle ... and far enough to eastward to leave room for ... the *Princess Louisa* to anchor astern of him for battering the westermost part'.[18] As the garrison's firepower diminished, a landing party would be sent ashore to capture the castle.

Vernon takes Porto Bello

On 20 November, having been delayed by contrary winds, the squadron arrived near Porto Bello and anchored overnight some nine miles offshore. At about 6am on 21 November, following Vernon's briefing on board the flagship an hour earlier, the squadron weighed anchor and formed a line of battle while raising a red flag to signal an attack. With the wind in a northerly direction, the squadron headed towards Porto Bello, with the six ships about 400 yards apart. After *Hampton Court* passed close to Drake Island and approached the harbour mouth, the wind changed suddenly to an easterly direction, forcing the squadron to confine its initial attack to the Iron Castle alone.

As Brown could no longer reach Gloria Castle, he was compelled to abandon the agreed plan of attack (a decision that Vernon later endorsed) and anchor off the Iron Castle at 2pm, when he received 'a very brisk fire from the Spaniards'. But, as William Campbell, purser on *Burford*, reported, Brown soon found he was unable to maintain his position: 'unluckily her anchor not immediately taking the ground, she fell over on the south shore, and by that means was rather at too great a distance, consequently the damage she did the less'.[19] This did not prevent *Hampton Court* from firing more than 500 shot against the castle in the space of twenty-five minutes, with the result 'that nothing was to be seen but fire and smoke, on both sides'.[20]

Within thirty minutes, *Norwich* and *Worcester* joined *Hampton Court* and anchored less than 200 yards from the Iron Castle, giving 'their broadsides so fast that [they] put the Spanish in great consternation'. They were followed by *Burford*, which 'anchored within half a musket shot of the castle'. The Spaniards greeted the flagship's arrival with 'a terrible volley; which, being at so short a distance, took place with almost every shot'.[21] Her foretopmast was hit, the mainmast narrowly escaped damage, and three seamen were killed, but this did not prevent Vernon from intensifying her fire and 'so plied them with

The Capture of Puerto Bello, 21 November 1739, a painting
by George Hyde Chambers (1803–40), 1838
(© National Maritime Museum, Greenwich, London)

the small arms and pouring in broadsides, that scarce anyone could show their heads on the battery'.[22]

Burford's concentrated small arms fire soon forced the gunners in the lower battery to withdraw to the upper fort, and, thirty minutes after his arrival, Vernon decided it was time to send his men ashore under the command of Captain Downing. Each longboat landed thirty seamen and a company of marines at the mole in front of the lower battery and the entire operation was completed in fifteen minutes with minimal casualties. As the fortifications were still intact, the seamen had to scale the battery walls before entering the structure through the gun embrasures. They 'then slung the soldiers and hoisted them up the platform' while striking the Spanish colours and hoisting the English ensign.[23]

Meanwhile, the surviving members of the garrison sheltering in the upper fort realised that further resistance was futile and quickly displayed a white sheet signalling their intention to surrender. Vernon answered by raising a white flag on *Burford* but, according to the official dispatch, 'it was some time before he could stop his own men ... from firing'.[24] When they reached the upper fort, seamen led by Lieutenant Thomas Brodrick discovered that the garrison had 'shut themselves up in a strong lodgement; but upon the Lieutenant's ... firing a gun or two thro' the door, they quickly opened it and very quietly yielded'.[25] Only five officers and thirty-five soldiers were taken prisoner as most of the garrison had either deserted or been killed during the assault.

When Don Juan Francisco de Garganta, the castle governor, surrendered on board *Hampton Court* he presented his sword to Commodore Brown, but Brown refused to accept it as the squadron's second in command. The governor was then taken to *Burford*, where he repeated his wish to present the sword to Brown in Vernon's presence, explaining that 'but for the insupportable fire of the commodore he never would have surrendered'.[26] Vernon then took the sword and presented it to Brown in recognition of his role in capturing the castle.[27]

Vernon had taken the Iron Castle in just under two hours with only four warships (*Strafford* and *Princess Louisa* did not arrive until the engagement was over), but Porto Bello was not yet in his hands. For the moment, he was unable to move forward because of the prevailing easterly wind and, as he remained in position, came under attack from gunners in Gloria Castle, who opened fire at extreme range. The flagship, which was the only British vessel in sight of the guns, suffered little damage as 'most of their shot fell short, or flew over the rigging', while the other members of the squadron were left unscathed.[28] *Burford* returned fire with her new chase guns, which had a longer range than the Spanish cannon and caused significant damage: 'though at so great a distance, almost 2 miles, the first shot carried away a corner of the westernmost bastion, the second the flagstaff and killed two sentinels, the third sunk a sloop lying near the castle'.[29] Several houses in the town, including the governor's residence, were damaged in the action, which continued at extreme range until nightfall.

On the following day, at 5am, Vernon called his captains to a meeting on *Hampton Court* where he consulted them about his plans to renew the attack. He had decided to delay advancing into the inner harbour until nightfall because of the danger of moving closer to Gloria Castle in daylight. He would then launch an attack early the following morning.[30] However, while the meeting was in progress, a white flag of truce was raised on Gloria Castle and a launch also showing a white flag was seen leaving the shore. The governor of Porto Bello, Don Francisco de Retez, had sent his adjutant to the flagship with the terms on which he would be prepared to surrender the town.[31] His proposals included handing over the three castles, permitting the garrison to leave Porto

Bello and ensuring the protection of the town and its churches. He also wanted to retain control of the ships anchored in the harbour.

Vernon was unwilling to accept an agreement that excluded the transfer of the ships and he set out his own six conditions for surrender, giving the governor until 3pm to accept them.[32] While the governor considered them, the squadron moved further into the inner harbour in case hostilities were resumed. But at 1pm, the governor confirmed his acceptance of Vernon's terms, which included permitting the garrison to leave Porto Bello and handing over the ships complete with their arms. Apart from the *guardacosta Astrea* (24) and *Triunfo* (20), the vessels now in Vernon's possession included four sloops and a schooner, which were 'the very individual ships, or rather pirates that committed all the depredations and carried our ships into the several Spanish ports'.[33]

Later in the afternoon, as the garrison marched out, Vernon sent his marines onshore to take possession of Gloria and St Jeronimo Castles, where they found large quantities of weapons and ammunition. Total Spanish losses are unknown, but English casualties were light, with eight men killed and nine wounded. Vernon issued orders prohibiting his seamen from plundering the town but Spanish seamen and soldiers who had deserted their posts were less disciplined. According to William Campbell, they 'went into the town, broke open the doors and plundered the whole place; so that in the morning of the capitulation you would be surprised to see every door open, all sorts of goods lying promiscuously; treasure and most valuable goods removed and what remained in the utmost confusion'.[34] However, they missed a store of 10,000 pieces of eight, which fell into Vernon's hands and he 'distributed them among his Majesty's forces for their encouragement'.[35]

Soon after the engagement, Vernon was reinforced by three more warships but he had already decided that he did not have sufficient strength to retain Porto Bello for more than a brief period while he destroyed the castles and removed their armament. Captain Charles Knowles, who arrived at Porto Bello in the fifth-rate HMS *Diamond* (40) on 27 November, was given responsibility (as chief engineer) for the demolition work.[36] He was assisted by Captain Edward Boscawen, who was serving as a volunteer at Porto Bello while his ship was being repaired at Port Royal.[37]

Over a three-week period, 'whole fortresses are reduced, so that there does not remain one stone after another, but the whole an entire heap of rubbish'.[38] The demolition of the Iron Castle proved to be particularly difficult because of the quality of its construction: 'the walls of the lower battery, which consisted of 22 guns, were nine feet thick, and of a hard stone, cemented with such a fine mortar that it was a long work to make any impression in it to come to mind at all'.[39] There were nearly 100 iron cannon to be destroyed, more than 60 brass guns to be shipped to Port Royal and 120 barrels of gunpowder to be blown up.

Before returning to Jamaica, Vernon considered repeating the successful raid on Panama carried out by the Welsh privateer Sir Henry Morgan in 1671, with the aim of seizing the silver that had recently arrived from Peru. But Panama was some 40 miles from Porto Bello across the isthmus and Vernon concluded that such a venture would be too risky. There was a danger of being ambushed as they marched through thick vegetation, they had no means of transporting cannon to attack Panama's fortifications and there was a risk that the Ferrol squadron might arrive in their absence.[40] He was forced to abandon the idea but corresponded with the president of Panama about the imprisonment of South Sea Company officials and secured their release.

News of Vernon's victory reaches Britain
Vernon, who left Porto Bello for Jamaica on 15 December, appointed Captain James Rentone, who had served as his pilot on the expedition, as captain of the *Triumph* prize, the captured *guardacosta* snow *Triunfo*, and sent him back to England with his dispatches and the articles of capitulation.[41] On 13 March 1740, Rentone arrived in London with news of the victory and was received by George II, who awarded him 200 guineas and promised him the command of a ship of the line.[42] A few days later, Thomas Pelham-Holles, First Duke of Newcastle, Secretary of State for the Southern Department, wrote to Vernon to convey the King's 'satisfaction in the courage and zeal which you, and the officers, and men, under your command, showed in this action; and in the humanity with which you treated the inhabitants of Porto Bello, after the reduction of it'.[43]

On 18 March, both Houses of Parliament joined in an address to the King offering their congratulations and Vernon was promoted to Vice-Admiral of the White. This official recognition was reflected in his public popularity, which 'reached a height almost unparalleled before or since, except in the case of Nelson'.[44] Poems, medals and prints soon appeared celebrating Vernon as a national hero who had achieved Britain's first success in the war against Spain. They included Richard Glover's anti-Spanish ballad, *Admiral Hosier's Ghost* (1740), which celebrated Vernon's victory and contrasted it with the fate of Hosier and his men in 1727.[45]

Vernon's success enhanced his professional reputation as a result of his thorough preparations, based on the effective use of intelligence, detailed planning and strong leadership during the operation. However, in time, his public reputation slowly declined as the hopes of further success against Spain faded and setbacks accumulated. Following his defeat at Cartagena in 1741 and an unsuccessful attempt to invade Cuba, Vernon was recalled to London in

1742. Despite these reverses, in 1745, at a time of national crisis, Vernon was appointed as commander of the Channel Fleet, but a succession of disputes with the Admiralty led to his dismissal from the navy in 1746.

At a time when it was deeply unpopular, the Walpole ministry had exaggerated the importance of Vernon's success for political reasons and there is little doubt that its wider strategic significance was limited. Neither galleons nor Peruvian silver had been taken during the attack and its main effect was to disrupt Spanish trade and undermine Panama's prosperity. Without any protection from a further British assault, the town's annual fair was permanently abandoned and the treasure fleets no longer called there. This brought Porto Bello's role as a major entrepôt for Spanish–American trade to an end after nearly two centuries and opened the town to British merchants. But trade between Peru and Spain continued by other means. Nearby Chagres, which served as a second port supplying goods from Spain and sending gold and silver to Europe, briefly assumed greater importance after the fall of Porto Bello until March 1740, when Vernon returned to destroy its fortifications. This severed Spanish trading links with the isthmus and her trade was diverted elsewhere, resulting in the stagnation of Panama's economy for more than a century.

The taking of Porto Bello, see colour plate 3

The Unwanted Coup: James Callander, Spiridon Foresti, and British Espionage in the Ionian Islands during the War of the Second Coalition

Nicholas James Kaizer

Not long ago, I was engrossed in a Navy Records Society-edited volume of the correspondence of Admiral Lord Keith, the British commander of the Mediterranean Fleet at the end of the French Revolutionary Wars. I was not there in search of anything relating to naval intelligence, until I stumbled upon a letter directed to Lord Keith from a British Colonel Callander,[1] which the editor described as 'curious reading'.[2] In it, Callander reports that the islanders of Zante, 'long attached to the British nation from esteem and commerce, hoisted the British flag and declared unanimously their firm desire to live and die under the protection of Britain'. Callander highlighted his own role in the uprising, rooted in his patriotic zeal as a British officer, and added that 'the proceedings ... have been detailed to your Lordship, according to Mr Foresti'.[3]

These particulars immediately piqued my interest; Zakynthos (commonly known by its Italian name, Zante) was one of the seven Ionian Islands, which in 1801 were organised into the newly established Septinsular Republic. This state, nominally self-governing with an aristocratic constitution, was in actuality under Russian and Ottoman suzerainty.[4] Why, then, did the islanders hoist the British flag? Doing so put them and the British in stark opposition to the Ottomans, a British ally in the war against France in Egypt. This coup also came at a dangerous moment in Anglo-Russian relations. As the islanders cast off Russian and Turkish rule, a Russian-led League of Armed Neutrality was formed in northern Europe. War with Russia brewed.

There is little discussion of this event in secondary sources, and what has been written is contradictory and generally uninterested. Of the sources that discuss the uprising, many claim that James Callander was a British agent, operating under the orders of Admiral Horatio Nelson. I was therefore left with several questions, which are to be addressed in this article: what exactly happened on Zakynthos in 1801? What role did the British play in the uprising? Was James Callander really operating as an agent of the British? It was in the

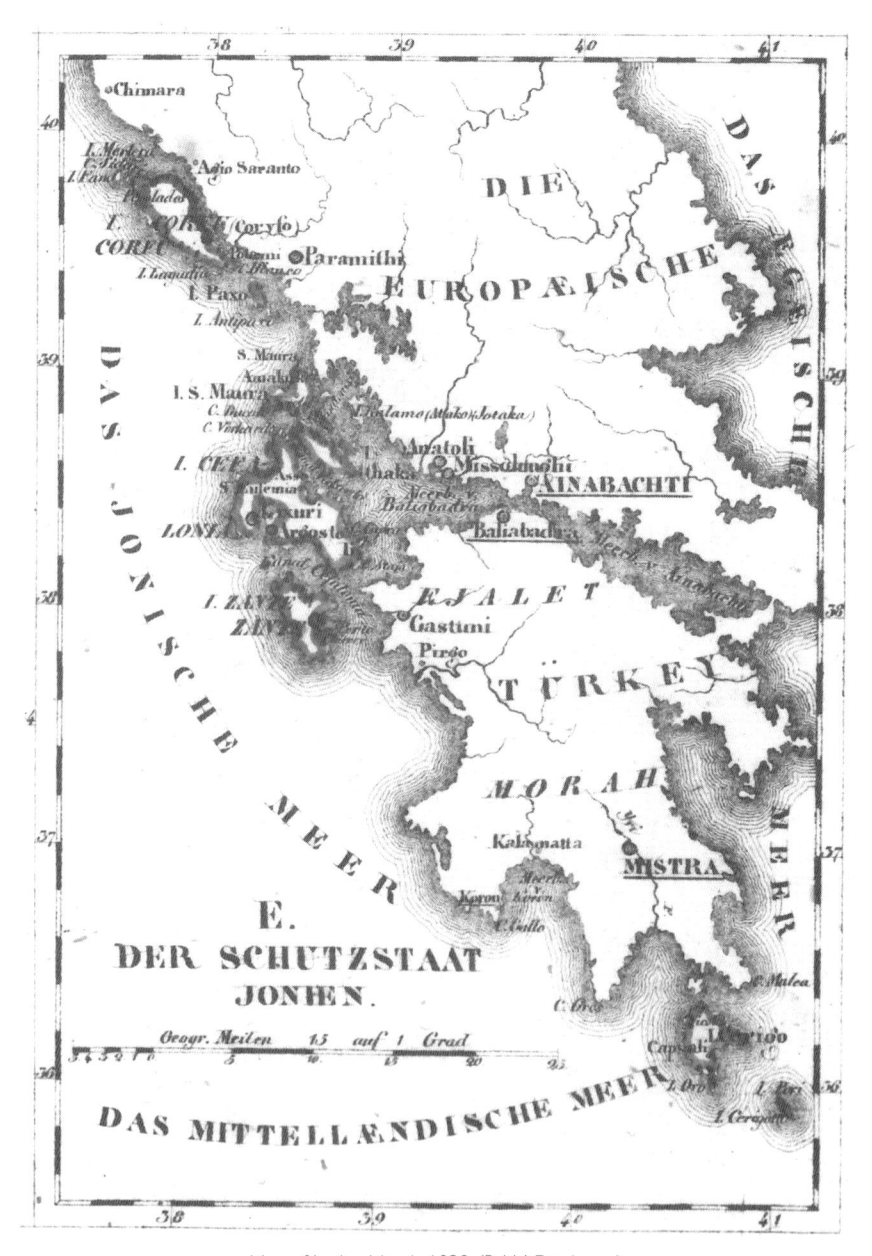

Map of Ionian Islands 1830. (BritishEmpire.co)

correspondence of an important but little-known British consul and intelligence operative that I found the answers: the aforementioned Spiridon Foresti.

Foresti was a native of Zakynthos who served as the British consul for the Ionian Islands throughout the Napoleonic Wars.[5] Consuls like Foresti were typically local, well-connected merchants, whose primary job was to support British traders and Britain's commercial interests.[6] Rather than professionals of later periods, 'intelligence officers' at this time, according to Captain Steven Maffeo, USN Ret, were primarily individuals for whom intelligence was a secondary role. Foresti was one of many diplomatic and commercial officials serving in what Maffeo described as a large but disorganised system of British intelligence during the Napoleonic Wars.[7] He was an invaluable source of intelligence to the Royal Navy in the Mediterranean, being at 'the centre of an active intelligence network in the Adriatic and beyond'.[8] Foresti was not alone in providing valuable intelligence in his role as a consul,[9] but, he was unique in that he took an active part in the Great Power warfare over the strategically important Ionian Islands.[10] His work was remarkable, and all the more so as he never received a salary.

Apart from two very interesting papers by C I Chassell,[11] little has been written about Foresti's career despite the important role he played both in the history of the Ionian Islands and the wider British commercial and naval sphere of this period. However, there is no shortage of archival evidence. Foresti's correspondence, official and personal, can be found in several archives in the United Kingdom. His letters reveal the complex and otherwise murky events on Zante, providing an interesting perspective on a relatively unknown event in an important corner of the world, during an uncertain time in the diplomatic history of Great Britain, Russia and the other Great Powers in the Eastern Mediterranean.

Ionian Islands at the turn of the century
Today a part of Greece, the seven Ionian Islands had been under the control of, and were heavily influenced by, the Republic of Venice, until its collapse in 1797. Italian names were common (and still are today) and much of the nobility came from Italian families, but much of the populace remained steadfastly Greek and adhered to Greek Orthodox Christianity. Catholicism and Orthodoxy coexisted, usually amicably, throughout the centuries of Venetian rule.[12]

As a result of France's annexation and subsequent forced dismemberment of Venice's lands and island possessions in 1797, the Ionian Islands became pawns in the Great Powers struggle throughout the 1790s and early 1800s. With extensive naval and commercial interests in the Adriatic Basin and the wider Eastern Mediterranean at stake, each of the Great Powers – Britain, France,

Russia, and the Ottomans – had complex interests and objectives in the region.[13] Russia's interest in the islands came from their commercial and religious ties. Most of the islanders were fellow adherents of Orthodoxy and the Russian Empire was the foremost Orthodox state. Trade between the islands and the Black Sea had grown considerably in the late eighteenth century.[14] In the late 1790s, fears of French control in the region and the possibility of restricted

Soldier of the Greek Light Infantry Regiment of the Duke of York by Denis Dighton (1792–1827), 1813. Many of the soldiers of this regiment were drawn from the Albanian mercenaries already present in the Ionian Islands. (Royal Collection Trust)

access of Russian naval and merchant vessels to the wider Mediterranean prompted the dispatch of a Russian fleet, which in 1799 captured the islands from the French.[15]

The British, too, had complex interests in the region. Apart from their strategic location, the islands were part of a very important currant trade.[16] As a result, the Royal Navy supported the Russians in seizing the islands from the French. When the Septinsular Republic was established, British Foreign Secretary Grenville instructed the ambassador to the Ottoman Empire, Lord Elgin, to state, 'His Majesty's willingness to acknowledge the Republic ... provided ... that the commerce of His subjects with the new Republic may be as free and as much protected as it was when the Seven Islands were under the Dominion of the Republic of Venice.'[17] Foresti played an important role in advancing British commercial interests in the islands and in cultivating the goodwill of the Ionian elites. As a major naval power in the region, the British offered a useful counterweight to the Russians and Turks in the new political context. This was particularly evident on Zante: when the French were driven from the islands, the aristocrats attributed the victory primarily to Admiral Nelson and the British.[18] Ultimately, the British were to establish full control over the islands at the end of the Napoleonic Wars, but in 1801 Great Britain was an ally of one of the Septinsular Republic's protectors, and on the verge of war with the other.

Britain and Russia had been allies until 1800, when Russian Tsar Paul

Ionian Flag showing the emblem of the Septinsular Republic (or Republic of the Seven Islands) based on Venetian symbols: the Lion of St Mark holding a Bible and seven bundled arrows. This flag was used between 1815 and 1864. (Wikipedia)

withdrew from the Second Coalition and made peace. Among Russian motivations was the failure of the British to hand over newly captured Malta to Paul, who was the Grand Master of the Order of Saint John (until Boneparte's invasion in 1798, the sovereign rulers of the island) and Britain's long-running habit of seizing neutral shipping in northern waters. As Anglo-Russian relations deteriorated, Paul sought friendly relations with the French and organised the other major powers of northern Europe into the League of Armed Neutrality, a military alliance determined to resist British naval force projection into the Baltic.[19] Early in 1801, a British fleet attacked Copenhagen, seized the Danish West Indies, and, under Admirals Parker and Nelson, were preparing to assault Russia in the Baltic. It was in this context, as the conflict at Copenhagen raged, that the islanders on Zante rose in rebellion and Colonel James Callander emerged.

Portrait of Emperor Paul of Russia by Vladimir Borovikovsky (1757–1825), 1800. (Museum of Fine Arts Academy, St Petersburg)

Coup d'etat of 1801: what happened?

On 19 February 1801, rebellious factions at Zante rose against the official regime of the Russo-Ottoman-backed Septinsular Republic and hoisted the British flag.[20] Today, this coup is known in Zakynthiot history as the *coup d'état* of Antonios Martinengos. As this event has attracted virtually no attention in English historiography there is little information about Martinengos or his motivations. We do know that tensions on the island were already high by 1801, in no small part due to the French Revolution. French annexation represented a major break with the Venetian regime, marked by the rule of Italian aristocratic families. Many of the island's merchant and middle classes supported the French occupation.[21] It is reasonable to assume that these individuals would have resented the aristocratic constitution, referred to as the 'Byzantine Constitution', imposed by the Septinsular Republic, which restricted power to the old nobility and shut out those of social classes who had been empowered under the French.[22] Many islanders had expressed their concern to the Russians in the early days of the Republic, and clashes occurred between social classes and rival factions across the islands.[23]

Corfu's authority in Zante and Cephalonia, a nearby island, had been waning by October 1800.[24] In a 26 February letter to Lord Elgin, Foresti described the chaotic state of affairs on the island, following the recall of the chief Russian official, Lieutenant Tesinghausen, on the 13th: 'Under his auspices the authority of the Senate has been openly and in the most violent manner set at defiance.' Days later, the rebels seized the city's fortress and hoisted the British flag. While the government, described by Foresti as firmly of the Russian party, stated publicly that they had attempted to oppose the rebels, Foresti reports that their forces, primarily Albanian mercenaries, did not oppose the uprising. In fact, they played a part in hoisting the British colours and then continued defending the now-rebellious island. He also accused the lieutenant, recently recalled for his failure to maintain control, of having known of the plans to overthrow the pro-Russian administration, stating that 'the Russian Lieutenant and his creatures would naturally countenance any measure that would produce a ferment and confusion'.[25]

What motivated the Zakynthiots to raise British colours specifically? The nobility on the island undoubtedly had British sympathies, in large part due to the currant trade. In 1800 they had given official thanks in the form of a golden sword to Admiral Nelson for his role in their liberation from the French, despite the fact that the Russians and the Ottomans did the fighting.[26] However, the islanders were not wholly devoted to Great Britain (as some accounts, including Callander's, have claimed): in 1797, under French rule, a crowd confronted the occupying French administration by raising the Russian flag and proclaiming 'Long Live Paul I!'[27] Foresti believed that they were to some extent motivated by a fear of retaliation by the Turks; with the withdrawal of the Russians, Britain was viewed as a reliable counterweight that could offer protection from the Turks.[28]

This was a shocking state of affairs, and a potentially dangerous escalation in the context of the brewing war between Russia and Britain. The Septinsular government decried these events but was helpless to respond. The regime in Corfu was disorganised and could muster fewer than 200 soldiers against the nearly 800 rebellious Albanians serving the Zakynthiot nobility.[29] The result was chaos and many months of upheaval, and both Cephalonia and Ithica were on the verge of a similar rebellion.[30] According to McKnight, in 1801 the Russian-nurtured Septinsular Republic 'was a state only in name'.[31]

The upheaval caused a great deal of trouble for Foresti as the British representative in Corfu. He officially denounced the uprising, but Foresti had to contend with the fallout of Callander's proclamation that Zante was 'to be considered as a component part of the British Empire'. Needless to say, this caused a great deal of tension between him and the local Turkish commandant.[32] Did the islanders in fact have the support of Great Britain? According to James Callander, they did.

The British role: Callander vs Foresti

The most detailed English language account of this coup comes from James Callander, a British army officer. Previously employed in Sicily, Callander had been present on Zante about two months before the 1801 uprising.[33] In a 4 March 1801 letter to Lord Keith, Callander suggested he did not instigate the initial uprising and hoisting of British colours, but that the islanders sought his advice because he was the only British subject on the island. He played the role of a mediator between the two parties on the island, owing to the intense distrust between them, and this he did out of 'my love for my country and the dictates of humanity'.[34]

In his memoir (under the name James Campbell), Callander claimed that he had been sent on the orders of both Lord Keith and Nelson on a mission to 'confirm the inhabitants of the Republic in their attachment to the interests of

His Majesty's Ship *Audacious* drawn by Richard Hawes, 1793. This painting shows the flagship of Lord Keith, Commander-in-Chief of the Mediterranean Fleet.
(© National Maritime Museum, Greenwich, London)

England …' and 'assure the inhabitants of the protection of the British government'. Callander asserts that, despite direct orders from Lord Nelson, he accepted the mission only upon receiving the support of 'my friend Lord Keith'. In more than sixty exhaustive pages he describes his very active role in the governance and defence of the island, beyond simply acting as a mediator. Curiously, he never once names any of the other leaders, such as Martinengos. He highlights the great enthusiasm for the British among the populace at Zante.[35]

Foresti's correspondence supports Callander's role as a leader of the rebellious government, where he described Callander as effectively in command of the Albanian mercenaries.[36] However, many of Callander's claims do not add up. He implies that he spent some time assisting with the governance of the other islands, particularly Corfu, despite the capital of the Republic never entering into a pro-British rebellion.[37] I am sceptical, too, of Callander's claim of receiving orders from Admiral Nelson, as there seems to be no evidence of correspondence between the two, and Nelson left the Mediterranean entirely half a year before Callander first went to Zante. However, there is no doubt that he did play a significant role there, and the islanders did raise a British flag in rebellion. The question is whether there was truth to his claim that he had the support of Lord Nelson and his self-described friend Lord Keith.

Discussions of Callander and the coup in secondary sources are few and far between, but of those that exist, a number take Callander at his word. These include the British *Dictionary of National Biography,* which stated that 'at the request of Lord Nelson he went to the Ionian Islands to confirm the inhabitants in their attachment to the English cause, remaining there until the peace of Amiens in 1802'.[38] More recently, Sakul's PhD dissertation described Callander as a 'British advanced scout from Malta', who had deviated from his official mission in declaring Zante a British protectorate.[39] A Zakynthos tourism website repeats a common understanding of the events of the 1801 coup: 'On 8 January 1801, James Callander, a British officer under the service of Nelson, arrived in Zakynthos to spread anti-French propaganda.'[40] In these sources, Callander is credited with serving as an intelligence agent under Nelson's orders.

This connection with Nelson is not likely, but Callander was certainly an acquaintance of Lord Keith. In a letter dated 16 June 1800, William Hamilton (ambassador to the King of Sicily and Naples) stated:

I have done all in my power to serve Col. Callender, whom your Lordship was pleased to recommend to me, but when I left Palermo it was not decided whether he would be employed in His Sicilian Majesty or not; but Gen. Acton seemed much inclined in his favour.[41]

This acquaintance, which amounted to Keith seeking a position for Callander, adds some credibility to the claims in his memoirs. The association with Nelson is understandable, given his wider fame, but if he was working for the British in some capacity in the Ionian Islands it would be for Lord Keith. And, this association was fruitful, as Callander did work for a time in Sicily with the Sicilian army.

As to Callander's mission in the Ionian Islands, there is little evidence either for or against, in part due to a lack of sources. The editors of the aforementioned volume of Keith's correspondence describe these events as 'the irresponsible behaviour of an adventurer',[42] and little else in Keith's papers suggest anything but official protest against his actions. However, other British officials were in some doubt as to Callander's status. In August 1801, Lord Elgin ordered Rear-Admiral John Warren to 'remove Col. Callender from Zante and put him under arrest til the King's pleasure be known upon his proceedings carried on in the King's name'.[43] While Lord Elgin was clear in his disapproval of Callander's actions in Zante, and wished for him to be detained, he was in some doubt on how the British government would view what he had done, suggesting he believed there was some possibility of clandestine sanction of Callander's actions from the government. For clear evidence regarding Callander's claim, and indeed for a more reliable account of the coup, one must turn to none other than Spiridon Foresti.

Foresti discussed the incident in both official and private correspondence, and he was regarded as a very credible figure by many in the British Mediterranean world. Admiral Nelson recommended him to many, such as Evan Nepean, Secretary to the Admiralty,[44] and to Lord Elgin.[45] To the former, he described Foresti as just one of two consuls who 'really and truly do their duty, and merit every encouragement and protection'.[46] In a

Right Honourable Lord Keith 1801, mezzotint by Samuel William Reynolds (1773–1835). (Yale Center for British Art)

letter to Foresti, Nelson stated, 'your letters are highly interesting, and continue to prove your unabated zeal in the cause of your King and Country. Be assured that there is not any man in Europe that estimates your services higher than myself.'[47] Nelson granted him considerable leeway and clearly respected his judgement, as he instructed a captain under his command to deliver a letter to Foresti and then, 'should Mr. Foresti request you to call at Zante on your return, to settle any matters at that Island, you will comply with his wish'.[48] Had Nelson dispatched Callander, it is highly unlikely that Foresti would not have known of it. However, when Foresti first met Callander, he did not know who he was.

Foresti described this first encounter in a letter to a longtime friend in Britain, John Hawkins.[49] It was long and likely composed over a great deal of time and discussed both personal and professional affairs. In it, he sought Hawkin's assistance in:

> Another matter of great moment to me. That is, proposals have been made to me by a Colonel James Callender, to marry my daughter. This officer arrived at Zante, from Malta, about the beginning of January. Mrs Foresti offered our house to him, & wrote to me that Lord Keith had sent him to Zante. He was afterwards taken in, & having experienced every attention from the family, soon recovered.[50]

This portion of the letter was likely written before the uprising took place, and before Callander had even visited Foresti in Corfu to discuss the potential marriage. Callander touted his pedigree and fortune, and Foresti was sorely tempted. He asked Hawkins to make inquiries about Callander before deciding on the matter.[51]

Before Foresti sent the letter, Zante rose in rebellion, and Foresti recounted what little he knew in the letter. It confirms Callander's involvement and credits him with preventing bloodshed. It also reports Callander's connection with Lord Keith, and that he was waiting upon orders from Keith.[52] Taken on its own, the letter lends credence to Callander's story. However, Foresti's later correspondence presents a very different picture.

By early June, Foresti no longer needed Hawkins' help in determining Callander's suitability as a husband for his daughter. His second letter, dated 6 June, sets out all he had since discovered about the British colonel. It certainly makes for *curious reading*:

> I am sorry that you will in consequence have had the trouble to inquire about a person, whose character I have of late discovered is such as to *preclude the most remote idea of his ever becoming my son-in-law*. I

allude to Colonel Callender. I have been pointedly informed by several respectable friends of mine that that person is really of the family, connections, and (originally) fortune, which he professes to be of, but that by extravagance he had been reduced to live by *sharking*.[53]

The report confirms an acquaintance between Lord Keith and Callander, and that the British admiral had sought employment for him (as suggested by Hamilton's letter), however with the caveat that:

He was certainly at one time in correspondence with Lord Keith, but I am assured that after the Colonel had been put into prison, but a few months ago, in Sicily, for debts & misconduct, Lord Keith expresses his concern that he had ever written to him & a doubt that he might make an improper use of his letters. In fact, he had made use of them so successfully at Zante, that the government & the people have totally disregarded the stigmatising disapprobation which Lord Elgin expresses upon the event of the hoisting of the British Colours at that island.[54]

Callander had used Keith's letters of recommendation, it seems, to convince the islanders at Zante that Callander had official sanction to act on behalf of the British government. He had hoodwinked them into giving him a position of authority. Even when official British protest came, the rebels on Zante continued in their rebellion due to Callander's assurances of Lord Keith's support.

Foresti's account portrays the actions of Callander as an embarrassment not only to the British state but also to Lord Keith personally. They also had significant repercussions for Foresti, who was gravely concerned, as Callander had effective control over his family home, that he might 'revenge himself upon my family'. His motivations, according to Foresti, were financial. He had profited from his leadership of the islanders, receiving a gold sword, but Foresti at least hoped that Callander would not 'obtain any money from any friends of mine'.[55] Of the two, Foresti is the more credible, and it is his insight into Callander's status and motivations that is most useful in understanding what transpired in early 1801.

War averted
These events left Zante in open rebellion, publicly siding with the British, at a time when war was brewing with Russia. Shortly following the uprising, the British defeated the Danes at Copenhagen, and a British fleet was preparing to sail into the Baltic and confront the Russians. Full-on war may indeed have broken out, were it not for the assassination of Tsar Paul in March 1801. This

was most opportune for the British, as Paul's successor Alexander immediately reversed his father's foreign policy. Rather than continuing to seek friendly relations with the French, Alexander made peace with Britain. However, none of this would have been known, and the British response to the rising at Zante should be seen in this dangerous context. Had war broken out, the continued supposed British presence in a rebellious island within a Russian protectorate certainly would have mattered. And, throughout the whole crisis, Britain remained allied with the Republic's other protector: the Ottomans.

In September 1801, the Admiralty dispatched a British ship to see that the 'indecent display of English colours in Zante finally ended'.[56] Captain Rickets of HM Brig *El Corso* (18) arrived in Zante with Foresti. In his memoirs, Callander claimed that he quitted the island only upon the orders of Lord Elgin, after the Peace of Amiens in 1802:

> Lord Elgin, the British ambassador at Constantinople, inform[ed] me, that, in consequence of the general pacification, his Majesty was to withdraw his protection from the Ionian Republic, and to leave the inhabitants under their own form of government. On receiving this communication, it only remained for me to haul down the English colours wherever they had been hoisted, and to withdraw myself from the islands.[57]

However, Rickets and Foresti found that Callander had already absconded from the island.[58] Following his flight, Callander retreated into relative historical obscurity. He published his aforementioned self-aggrandising memoirs as part of an attempt to counter accusations of 'numerous offences against the dictates of prudence and good management'.[59] Among these, it seems, was an alleged liaison with a Frenchwoman, Lina Sassen, who alleged Callander had promised to marry her while he was a prisoner of war in France during the Napoleonic Wars; she pursued this legal case for the remainder of her life.[60]

Foresti, however, remained an important player in the region. He was praised by Captain Rickets for his 'zeal, influence, and abilities', and was just as instrumental in resolving the crisis on Zante as he was in helping historians understand what had taken place there.[61] When Russia's involvement in the islands ended with their handing over to the French in 1807, Foresti again played a role in assisting the Royal Navy in a campaign to liberate the islands, both as an intelligence officer and a fighter.[62] His efforts were successful and the islands were incorporated into the United States of the Ionian Islands, a British protectorate from 1815, until they were ceded to the Kingdom of Greece in 1864.

Admiral Arthur Phillip, 1738–1814: Naval Officer, Explorer, Spy, Mercenary, Administrator

Tom Fremantle

Arthur Phillip was born a Londoner. Little is known of his parentage, but his father appears to have originated on the Continent and, perhaps, been a language tutor who served in some capacity in the Royal Navy. There is circumstantial evidence that the young Phillip first went to sea at the age of nine in 1747, but when he was thirteen he was taken into the Greenwich Hospital School for the sons of poor seamen.[1]

After two years of instruction in the basic knowledge required for a life at sea, Phillip was bound as an apprentice in 1753 for seven years to William Readhead, master of a ship built for the Greenland fisheries. In April the following year Readhead's ship left the Greenland Docks on the Thames with around forty others to head northwards to the Arctic seas, where whales were to be found. They fished for about two months and then returned to the Greenland Docks, where their cargoes were processed into oil to satisfy a growing market that was driven largely by the lubricant demands of the industrial revolution. Once Readhead had cleared the cargo and carried out any necessary repairs, he set off with a cargo probably of cloth and other manufactured goods for Spain and

Arthur Phillip (1738–1814), 1786, oil on canvas by Francis Wheatley (1747–1801). (National Portrait Gallery, London)

Greenland Fishery: English Whalers on the Ice, 1750, oil on canvas by Charles Brooking (1723–59). (© National Maritime Museum, Greenwich, London)

Italy. So, within a year the young Phillip had experienced the physical demands and challenges of the Arctic Ocean and the Mediterranean as well as being exposed to trading in Spain and Italy.

After one additional whaling voyage, Phillip found a way of ending his apprenticeship and in October 1755, aged seventeen, he joined his cousin Captain Michael Everitt aboard the third-rate *Buckingham* (68) as an able seaman. The following year saw *Buckingham* joining Admiral Byng's fleet bound for Menorca. On 20 May 1756 she was fourth in the British line opening fire on the superior French fleet. After a brief action the French sailed off and Byng did not pursue them, which ultimately resulted in his conviction and execution for cowardice; a very dubious charge, but one that had a profound consequence on the future navy. There is no record of Phillip's role in the battle but it must have given him first-hand experience on board a ship of the line in a major fleet action.

For the next few years Phillip moved from ship to ship, most particularly re-joining his cousin and patron Captain Everitt aboard the second-rate *Neptune* (98), where he was rated midshipman. During the Seven Years' War in 1760 he rejoined Everitt aboard the third-rate *Stirling Castle* (70) bound for the West Indies. After two years cruising with little action, Everitt left the command to Captain Campbell, but Phillip stayed on and was then involved in the taking of Martinique and the attack on Cuba under Admiral Rodney. Following the assault on Havana, Captain Campbell was court martialled and dismissed from the service for disobeying his admiral's orders. Not long afterwards *Stirling Castle* proved to be such a wreck that she was scuttled, and her entire crew moved into the third-rate, 70-gun Spanish prize, *Infanta*. By March 1763 *Infanta* was back in Portsmouth and on 24 March the Navy Board confirmed Phillip's appointment as a lieutenant. While there is little definitive record of specific exploits, it is certain that Phillip had acquired extensive and varied experience of every aspect of life at sea.

With the end of the war in 1764, Phillip was immediately placed on half-pay, insufficient to maintain anything like the life of a gentleman. However, within a few months he had married a wealthy widow, Margaret Charlotte Denison, sixteen years his senior. The couple appear to have lived in London for about two years but then moved south to Lyndhurst in the New Forest, where Phillip could live as a country gentleman with an interest in agriculture, supporting his local community. For some reason, unknown, his marriage was dissolved in 1769 and in accordance with a pre-nuptial agreement he did not benefit in any way from his wife's wealth.

He used the next year or so with permission from the Admiralty to go to Saint-Omer in France 'for his health' and, no doubt, to improve his French. After a brief spell in the third-rate *Egmont* (74) as fourth lieutenant, he applied for another year in France in a village not far from Lille. He appears to have remained in France until 1774. What he did there can only be a matter of speculation but may well have included some engagement with the Flanders textile trade and the mining industry, and even attendance at lectures given by the Professor of Artillery and Fortification at the *École Militaire* in Paris, a German named Isaac Landmann, with whom he was later identified as an old friend. At some point it is very likely that he travelled to Toulon to see what the French were doing there with their fleet. Phillip was certainly not idle and was making a good living as well as extending his knowledge and experience, and, no doubt, enhancing his reputation within the corridors of power in England.

Phillip joins the Portuguese navy

On his return to England in 1775 he might have been faced with further years of boredom on a lieutenant's half-pay. However, he had come to the notice of influential people at the Admiralty, presumably as a result of the information he had provided. Spain and Portugal had again gone to war with each other over their various spheres of influence in South America, and Portugal had asked for assistance from Great Britain. In such circumstances one of the Lords of the Admiralty, Augustus Hervey, who had come across Phillip at the battle for Havana, recommended him for employment in the Portuguese navy. The recommendation commended him for his theoretical knowledge and experience and his knowledge of French, and confirmed that he deserved promotion. Phillip's biographer, Professor Alan Frost, speculates that 'what Hervey alluded to was Phillip's character of a "discreet officer", one of those whom the Admiralty and the state departments from time to time employed either to travel observantly in Europe, or sent to distant waters on special missions'.[2] In other words, he was a practised spy who would observe and record objectively what he saw and experienced. Sending him to the Portuguese navy to operate along the South American coastline from Rio de Janeiro to the River Plate could be

Maritime Procession, in front of Lazaro Hospital, c1750–98, oil on canvas by Leandro Joachim (1738–98). (Museo Historico Nationale, Rio de Janeiro, Brazil)

expected to yield much useful information for the British government without exciting suspicion or animosity.

He left England in December 1774 and the following month received a commission as captain in the Portuguese navy. He was appointed second captain of the fourth-rate *Nossa Senhora de Belem* (54) and on 9 February sailed from the Tagus to Rio de Janeiro. The Portuguese fleet stationed in Rio was commanded by another Englishman named Robert M'Douall, whose bombastic behaviour as commodore had alienated him from many of his officers as well as the Viceroy, the Marquis de Lavradio.

Phillip's tactful discretion evidently impressed Lavradio from the start and he quickly became a well-trusted confidant. As a result, Lavradio soon took Phillip out of the *Belem* and gave him command of the sixth-rate frigate *Pilar* (26) and a small squadron, which was fitting out, with orders to defend the Portuguese settlements on the northern littoral of the River Plate. This gave Phillip four months in Rio, during which we can be sure he would have observed much of the exotic natural life surrounding the city as well as enjoying the delights of the opera and society that it could offer, whilst perfecting his knowledge of the language. Through the latter months of 1775 and into 1776 Phillip was operating between the island of Santa Caterina and the Plate estuary imposing Portuguese authority around its little settlement at Colonia against Spanish prevarication and, once again, impressing Lavradio with his decisiveness and courage.

Despite a truce having been declared, Lavradio sent Phillip back to Colonia with a small squadron to ensure the Spaniards were not tempted to harass the settlement. There he continued to ensure the Portuguese colony could operate safely, earning the respect of the Spaniards as well as further accolades from Lavradio. He was continually on the lookout and reported on the Spanish establishment at Buenos Aires, the details of ports and inlets, the defences of Montevideo and the method of producing cochineal – a dye for which demand in Europe had soared and which Phillip believed might be produced in the West Indies.

After the truce ended, Phillip was involved in yet another situation in which his superior lacked the stomach for a fight and failed to give battle to the Spaniards. Despite having only 26 guns he took the initiative, attacking a Spanish third-rate, 70-gun ship, and with a little help from the rest of his squadron was able to force a surrender. The ship, *San Agustin*, was immediately taken into Portuguese service and Phillip was rewarded with the command. He remained in that position, mostly in harbour in Rio, after the next declaration of peace between the two countries. He used some of his time learning about the diamond and gold mining and production about 500km north of Rio, although it is not absolutely clear that he visited the closely guarded mines himself. Sir Joseph Banks wrote notes on Brazilian mining with accompanying drawings that must have been made on the spot and were probably drawn by Phillip. The spy in Phillip was keeping his hand in and his eyes open.

By the middle of 1778, with his own country at war with the French and his services no longer required by the Portuguese, Phillip resigned his commission and made his way back to England. Lavradio wrote a fulsome report about him as an officer of 'distinct merit', even tempered and of great discretion; he was sad to see him go. Queen Maria (1777–1816) of Portugal specifically asked that he should be advanced in the Royal Navy. In the true character of the observant officer he was, he reported his arrival in London to the Secretary to the Admiralty, adding that he had sighted a French fleet of about thirty ships sailing southwards from Brest.

Phillip returns to the Royal Navy
Phillip spent about eight months as first lieutenant aboard the third-rate *Alexander* (74) before being appointed master and commander of a fireship, although it could not be made sufficiently seaworthy to go to sea. He volunteered to spend some months in the first-rate *Victory* (100) as a supernumerary, which usefully introduced him to the purser Evan Nepean, later to become Under Secretary at the Home Office and then at the Admiralty. Various gaps in his recorded activity emerge in the subsequent months of 1781 but he certainly met Lord Sandwich, the First Lord, who may have drawn on Phillip's knowledge and experience of Brazil and Argentina, leading to some sort of undercover assignment.

In October 1781 Phillip was appointed to command the sixth-rate *Ariadne* (24), being promoted to post-captain on 30 November, and at the end of that year took her to the Elbe to escort a shipload of Hanoverian soldiers to England. It proved too late in the season and he found himself obliged to spend a challenging winter iced into that river. After he arrived home in 1782 and paid off *Ariadne*, his activities are not recorded, but Frost has drawn together a considerable weight of circumstantial evidence suggesting that in that year he was engaged in some sort of undercover scheme, possibly for the invasion of the River Plate or in support of the Portuguese in their quarrels with the Spanish. As you might expect, records are sparse regarding someone trusted to undertake such covert exploits. One of the people who recommended Phillip to Lord Sandwich was Robert Shafto, a member of Parliament, who is known to have been involved in the British Secret Service.

At the end of 1782 Phillip was appointed to command the third-rate *Europe* (64), then fitting out to join two other ships of the line and a frigate under the overall command of Captain Robert Kingsmill to go via South America to India. Phillip's *Europe* was the only ship of the squadron to successfully weather a storm in the Atlantic, which drove the others to return home, and after refitting in Rio he continued to India. There he joined Sir Edward Hughes' India squadron briefly but remained only long enough to make the ship fit for the return voyage to England accompanied by eleven others, no longer required because the war had ended. When this squadron arrived at Cape Town the Dutch governor, having received no instructions to the contrary, assumed his country was still at war with Great Britain and refused them entry.

Phillip was given the task of meeting the governor and persuading him that the orders they had from Sir Edward Hughes confirming that the Dutch were no longer adversaries were genuine. Only then were the ships allowed to carry out the major repairs that were necessary to give them the chance of reaching home. Phillip lived ashore and was able to observe and record the workings of the colony; information that would serve him well in the future. *Europe* sailed ahead of the remainder of the squadron, suggesting that Phillip was seen as a particularly reliable officer, with orders to deliver Hughes' dispatches, and in May 1784 *Europe* was paid off.

At this point Evan Nepean, Under Secretary at the Home Office, which curiously remained responsible for espionage in France and Spain, turned to Phillip upon receiving news that the French were rebuilding their fleet in Toulon. Nepean gave orders to Phillip to 'undertake a journey to Toulon & other ports of France for the purpose of ascertaining the naval force and stores in the arsenals'.[3] Phillip formally requested permission from the Admiralty to travel to France 'on account of my private affairs'. When he reached Toulon he observed activity that might indeed have been considered somewhat threatening and he confirmed that the arsenal was better supplied than when he had seen it previously. That comment, if nothing else, confirms that he had visited Toulon during his earlier spell in France in 1774.

There is no record of other ports he visited but he returned to England in October 1785. Nepean paid him another £160 from the espionage budget and Phillip applied to spend a further twelve months at Hyères in Provence, not far from Toulon, for his 'private affairs'. It is inconceivable that he did not use that time to keep a very close eye on all the developments within the French fleet and dockyard.

In 1786 he was back in England and his work must have pleased his superiors. Not long after his return, he was recommended by Lord Sydney, the Secretary of State for the Home Office, who would have been well aware of his activities in France and who could refer to Evan Nepean for details of his earlier career, to lead the project to take convicts from the overcrowded gaols to Botany Bay and there create a colony. Admiral Lord Howe, First Lord of the Admiralty, suggested that Phillip was not the best man for the job,[4] but he was overruled and Phillip was ordered to prepare a fleet and to secure the necessary stores to take possession and establish the colony. The government was very uncertain about how to undertake the task and Phillip found himself having to think through every detail, to ensure he could defend any settlement against the French or other aggressor as well as provide sufficient clothing and food for men, women and children, and the equipment to clear and work an unknown land.

One of the significant appointments Phillip made was Lieutenant Philip Gidley King, as second lieutenant in *Sirius*. They had first met when Phillip commanded *Ariadne* and King had accompanied him when he moved to *Europe*. The two men clearly enjoyed a very close relationship and shared the same values based on total loyalty to the King and deeply held Christian belief with its respect for every single human being. These characteristics were later manifested in both men's attitude to the native populations and to the convicts.

Establishing colonies at Port Jackson and Norfolk Island
It took until May 1787 for the little fleet of nine hired transports, one Admiralty armed tender, *Supply*, and the converted frigate *Sirius* to be gathered and prepared, carrying 750 convicts, with a company of just under 200 marines, and a few free settlers and officials.[5] The fleet called at Santa Cruz de Tenerife, Rio and the Cape before setting off eastwards across the Southern Ocean. They arrived at Botany Bay in January 1788 but after a few days of exploration Phillip decided it would be unsuitable for a settlement and he set off to search for a better solution. Within a day's sail he had found the entrance to Port Jackson and immediately declared that it was 'the finest harbour in the world, in which a thousand sail of the line may ride in the most perfect security'.[6] The fleet moved to Port Jackson and began to disembark at Sydney Cove, where the British flag was ceremonially hoisted on 26 January 1788. Phillip's exploration of the surrounding countryside began at once and his early reports paint a positive picture of the prospects for the colony. Within two weeks he had sent Lieutenant King, 'a very steady, good officer', to take possession of Norfolk Island, 1,000 miles to the east, and to create a settlement there to exploit the timber and flax that had been recommended by Captain Cook, and to deny it to the French.

Phillip was anxious to demonstrate that his benevolent and Christian attitude towards the natives was precisely in accordance with the orders contained in his commission. 'The natives have ever been treated with the greatest humanity and attention, and every precaution that was possible has been taken to prevent

The Founding of Australia by Capt. Arthur Phillip RN, Sydney Cove, Jan. 26th, 1788, oil sketch painted in 1937 by Algernon Talmage RA (1871–1939). (State Library of New South Wales)

their receiving any insults ... every means shall be used to reconcile them to live amongst us ... to teach them ...'[7]

Shortly after arriving he began experiencing trouble from the marine officers, and most especially their commanding officer Major Ross, who for the next three years proved to be one of Phillip's most difficult challenges.[8] It may have been that Ross felt he was not being given the authority he expected as

Captain Philip Gidley King, Lieutenant Governor Norfolk Island, 1788–96, Governor New South Wales, 1800–06. Artist Unknown.
(State Library of New South Wales)

Lieutenant Governor, but he quickly demonstrated that he was unable to resolve tactfully any of the difficulties and disputes that arose between his officers. Unnecessary courts martial became a significant distraction and irritant.

From the outset Phillip was concerned about food supplies. He well understood that it would be some years before the colony could possibly become self-sufficient – the land had to be cleared for crops and the farmers must work out how to manage their agriculture and horticulture contending with the seasons, climate and soil. He also needed to establish some form of market that could allow those engaged in farming to sell their surplus to the government store to help feed the convicts. Phillip's intention was also to retain sufficient land under cultivation in government ownership to feed the convict community, but he acknowledged that all this would take time and, in the meantime, he was 'surrounded by the most infamous of mankind'.

The challenges were many. Storms wrecked some of the early crops, cattle from which it was hoped to breed escaped, the natives were not always as friendly as he had hoped, and a vital store ship was wrecked off the Cape with the loss of essential supplies, which brought the colony close to starvation. The second fleet of convict ships that might have brought reasonably healthy bodies to support the work in the colony arrived with a majority of sick and dying people who had been treated appallingly on the voyage and proved an added burden.

He was continually harassed by Major Ross and eventually devised a plan to move him to Norfolk Island, recalling Lieutenant King so that he could return to London as Phillip's personal envoy to request more supplies of food and other necessaries. In disembarking Ross and others at Norfolk Island, *Sirius*, Phillip's main link to the outside world, was wrecked following a lack of judgement on the part of her captain, John Hunter. On Norfolk Island Ross turned the relatively benign and permissive regime established by King into a dictatorial state under martial law. In London King passed Phillip's messages, written and verbal, to the Secretary of State before sailing back to Port Jackson to resume his position on Norfolk Island.[9]

Phillip requested the relief of the marine detachment, to achieve that which the authorities in London raised as the New South Wales Corps, appointing Major Francis Grose in command. Recruitment was not easy and inducements had to be offered; some offenders under sentence or already convicted were given the option to enlist. Grose himself set the tone as one whose motivation appears to have been much more the lining of his own pockets than service to the King in establishing the colony. When he arrived in Port Jackson he was immediately critical of what he found and did nothing to support Phillip.

Phillip remained steadfast in his intentions and civilian settlers praised his efforts, but by February 1791 his health was suffering and he was anxious to return home. A sad demonstration of the length of time it took for such requests to be answered, he received no response to his request until the middle of 1792. After he handed responsibility for the colony to the Lieutenant Governor, Major Grose, the morale of the colony that Phillip had worked so hard to maintain collapsed as the military exploited every possible opportunity to squeeze money out of the government, the free settlers and the convicts. Many settlers and convicts found their only solace lay in consuming large amounts of rum, which the officers sold at exorbitant mark-ups. For the following eight years many of those who had made their lives in New South Wales regretted Phillip's departure and longed to return to the principled and relatively well-ordered, though tough, environment that he had created successfully.

Returning to England
Having arrived in London in May 1793, not long after war with France had been declared, he formally asked to resign his position as governor on 23 July and to receive permission to leave London to take the waters at Bath. The resignation became official in October 1793 and Phillip expressed his gratitude for the award of a pension of £500 a year in recognition of his seven years under the Colonial Office preparing for and establishing the colony. The question of a successor arose at once and Phillip had no hesitation in recommending Lieutenant Governor King, whom he had much relied upon and who shared his beliefs and standards. Nevertheless, Captain Hunter who had served as second captain under Phillip in *Sirius*, was appointed instead and it was another seven years before King succeeded him.

By May 1794, after having confirmation that his first wife had died, Phillip married Isabella Whitehead and with her he appears to have lived the life of a gentleman near London. As war developed, Phillip's offer to serve again was taken up in 1796 when he took command of the third-rate *Alexander* (74), which had completed a major refit after being captured from the French. Later in the same year he transferred to the third-rate *Swiftsure* (74) and escorted a convoy with much-needed supplies to Gibraltar shortly after the Battle of Cape St Vincent (1797). His style of leadership was such that his crew was not infected by the mutiny that swept through much of Jervis's fleet during that year. In June he joined Nelson's squadron blockading Cadiz, where he remained after Nelson left for Tenerife in July. In September he left what was, in his opinion, 'one of the best ships in His Majesty's service', to take command of the second-rate *Blenheim* (90) after St Vincent (Jervis) had experienced a serious rift with his second in command Admiral Thompson, leaving the vacancy in *Blenheim*.

St Vincent was working on a scheme to provide a squadron of three British ships to operate with a Portuguese squadron patrolling between Lisbon and Cape St Vincent. Phillip was the obvious choice to lead it. But *Blenheim*'s need for urgent repairs led to Phillip going ahead into Lisbon, where in three months he re-established his close links to the Portuguese regime. However, the expected declaration of war and attack by France and Spain did not materialise. Then, in February 1798, Admiral Frederick arrived as St Vincent's new number two, bringing his own flag captain and insisted on raising his flag in *Blenheim*. St Vincent, sadly but correctly, felt he could not remove Captain Benjamin Hallowell and return *Swiftsure* to Phillip, who was left with the very sad and unappealing option of returning home. What had seemed for a while like the perfect opportunity as commodore of an Anglo-Portuguese squadron to do battle with French and Spanish and secure some prize money had suddenly faded like a mirage.

On Phillip's arrival in England he was rewarded, though not exactly as he would have liked, with command of the Sea Fencibles in Hampshire. This body of men, who were being similarly recruited in the other counties around the south coast, were to be trained to man the defensive Martello towers and the chain of signal stations, and in the event of an invasion, put to sea in small boats to drive the invasion force away. In 1799 he was promoted at the age of sixty-one, by seniority, to Rear-Admiral of the Blue, but despite offering his services for another sea command, even St Vincent, by then First Lord of the Admiralty, was unable to find anything with which he could suitably repay Phillip after his disappointment off Portugal.

In July 1801 the Admiralty ordered Phillip to carry out a review of the system and workings of the press gangs that operated all around Britain's coasts, especially in the major ports. St Vincent and his fellow commissioners were concerned that officers of the impress service were failing to use the resources they were given with full effect and that many of them were adopting fraudulent practices to line their pockets. Not surprisingly, Phillip undertook the task with customary diligence, no doubt finding useful his experience of dealing with similar dubious practices in New South Wales. After visiting ports up and down the length of the country his report was full of imaginative proposals; it is not clear whether the Admiralty took any notice of them.

There seems to have been some consideration given to appointing him to the naval command in the Leeward Islands and to the command of the warships based in Ireland, but neither of these came to fruition. As the country renewed its war with France in 1803 Phillip was appointed Inspector of the Sea Fencibles and the Impress Service and again spent much time travelling between the seaports. The possibility of invasion was a significant worry to the government, which was torn between recruiting fit young men into the Fencibles or pressing them into full naval service. Little was done to provide the Fencibles with the gunboats necessary to mount a defence, and the land-based forts were generally far from adequate. Phillip must have found this work very frustrating, but in due course he advanced to Rear-Admiral of the White in 1804. By 1805 he had recognised that his seafaring days were over.

During his peregrinations Mrs Phillip had based herself at a house in Bathampton on the eastern fringes of Bath, but records exist of them buying a property in Bath itself. There is no record of how he occupied his retirement there but in 1808 he suffered a series of strokes that left him partially paralysed. He lived on until 31 August 1814, by which time he had advanced to Admiral of the Blue. He was buried a week later at the parish church in Bathampton.

Phillip epitomised the best aspects of the Royal Navy at the end of the eighteenth century. He came from a humble background and worked through many of the toughest experiences a young sailor might encounter. He taught himself the breadth of knowledge he needed to draw on as each opportunity occurred during his career. He was an accomplished linguist and a meticulous observer of the coastline and countryside, flora and fauna. With his first-hand experience of agriculture in the New Forest he was able to set the early colonists onto a path towards self-sufficiency, despite the nay-sayers who were determined to undermine both his efforts and those of other loyal servants of the Crown.

He was humane and while he undoubtedly used punishment, he avoided excess, and won the loyalty of those who served under him. Whilst there is no specific evidence of religious belief, he followed the Christian principles of a just and loving God who allowed that all humanity was valuable; there are many examples of how he protected the aboriginal population from the excesses of angry settlers and did as much as he could to understand them and care for them. He was scrupulously honest in his dealings and there is not the slightest whiff of the self-seeking corruption and fraud that poisoned so much of the early effort in the colony in New South Wales. He showed how it was possible for someone of humble origin and without patronage to rise through the ranks, enjoy a full and varied service to the Crown, achieve flag rank, the status of a gentleman and financial security. He was a leader, manager, spy, diplomat and a man of exemplary character.

Queen Maria I of Portugal (1777–1816), see colour plate 4

Plate 1. Lloyd's Coffee House, London 1798, by William Holland (1757–1834), publisher. (Alamy)

Plate 2. Destruction of the French fleet at Toulon, 18 December 1793. An 1816 engraving by Thomas Whitcombe (1763–1824). (Naval History and Heritage Command, Washington, DC)

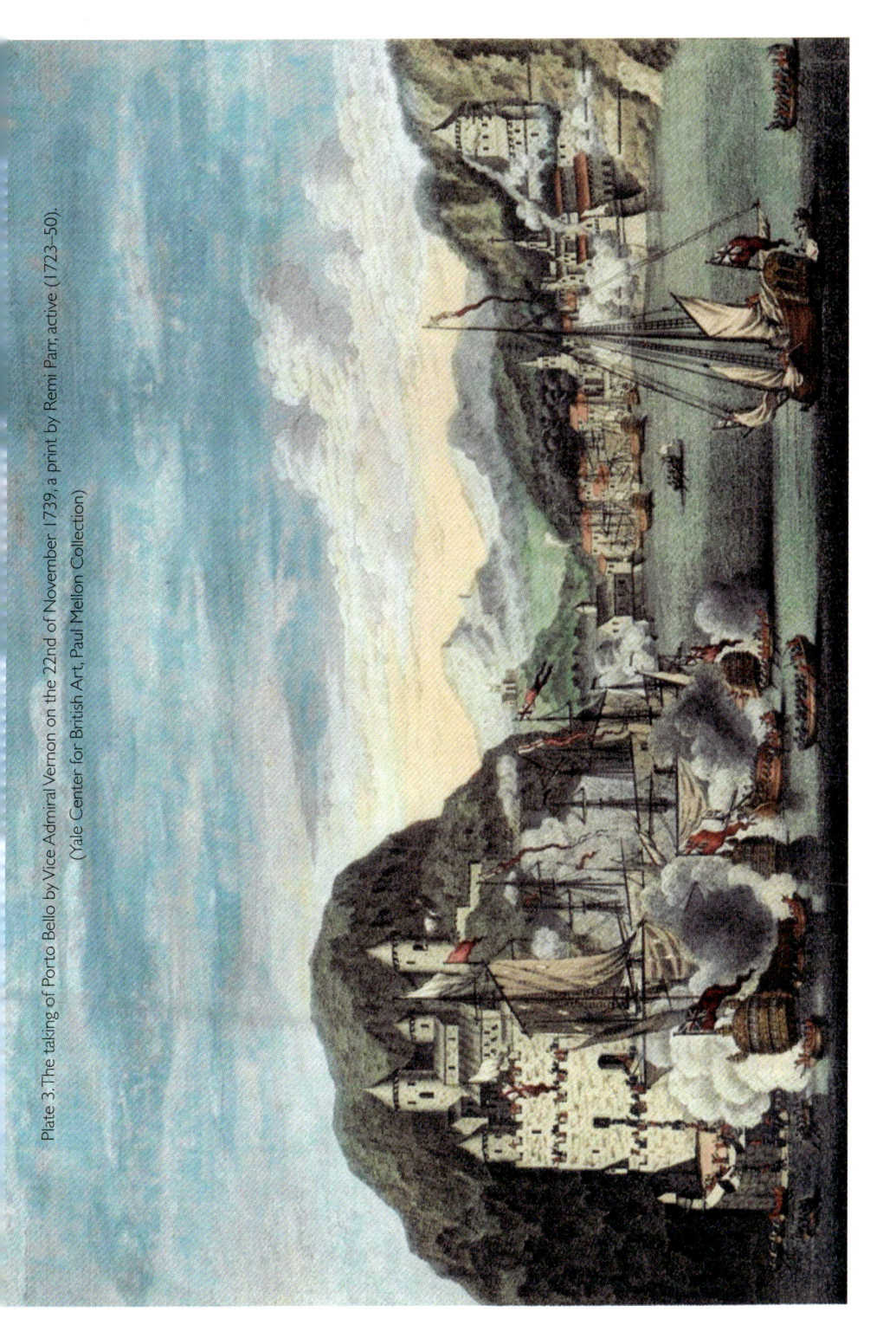

Plate 3. The taking of Porto Bello by Vice Admiral Vernon on the 22nd of November 1739, a print by Remi Parr, active (1723–50). (Yale Center for British Art, Paul Mellon Collection)

Plate 4 (above). Queen Maria I of Portugal (1777–1816), 1783, oil on canvas, attributed to Thomas Hickey (1741–1824) or Guiseppe Troni (1739–1810).
(National Palace of Queluz, Portugal)

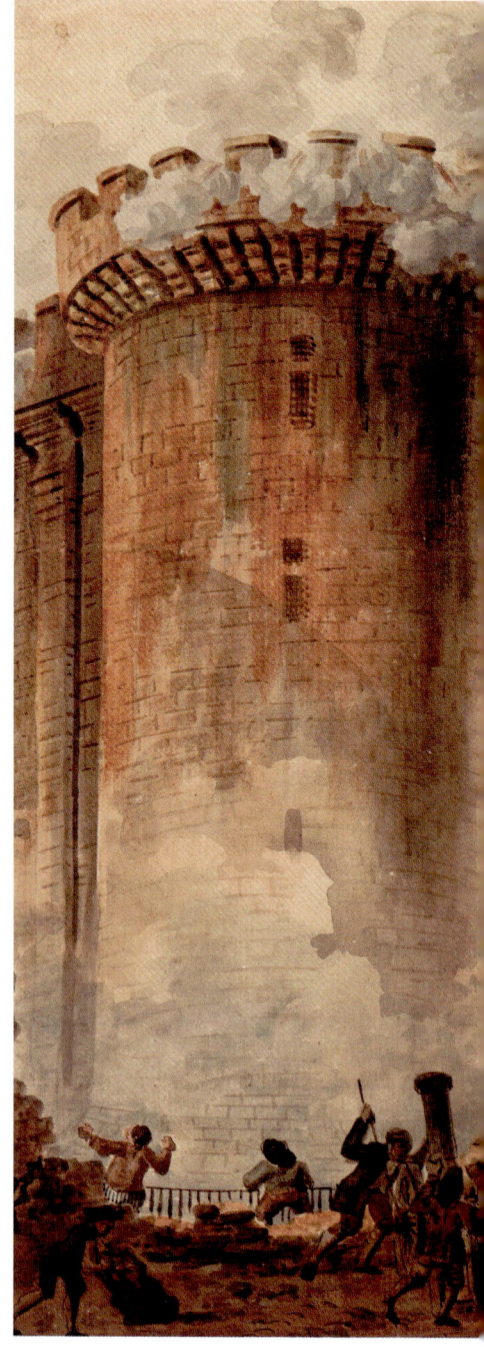

Plate 5 (right). The Storming of the Bastille, 1789. Watercolour by Jean Pierre Hou I (1735–1813).
(Bibliothéque Nationale de France)

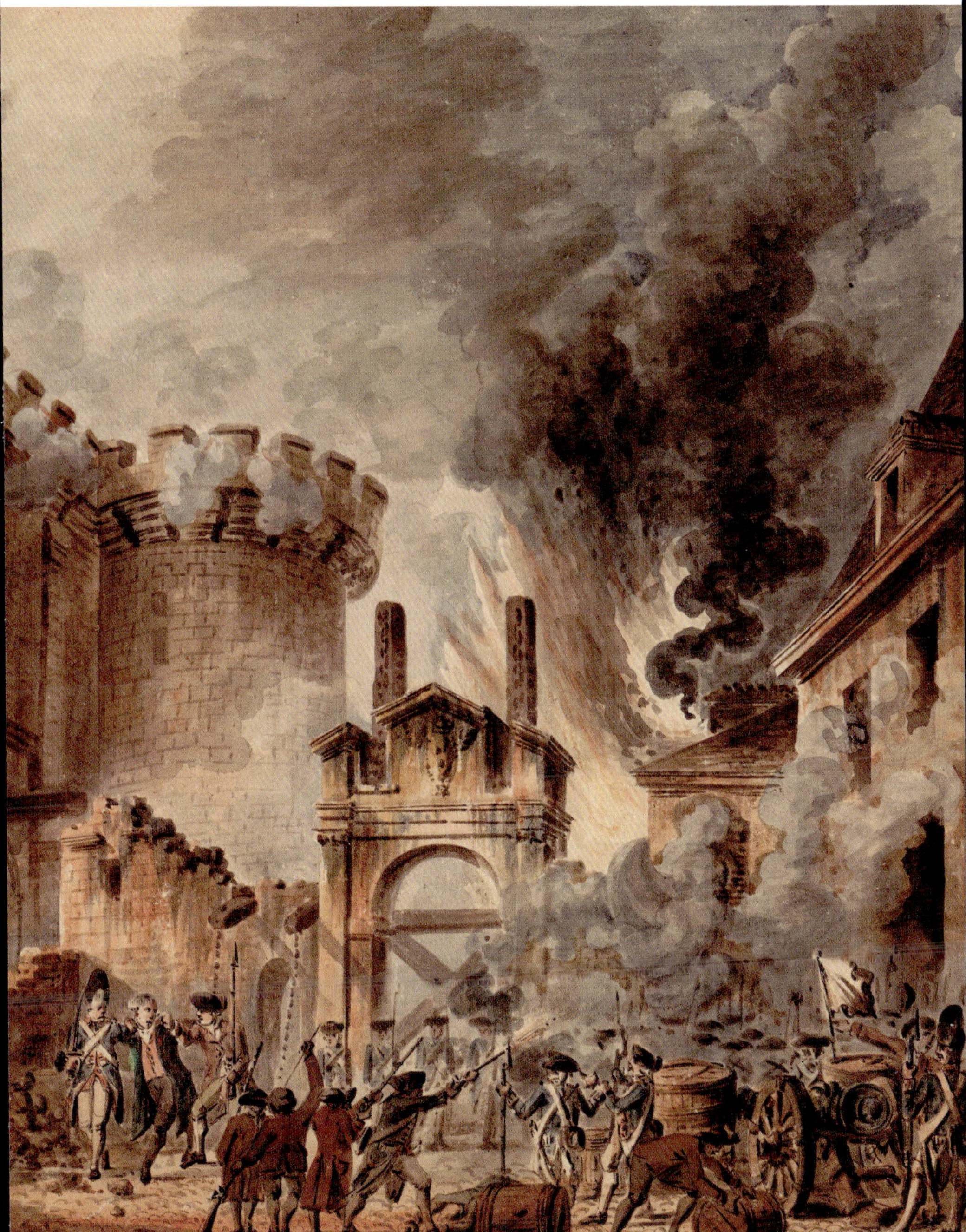

Plate 6. North East View of Fort Louis in the Island of Martinique, by Samuel Alken (1756–1815), British, 1796. Coloured aquatint. (Yale Center for British Art, Paul Mellon Collection)

Plate 7. HMS *Formidable* careened in Malta Dockyard, 31 January 1843, by J Quintanas, Schranz Brothers engravers. (Wikipedia)

Plate 8. Venice: the Basin of San Marco on Ascension Day, c1740.
Oil on canvas by Giovanni Antonio Canal (Canaletto, 1697–1768).
(National Gallery, London, Lord Revelstoke bequest)

The Fortunes and Misfortunes of Baron d'Imbert, 1760–1844: French Naval Officer and Royalist Agent

Natacha Abriat

As the French Revolution was a catastrophe for the 'Grand Corps' of naval officers, who were from the nobility, and, in their vast majority, Catholics and royalists, they emigrated *en masse* in 1792 after being subjected to arbitrary arrests, abuse and even massacres in French harbours. As soon as they left France, they no longer had any means of subsistence and sought employment, in foreign armies or navies. Or they became intelligence 'agents'.

The lifeblood of war and intelligence is money. Although English money played a role at the start of the Revolution (in particular to corrupt French ministers and deputies[1]), it was in 1793, with the creation of the War Office, that England set up an intelligence network that relied in particular on *émigrés*. England employed French officers to obtain military intelligence, especially naval intelligence – because the English constantly feared invasion – but also to carry out 'counter-revolutionary' actions from within France, designed to destabilise the enemy.

Xavier de Lebret, 'Chevalier' then 'Baron' d'Imbert, is remembered as one of the main architects of the negotiations that led to the port of Toulon surrendering to the English and Spanish fleets in 1793. So, what was it that led a naval officer, who had fought against the English during the American War of Independence, to find an ally in the 'hereditary' enemy, even going so far as to become a spy 'in the pay' of England?

A penniless cadet, he was not part of the high aristocracy who, even in exile, still had the means to subsist or to use their fortune to defend the royal cause. Introduced to intrigue and the art of secrecy, and gifted in the art of circumventing men, he served the counter-revolution from an early age. He loved nothing more than devising plans, but the lack of financial resources and, above all, the inertia and failures of the cause he was defending would place him in the position of many royalist agents suspected (rightly or wrongly) of having been double agents and who, on the King's return in 1814, would never be rewarded for their actions.

Why d'Imbert? Because, unlike other 'adventurous' spies who died in oblivion, Baron d'Imbert's legal wrangling, his dogged determination to claim what was owed to him and the *factum* he published to justify himself and obtain justice have left traces that historians must handle with care, but which illustrate this very special period when spies abounded and conspiracies multiplied.

An exemplary naval officer 1760–89

A gentleman from Provence

Thomas-François-Antoine-Xavier Imbert de Lebret was born in Le Canet, near Marseille, on 5 November 1760. His father, Claude Imbert,[2] came from Aix and settled in Marseille, where he married Rose d'Artuffel. The d'Imbert and d'Artuffel families became nobility by acquiring the offices of 'Secrétaire du Roi' and 'Juge des Ports'. The family's fortune, of bourgeois origin, came from the inheritance of a great-uncle from Aix, whose name they took as 'Lebret'. It was his elder brother, Jacques-Anne-Magloire, born in 1749, to whom Xavier owed his career, his network and his title of Baron: this brilliant officer of the regiment Royal-Roussillon covered himself in glory during the Corsican campaign (1768–70) and received from King Louis XVI, as a reward for his services, the cross of knighthood in the military order of St Louis and the title of baron (which transferred to his brother Xavier d'Imbert after Jacques' death).

Jacques also married well, which enabled him to enter the sphere of influence of the families of royal galley officers from Marseille: the de Cambray and the d'Heureux.[3] Among the witnesses, Joseph-Gabriel de Cambray, captain with the regiment Reine-Infanterie, undoubtedly facilitated the entry of young Xavier into this regiment of infantry in 1774. At the age of fourteen, Xavier was trained as a soldier in Italy and Spain.[4] His older brother helped him obtain a place as an aspirant guard in the Marine Royale.[5]

Under the impetus of Richelieu and then Colbert at the end of the seventeenth century, the State undertook the training of future naval

Imbert family coat of arms, found in Artefeuil's genealogy in 1786. Motto: Nullis parcendo periculis (Sparing no danger).
(Wikimedia Creative Commons)

Stamp with the arms of the 'd'Imbert' family, on a certificate issued to one of his agents, Malus du Mesnil, by the Baron d'Imbert in 1815. (Service Historique de la Défense, Vincennes)

officers, the Gardes de la Marine, in order to create a homogeneous 'corps'. The 'Grand Corps' underwent vicissitudes throughout the eighteenth century, but nonetheless remained a source of social advancement because, unlike the army, there was no venality in office and, even if one had to be a 'gentleman' to enter, very recent nobility was not an obstacle. Inheritance practices placed cadets in a situation of dependence and insecurity,[6] which is why joining the Marine Royale offered them an advantageous prospect: they received a salary (which was modest and paid irregularly, hence the indebtedness of the poorest officers – as in the case of the Chevalier d'Imbert) and, above all, the prospect of a retirement pension.

Xavier d'Imbert was appointed to the Gardes de la Marine on 9 December 1778 in Toulon, at a time when France had just joined the Americans in their War of Independence. In 1779 he embarked on *La Bourgogne* (74),[7] which was to sail from Toulon to Brest: off Gibraltar, she engaged two English fifth-rate frigates, HMS *Thetis* (32) and HMS *Montreal* (32), the second of which was captured. *La Bourgogne* then reached the English Channel as part of Comte d'Orvilliers' squadron, which, combined with Admiral Cordova's Spanish fleet, was to support a planned landing in England, an operation that ended in fiasco. On *Le Citoyen* (74) he cruised not far from the Straits of Gibraltar, staying in Malaga, La Coruña, Ferrol and Cadiz, an experience he would later use to devise a landing plan at Ferrol with Sir Home Popham.

The American War of Independence
On board *Le Citoyen*, part of the Comte de Grasse's squadron, d'Imbert sailed for America and took part in numerous battles: the battle of Martinique (29 April 1781), the capture of Tobago (24 May 1781) and the capture of Yorktown (28 September–19 October 1781). As a midshipman in 1781, he took part in the Battle of Frigate Bay, off the coast of St Kitts in the West Indies, in January 1782. During the Battle of The Saintes, off the island of Dominica, on 12 April 1782, all the senior officers on his ship were killed. Finding themselves alone on the forecastle, the two young midshipmen, Xavier d'Imbert and Marie-Gabriel de Chieusses de

Combaud,[8] took command of *Le Northumberland* (74), which was dismasted in the middle of the battle, and brought it safely back to port.

When peace was signed, he was in Porto Bello, embarked on *Le Souverain* (74), which was disarmed in Toulon in August 1783. He was then summoned to Lorient to testify at the council of war for Admiral de Grasse, who was on trial for his defeat at The Saintes: d'Imbert's logbook[9] has been preserved and bears witness to his seriousness and the quality of his observations.[10] One of the jurors on the council of war was Captain Antoine Bruny d'Entrecasteaux, who later asked the King to reward d'Imbert for his conduct during the battle.

Counter-monsoon expedition with Chevalier d'Entrecasteaux

In 1784 d'Imbert joined the frigate *La Vénus* (38), which accompanied *La Résolution* (50), commanded by Chevalier d'Entrecasteaux, on a hydrographic mission to the Indian Ocean. He transferred to *La Résolution* in October of that year. The frigates were ready to leave in March 1785, but the order to sail was late in arriving and they did not leave Brest until 9 May. The peace agreement signed with England stipulated that no ships of the line were to be stationed in the Indies. However, the presence of the powerful English East India Company gave the English a major advantage (the French had trading posts there and only one port: Trincomalee, a Dutch base with no resources). Political considerations undoubtedly delayed the departure order, as the Minister for the Navy, Maréchal de Castries, was afraid of a resumption of hostilities with the English and wanted to entrust d'Entrecasteaux with a genuine naval intelligence mission in India.[11] The many reports that d'Entrecasteaux sent to Castries show that the latter took the training of young midshipmen very seriously, and he promoted some of them, in particular d'Imbert, whom he promoted to lieutenant 2nd class on 1 May 1786.

Two memoranda from the King, arriving in June 1786, tasked d'Entrecasteaux with a mission to China to promote French trade. He sailed a 'counter-monsoon' course through the Sunda Strait (Indonesia) and arrived at Canton, China.[12] This voyage was formative for the young man, who was learning about naval intelligence. D'Imbert's later accounts distorted certain facts to give himself greater credibility. For example, he said he had met the explorer Jean François de Galaup, Comte de Lapérouse, but *La Résolution* arrived in Macao on 7 February 1787, whereas Lapérouse's expedition had left Macao for Manila on 5 February, two days earlier: d'Entrecasteaux himself regretted this.[13] *La Résolution* arrived in Pondicherry (Puducherry), India on 26 April 1787 after a five-month voyage against the monsoon. D'Imbert fell ill and returned to France.

In the service of the counter-revolution 1790–1800

When d'Imbert disembarked in Lorient on 2 April 1788, France was in the throes of a serious political and financial crisis and King Louis XVI was preparing to convene the Etats Généraux. But, in July 1789, the Etats Généraux were transformed into the National Constituent Assembly. Unrest broke out in the countryside during the 'Great Fear': the King's brother, the Comte d'Artois, fled to Turin and many nobles followed suit.

The troubles of the Revolution broke out early in the harbours, particularly in Toulon, with massacres in August. In December 1789, an insurrection led to the imprisonment of the Commander of the Navy, Comte d'Albert de Rioms, and triggered the first wave of departures of officers, initially in the form of leave. The naval officers of 1789, 'educated, cultured, polite, open to new ideas, attached to the king and Catholic',[14] were not opposed to the reforms, but the impunity of the mutineers in the ports called into question any exercise of authority. Anarchy spread throughout the navy[15] and sailors disobeyed orders and refused to 'weigh anchor for any operation of any significance'.[16] Faced with insubordination and a permanent state of insurrection, some officers simply resigned, while others joined the army of the Princes (the brothers of King Louis XVI) and in particular the 'Regiment d'Hector',[17] in whose service many naval officers died during the disastrous Quiberon Expedition of 1795.

The Assembly passed a law to remedy absenteeism and oblige all officers who were absent or outside the kingdom to return to their posts. The decree of 29 April 1791 abolished the Marine 'Grand Corps' and reorganised the 'cadres' by including officers from the Merchant Navy. D'Imbert[18] did not attend the General Review decreed on 15 March 1792.[19] He would later say that it had 'brought about the destruction of this ancient and respectable Corps of the Marine Royale'.

The authorities were aware that the flight of officers to foreign armies posed a security problem, so measures were taken: a 'penal code for ships' (22 August 1790) associated treason with 'perfidious intelligence with the enemy'. The decree of 9 October 1792 punished by death any *émigré* caught carrying arms.[20] Finally, a decree dated 16 June 1793 legislated on 'French or foreigners convicted of spying in places of war or in armies'.[21]

The first wave of emigration mainly affected general and flag officers: 67 per cent of navy lieutenants were still active, as they hoped for quick promotions. The Tuileries insurrection on 10 August 1792 (which changed France from a constitutional monarchy to a republic) marked the start of mass emigration of naval officers, who were persecuted, arrested and summarily executed.[22] Nobility who chose to serve the Revolution lost their titles in 1793.

In 1789, Chevalier d'Imbert was twenty-nine years old. After spending

The Storming of the Tuileries, 10 August 1792. Oil on canvas by Jacques Bertaus (1741–1813). (Musée de l'Histoire de France)

almost ten years at sea, he had taken leave and was in Paris, where he frequented a club, the Salon Français, a veritable 'school for royalist spies'. Its members were young aristocrats, mostly from the southern nobility. The police court closed the club in April 1790, but its members continued to meet in secret to prepare counter-revolutionary actions in liaison with emigrants in Turin.[23] They drew up a plan for an insurrection in south-eastern France, but they quickly abandoned the plan because Louis XVI and the Princes (the King's two brothers in exile) considered it too dangerous.[24] They also tried to make the King flee, but without success.

D'Imbert was involved in all the young nobles' attempts to 'save the king'. On 28 February 1791, he took part in what the Jacobin press called the 'conspiracy of the Knights of the Dagger'.[25] After the King's arrest at Varennes in June 1791, the members of the Salon dispersed to work more or less independently of each other for the restoration of the monarchy, crossing paths as events unfolded. Some, like d'Imbert, remained in Paris to take part in the demonstrations of 20 June and the insurrection of 10 August 1792.[26]

After all these setbacks, he was tempted to emigrate but thought he could be useful to the royalists in the Midi organised around the Marquis de Miran, who needed accomplices in the military. D'Imbert chose to rejoin the navy,[27] from which he had been struck off the rolls following his absence from the General Review:

> I had to try to raise the throne as an officer, as head of the corps, and as someone who had received secret instructions from Louis XVI's ministers to direct maritime operations in the interests of the monarchy. I did so.

He was promoted to captain on 1 January 1793 and, above all, was appointed by Monge, Minister of the Navy, to lead a squadron destined to collect wheat in Algiers. This surprising appointment for someone, who was suspect and compromised with the most extreme royalists, leaves no doubt that he benefited from complicities in the Ministry of the Navy.[28] With the 'delivery' of Toulon to the English, the revolutionary Paul Barras reported to the Committee of Public Safety his suspicions of d'Imbert:

> I must remind you of a fact, fellow citizens, which may throw some light on the treachery with which we are surrounded. In January or February last, I learned that the Minister of the Navy had just promoted to the rank of captain and given command of a vessel to the scoundrel Imbert, from Marseille, whom I had lost sight of a long time ago, whom I even believed to have emigrated, and who was nevertheless in Paris; after inquiring about this Imbert, whom I considered to be suspicious, I ascertained that members of the Military Committee had issued a decree in favour of this vile brigand, who had long since been struck off the naval roll.[29]

This document, produced at the very time of the events and emanating from the opposing camp, is all the more interesting as it proves the 'Intelligence' prior to the Toulon event, whereas d'Imbert has often been criticised for exaggerating his role and had later difficulty proving that he had really been an agent with 'secret orders'.

At the same time, Antoine-Claude Rey, a former lieutenant general of the police in Lyon, was setting up one of the first networks of French spies in the pay of England. Indeed, before their expulsion in 1792, it was the English ambassadors who sent the War Office reports on the state of the ports and the fleet of the kingdom of France.[30] After that, spies had to be maintained. Rey provided England with a *Mémoire sur les ports de France* dated 5 January 1793.[31] Like d'Imbert, he was in Paris at the start of the Revolution and, more importantly, was a member of the Salon Français. Rey proposed to indicate the state of the garrisons and ships in the ports of Brest, Toulon, Rochefort and Saint-Malo. Above all, in this memorandum, he proposed organising a spy network and indicated that he would delegate trusted agents to the ports. The British Foreign Office accepted this plan and sent agents to the ports with the task, in addition to providing intelligence, of 'warming the spirits with money underhand'.[32]

Although his naval knowledge may have provided information or ideas for the *Memoire*, d'Imbert was not an agent in Rey's network. William Huskisson,[33] assistant to the British Ambassador to France, was critical of Rey and his network for hiding behind the cloak of secrecy, causing the English to doubt their existence. [34]

In January 1793, d'Imbert was still in Paris and postponed his mission to Toulon 'to try to save the king'. After Louis XVI's execution, he left for Toulon.

The 'delivery' of Toulon to the English

When d'Imbert arrived in Toulon, the mission the Republic had entrusted him with to the Dey of Algiers had been given to another,[35] which no doubt saved his life. On 12 May, Rear-Admiral Trogoff appointed him to command a third-rate ship of the line, *L'Apollon* (74),[36] whose crew, most of whom were from Ponente, were particularly undisciplined. Toulon was still run by Jacobins who, on the night of 19 to 20 May 1793, imprisoned seventy-two notables in Fort Lamalgue, including twenty-five captains (among them d'Imbert) and twenty-five other military and civil officers. This provoked indignation among the population and, just as the prisoners were about to be executed, they were finally freed by an anti-Jacobin revolt that dismissed the revolutionary club and reopened the 'Sections'; civil committees that met to make decisions on behalf of the town.

In the spring of 1793, several so-called 'federalist' uprisings broke out in the south of France.[37] Initially, the reaction in Toulon was not royalist, and the sectionnaires protested within the framework of republican institutions by addressing grievances to the Convention. Royalist sympathies did not manifest themselves 'openly', but d'Imbert 'worked' – conspired – to transform this anti-Jacobin revolt into a royalist revolt, as Gauthier de Brécy, then director of customs in Toulon, and who took an active part in the events, wrote:

> Baron d'Imbert, one of the commanders of the squadron, who had known my principles for a long time, secretly opened up to me. He believed that

the moment had come to arouse the spirits, to excite the royalists, and to prepare all the necessary arrangements for the return of the monarchy. We agreed to direct all our movements in this single spirit, and we found many collaborators in this great work.[38]

D'Imbert added: 'We sought to intimidate some and bring back others. We worked tirelessly and in concert to direct public opinion.'[39] One of d'Imbert's main qualities was his ability to seduce and convince: it is hardly surprising that he succeeded, as he claimed, in overcoming the indecision of the head of the navy, Rear-Admiral Trogoff, who was overwhelmed by events and who asked the Minister of the Navy in vain for his recall.

The Toulon royalists were strengthened by the arrival of federalist leaders from Marseille, whose revolt had just been crushed by General Carteaux's armies. The Marseillais had already attempted negotiations with Admiral Samuel Hood's English fleet, which had been cruising off Marseille and Toulon since April and had been joined by Admiral Juan de Langara's Spanish fleet.

First, the inhabitants of Toulon had to be won over to the cause. According to William S Cormarck, 'Toulon's alliance with the British and its declaration of the monarchy was less a royalist coup than an act of desperation.'[40] That 'desperation of the Toulon people' was due to a 'programmed famine' brought about by another member of the Salon Français, the merchant Regny,[41] who maintained a network of speculators, causing a rise in the price of wheat in Genoa and rumours of an imminent famine in Toulon. D'Imbert confirmed this 'plot' in a note he later wrote for the English government, who wanted to know, in August 1803, whether the Toulon operation could be repeated at Rochefort:

> It is essential to note that the English did not use any means of seduction in Toulon. Discontent and famine determined the insurrection […] Circumstances are not the same today in Rochefort and the same means will not be used there. There are undoubtedly many discontented people, but they are much more timid, and their tired energy, compressed by ten years of revolution and tyranny, needs to be powerfully stirred up. These always infallible motives for popular insurrections do not exist in Rochefort and it is therefore necessary to resort to other means.[42]

D'Imbert also manoeuvred the Sections so that Louis XVII, 'the child of the Temple', would be recognised as the legitimate sovereign. He drafted a proclamation to this effect.[43] However, the squadron was not in the same frame of mind as the people of Toulon and d'Imbert himself was challenged on his ship *L'Apollon* when he made his crew wear the white cockade (a symbol of the royalists). The royalists worried, not only about the inhabitants of Toulon, but also about the crews of the fleet: the sailors from the Ponant region were reputed to be much more republican (and especially anti-English) than the sailors from Provence, most of whom had their families in the town. Rear-Admiral Saint-Julien had taken command of the Escadre de la Méditerranée and opposed the decisions taken by the Toulon General Committee, which preferred to cooperate with Admiral Hood. Saint-Julian had people arrested who were on flag-of-truce boats.

Jean-Baptiste Pasquier, flag captain of *Le Commerce de Marseille* (118), judged, 'the large number of crew from outside our region […] greatly diminished the strength of the royalists due to the impossibility of knowing the pure feelings of each person …. On 24 August, surrounded by all sorts of dangers, we proclaimed our legitimate sovereign, King Louis XVII, son of Louis XVI.'[44] As a member of the General Committee, Pasquier led a delegation of Toulon residents onto the ships in the harbour to invite them to swear loyalty to the King, provoking the anger of the fiercely republican *Ponant* crew. *L'Apollon*'s doctor, Pierre Bonvalet, described the scene as follows:

> The unrest was so great that on board several ships, gantlines had been hung from the ends of the yards for their captains, who were suspected of belonging to the city's party, and if General Trogoff had appeared on board, he would have been done for.[45]

In fact, it was a diversionary manoeuvre that had been d'Imbert's idea: he set sail from the nearby town of Hyères with the mayor of the town,[46] the doctor Geay and the Marseillais Jean-Joseph Abeille to go on board HMS *Victory* to negotiate the surrender of the town with Lord Hood. D'Imbert gave Admiral Hood 'a moral and material picture of the French squadron',[47] without concealing from him the resistance of the *Ponant* sailors and the existence of powerful Jacobins in Toulon. It was agreed that a blue flag would be raised at the top of Fort Lamalgue once the situation was under control.

On the evening of 24 August, Lieutenant Crook brought Admiral Hood's offer to the General Committee. He promised to come to the aid of the Toulon people on condition that the ships were disarmed and the forts placed at the disposal of the English. The General Committee deliberated and decided to accept the English offer. A tug-of-war between the town and the squadron began: it was to last three days.

Finally, on 27 August, d'Imbert, Barallier and Deydier de Pierrefeu guided the Anglo-Spanish troops who had landed under the command of Lord Keith at Fort Lamalgue, where they took possession. The blue flag then flew over the

Introduction des Anglais dans le port de Toulon. Le 28 août 1793, engraving from a painting by François Feraud, c1795. On 28 August, the Toulon roadstead was opened to the English ships commanded by Admiral Hood and to their allies; on 15 September, Hood received the keys to the city and the French fleet. (Private collection)

Grosse-Tour and the fort: on 28 August 1793, the Anglo-Spanish fleet entered Toulon harbour. There, English, Spanish, Sardinian and Piedmontese troops disembarked and Lord Hood took possession of the town and the arsenal in the name of 'Louis XVII'.

Officers and sailors from *Ponant* who wished to return home received their wages and were allowed to embark on four ships bound for Brest, Lorient and Rochefort. *L'Apollon* was part of the voyage, and d'Imbert put his second in command and stayed behind in Toulon. He later wrote:

> The officers who were sent on board the four ships of Rear Admiral Bouvet were charged (and principally this worthy admiral) with restoring the spirit of the sailors to the principles of the legitimate monarchy and bringing about a great movement on all the coasts of western France.[48]

It does not seem that these officers and sailors left with such intentions. Nevertheless, the revolutionary courts sentenced most of them to death upon their arrival in the western ports.

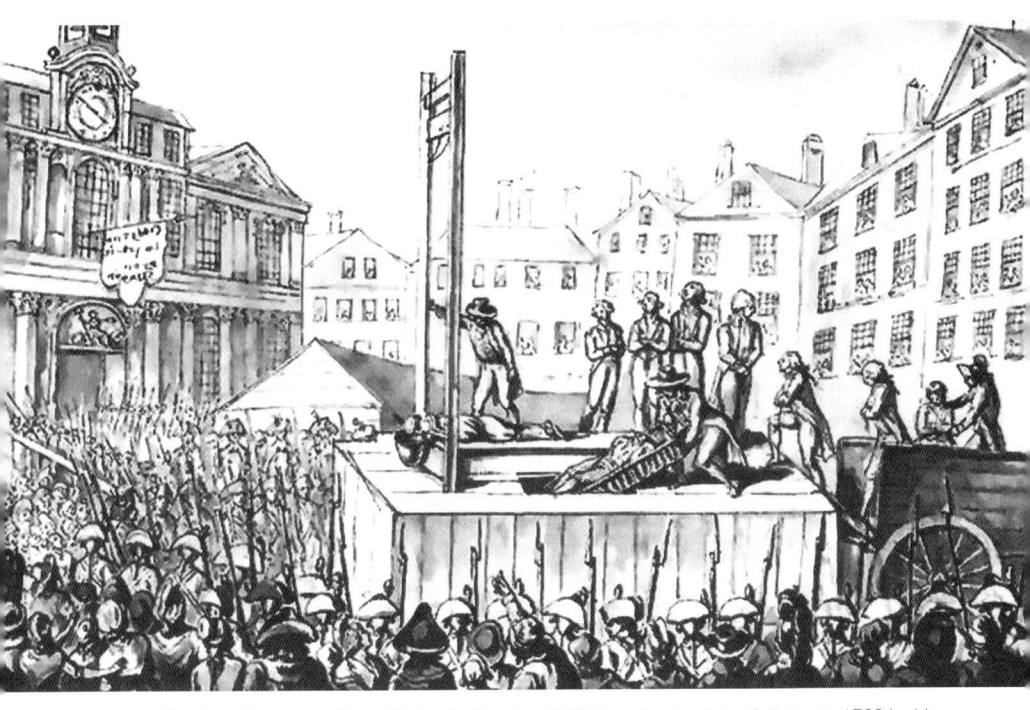

Nine émigrés executed by guillotine in October 1793 from the book *La Guillotine in 1793* by H Fleishman (1908). Artist unknown. (Wikipedia)

From Toulon, d'Imbert and Gauthier de Brécy attempted to provoke a royalist uprising in Languedoc, but letters addressed to the inhabitants of Cette (now Sète) and Agde containing proclamations in the name of Louis XVII were seized.[49]

The occupation of Toulon ended with the strategic takeover of the forts and redoubts by the Republican armies of Bonaparte and Dugommier. As the safety of the allied vessels anchored in the roadstead was no longer guaranteed, the port was evacuated on 18 December 1793.

In his *Précis historique sur les événements de Toulon en 1793,* published in 1814 at the time of the Restoration of the Monarchy, d'Imbert went against the official line that the Toulon revolt was an outright popular royalist revolt. By publicising his role as an agitator, he was going to upset public opinion, because any manipulation of the citizenry, even if the end goal was laudable, was morally degrading. This is the paradox of the secret agent. However, in his mind, contrary to what many historians have likened to 'treason', d'Imbert did not 'deliver the port and the ships to the English' but 'returned them to his

King'. Gauthier de Brécy, for his part, said that they had opened the gates of Toulon, not to foreigners but 'to the friends of the Bourbons'.[50] They had 'not betrayed France, but the Republic'.

As Jennifer Mori has written, it was the Toulon revolt and Lord Hood's agreement to retain Toulon 'in the name of the Bourbons' that led the English government to clarify its political position towards the princes in exile and to formalise its support for the counter-revolution:[51] 'The Pitt ministry was moving towards royalism but was not yet prepared to make public statements to this effect. Hood was rebuked for having taken Toulon in the name of Louis XVII.'[52] Indeed, the English Parliament had rather welcomed the Revolution in as it weakened France; the notable exception was Edmund Burke, who feared the spread of the anarchic principles of the French Revolution.[53] Burke's warnings were increasingly echoed after the insurrection of 10 August, the massacres of September and the death of Louis XVI. However, even after France declared war on Great Britain and the Netherlands on 1 February 1793, ambiguity remained. George Grenville, the Foreign Secretary, for example, preferred to wait and see: he thought that 'the best prospect of destroying the Revolution lay in leaving it alone'.[54]

Support for the royalists at home was tactical rather than ideological. Hence the distrust of the royalists towards the British government: the vast majority were not fooled but lacked the logistical or financial means to work towards the restoration of the throne without British financial and logistical support, hence the sometimes biased reports of certain royalist *émigrés*. Francis Drake for example, a British diplomat to Genoa, had come to distrust, quite rightly, the information obtained by the d'Antraigues network[55]. Mutual distrust – justified since the aims were obviously not the same – was not likely to encourage reliable and therefore effective intelligence.

It should be noted that it was only at the end of December 1793 that 'the destruction of the atrocious system now prevailing in France had been added to the government's list of official war aims'.[56] But it was too late, and David Hannay, in 1898, writing a review of Cottin's book,[57] clearly expressed Pitt's monumental error at the time:[58]

When Hood's request for reinforcements reached England there were no men to send, because our little army was scattered all over the world on small expeditions employed in nibbling at the colonial possessions of France. The same number of men concentrated at Toulon and used with spirit would have raised the siege and would have served as a rallying-point for the Moderates and Royalists of the South. Then the destructive career of the Jacobin Republic might have been cut short in the beginning and Europe might have escaped Napoleon, – for the greater good of herself and of France.

The Toulon affair was a missed opportunity. From January 1794 onwards, France would sink into the bureaucratisation of the Terror. In his writings, d'Imbert never ceased to regret the failure at Toulon. At the time, he had had the impression that the royalist victory was within reach, that it would have spared France '20 years of misfortune': the people of Toulon, the naval officers and the royalist agents would have been heroes and not traitors accused of having delivered 'Toulon to the English', a stain from which they would never rid themselves, even once the monarchy had been re-established – thanks to the English, incidentally!

Fugitive in Italy
The failure at Toulon really 'turned him around': d'Imbert became an 'adventurer' desperately seeking funds to 'conspire' to re-establish the monarchy, but also to ensure his survival and that of the henchmen he liked to surround himself with.

The evacuees from Toulon were landed at Mahon, Porto-Ferraio or Livorno. The Chevalier d'Imbert joined his brother and cousins, naval officers who had emigrated to Turin in 1791 to join the future Louis XVIII, where they died 'as a result of the misfortunes of their long exile'.[59] Even though, at the end of 1793, Pitt saw the need to re-establish the monarchy in France, his conception of the monarchy did not coincide with that of the Bourbon Princes in exile. Pitt did not want the return of an *ancien régime* monarchy and 'the Parliament disliked the French Bourbons intensely'.[60] It is easy to imagine the conflict of loyalties and consciences of the French royalist secret agents. In 1795 the English government devised a plan to carry out coordinated attacks in France with insurrections fomented by royalist agents paid by the English: the idea of William Widham, Secretary at War, was to provide armed support for these actions from within, and above all to 'turn' a republican general and his army. But, as Elizabeth Sparrow explained, 'The weakness of the system was that agents provided information with more regard for their salaries than the truth. Espionage was a lucrative business.'[61] At the end of 1795, with the advent of the Directoire, the British fear of the spread of anarchy diminished and 'the war of principle' was abandoned in the belief that it would be possible to find reasonable common ground with the new French government. However, negotiations broke down in December 1796 and the Directoire's warlike tendencies led to fears of an armed French invasion rather than the spread of the principles of the Revolution, although some in Ireland used these to destabilise England.

During his long stay in Italy, d'Imbert sought employment, particularly with the English ambassadors: he went to Verona, Venice and then Florence, but was driven out by the arrival of French troops. He went to Rome, then Naples and finally Palermo. He tried to obtain command of an artillery company in Corsica, but Lord Minto preferred another naval officer, Chevalier de Sade. Mr Reboul, former president of the General Committee of Toulon, summed up d'Imbert's activities in Italy as follows: 'Since the evacuation of Toulon, he has always sought to be useful to the British government. However, if he sought to be useful, he could not be and certainly was not useful.'[62]

In 1800, d'Imbert embarked on the corvette *L'Espérance* with Marquis de Colbert-Cannet, who was sailing the Mediterranean under the royalist white flag. Colbert-Cannet, who had joined the Russian Navy,[63] worked with Chevalier de Vernègues on an attempted insurrection in Provence instigated by the former revolutionary General Amédée Willot, whom Louis XVIII had appointed 'Governor of the Southern Provinces' in 1800.[64] The conspiracy failed due to internal quarrels.

After the failure of the various conspiracies and landings, largely due to differences of opinion between the princes in exile and the allied foreign powers, and with the prospect of the restoration of the monarchy receding, the Bourbons developed a strategy of political waiting which 'consisted of fuelling the feeling of attachment to royalty in the population, but, *de facto*, discouraging action'.[65] It is easy to see how this placed our royalist 'activists' in a highly ambiguous position, foreshadowing the way in which they would be (dis)regarded at the time of the Restoration.

Finally, the Directoire (1795–99) had encouraged the return of fourteen thousand emigrants (who mainly returned for economic rather than political reasons). After his *coup d'état* in November 1799, Bonaparte promised further amnesties, particularly for the rebels in the Vendée and Brittany. In 1800, many *émigrés* asked to be struck off the List of *Émigrés* (those who left France and were condemned as traitors to the Revolution), tired of exile and poverty and convinced that Bonaparte would favour the return of the Bourbons. Joseph Fouché, Minister of the Police, established a system of controlled amnesties[66] to prevent dangerous activists from spreading throughout the country. D'Imbert, with his action in Toulon, was still an 'undesirable' and his amnesty was unthinkable: in charge of his two orphaned nephews, having exhausted all his resources, he decided to go to England from Lisbon: 'Sir Sidney Smith having arrived in this port towards the end of November, I went with him on the frigate which took him to England, I arrived in London on 18 December 1801.'[67]

In the pay of England 1801–07
When d'Imbert arrived in England in December 1801, his aim was to find a means of subsistence in line with what he loved and knew how to do: devise plans and conspire. The failure of the Second Coalition and the signing of the Peace of Amiens on 25 March 1802 brought this type of activity to a halt and d'Imbert analysed it well himself:

> Soon the breaking of the treaty of Amiens seemed to change the negative dispositions of the English treasury. I was known to the English Ministry as one of Louis XVIII's most zealous servants and an essential man to employ either because of my ascendancy over a host of brave French officers or because of my experience as a sailor and my connections in the various ports of France or on the French coast. Towards the end of 1803, the noble MacArthur, whom I had once known as secretary to Admiral Hood, was sent to me by the Ministry of War to invite me to draw up a plan for invading France in the interests of the King.[68]

Indeed, d'Imbert teamed up with Sir Home Popham to draw up the plan in question, and the two of them raised the initial funds for the first expedition.[69] It is hardly surprising that these two found each other: d'Imbert and Popham were exactly the same age,[70] had the same controversial personality and the same taste for intrigue.[71] Their plan called for a major expedition to the Ferrol, supported by a squadron commanded by Sir Home Popham. Mr MacArthur was to be employed as administrator and d'Imbert as chief officer.

Advance funding had made it possible to send, in 1803, two Toulon midshipmen, Rossolin and Cocampot, to find out about the Ferrol fleet and to travel to France to sound out the opinion of the inhabitants of Bordeaux. However, in the report of the expedition,[72] we learn that the plan was already known to the French and the two spies were immediately arrested and suspected:

> by the last notices we had received from Ireland, we were warned that the English were sending spies on all sides with the aim of raising new *Vendées*, and that the same notices announced that Admiral Popham was in charge of a secret expedition to the coasts of France, all that came from England had to be regarded as suspicious.

They managed to escape, thanks to the royalist sympathies of the locals, and even managed to obtain a recommendation in Bayonne to join the fleet of Rear-Admiral Bedout, commander of the French division at Ferrol. However, the two agents were denounced and were unable to reach Bordeaux. They boarded Sir Edward Pellew's second-rate HMS *Tonnant* (80) and asked to return to London. They reported on the French naval forces (and in particular the construction of flat-bottomed ships – therefore intended for a landing – at Bayon), of which Rossolin wrote, 'The general opinion is that they are nothing but scarecrows to keep the people entertained with the idea of invasion.'

Like Popham, d'Imbert had a talent for making lots of enemies. He upset the small group of Toulon refugees settled in England and proclaimed himself their leader, negotiating an increase in their salaries with the Treasury on their behalf: his purpose was to recruit future agents for his network. He gave his opinion on each emigrant, measuring their zeal and whether they were capable of fulfilling any mission of trust.[73]

Former Toulon officers who had taken refuge in London wrote to the Treasurer to complain about d'Imbert's manoeuvres: he had been sowing discord among them for two years. They described him as 'a junior officer born with a vivid imagination and perhaps too much ambition' who did 'not respect age and seniority'.[74] They gave accounts of the methods of intimidation that d'Imbert and his recruit, Midshipman Rossolin, used against them.

Comte d'Artois was in London at the time and maintained a spy agency run by Dutheil, who had the confidence of British spymaster William Wickham and Lord Grenville. Louis XVIII, who also had his own 'agency', wanted to supervise spying activities so that they did not damage the image of the royalty, especially among the royalists at home. This is why d'Artois had proposed a

> plan approved by the King, who alone knows the totality of it [...] the agents will have to make themselves always independent of the instructions which could be given to the English; the second object of the English correspondence will be to give them all the intelligences which tend to the service of the cause, but never those whose result could be to facilitate to them the capture of some of our maritime places, and in general none which would have utility only for them.[75]

It is clear that d'Imbert's plans put him at odds with the King's recommendations.[76]

The reorganisation of the French police under the Directoire and then the Consulate made them much more efficient, and they could now track down royalist agents as far away as England. One of the spies employed by Talleyrand, Nicolas-Etienne-Charles Sandillaud du Bouchet,[77] arrived in London in April 1804. This former agent of the princes in exile, who returned to Paris on 6 November of the same year, described the London 'conspiracy' milieu that he had managed to infiltrate by renewing old acquaintances:

It took me few days, in these various coalitions, to convince myself of the imperialism, the extravagance, the vanity, and above all the greed of some of these individuals, who believe themselves to be in London the most important spring of the counter-revolutionary political machine. A few days after my arrival, the English Ministry asked for details of the position of the coasts of France, which I said I had visited as an observer [...] The way in which this note was received convinced me that this Ministry was very little or very poorly informed about the nature of the forces gathered on the coasts of France, since what I said at random was taken for real. [...] Among the individuals who exhausted the heat of their imagination on finesse for projects that had no follow-up and contradicted each other, the most cited were the Baron de Roll, Dutheil, Willot, the former minister Bertrand [de Molleville] and the Baron d'Imbert [...] Captain of a vessel of the Republic, one of those who fetched the English to bring them to Toulon in 1793. Because this individual has from time to time sent a few lost children to sail along the coasts of Rochefort and the port of Ferrol, and because they have returned to England, he believes he has been transplanted to [do] great things. He also claims to have great connections in Marseille and Toulon, but I am sure of the opposite. It was between him, Admiral Popham and another English officer that the plan was made to set fire to the French ships in Ferrol.[78]

The failure of his first plan did not discourage d'Imbert and he devised a new one, which was approved by the English government in October 1804 in the person of Edward Cooke, Under-secretary of War, who was to provide the funds. The plan called for an invasion with a landing of troops (requiring accurate information on the defence of the coasts), a plot for an internal uprising (requiring knowledge of the attitudes of the inhabitants) and the corruption of a general (or naval officers).

The activities of the 'Imbert network' were documented in French police bulletins. The chief, Fouché, had reorganised the general police force. Pierre-Marie Desmarets directed the secret agents in France and abroad, receiving reports from them and producing a daily intelligence bulletin for Fouché. Then, Fouché gave Napoleon a copy, annotated in his own hand.[79]

At the end of 1804, Pierre-Paul Dubuc and Jean-Jacques Rossolin, d'Imbert's two agents, disembarked in France with the mission of providing information on French forces and plans, obtaining intelligence in Boulogne and Rochefort

The Coronation of Napoleon, by Jacques-Louis David (1748–1825), 1804. (Louvre, Paris)

in the offices and army, identifying friends loyal to the Bourbon cause and approaching generals and civil officers and making proposals to them. D'Imbert set up a network with all the subterfuge of spies: false names and the use of sympathetic (invisible) ink in correspondence, the recipe for which was supplied to him by the former Minister of the Navy, Bertrand de Molleville, who liked to try out recipes[80] and whose code name was 'Mme Cholet'.

Dubuc[81] was a former merchant navy officer who had been taken prisoner in England after the surrender of Pondicherry, where he had been stationed. D'Imbert was staying with Sir Rupert Georges, President of the Transport Office, when he recognised the name Dubuc, whom he had met in India. He approached him, mentioned their relationship and asked Dubuc to serve the Bourbon cause. Dubuc was the ideal person to approach the generals of the Empire to 'corrupt' them. He would be sent to France under his real identity on a flag-of-truce boat, taking advantage of a prisoner exchange. However, the English were suspicious of Dubuc and demanded that d'Imbert send one of his most trusted men to keep an eye on him: this would be Rossolin's mission, and he embarked with Dubuc as a merchant.

The manoeuvre was clever, because when they landed in Morlaix in November 1804 the French did not suspect Dubuc, and even asked him to vouch for Rossolin. The deception was perfect and the two agents settled in Paris, where Dubuc even managed to obtain a passport for Rossolin, who was due to travel to Marseille. Unfortunately, Rossolin trusted the 'double agent' Sandilleau du Bouchet,[82] whom he believed to be one of them because he had seen him in London with d'Imbert. Du Bouchet denounced him and the *Bulletin* of 2 May 1805[83] informed Napoleon that 'Dubuc and Rossolin, spies for England, have been arrested in Paris'. Their correspondence and the funds they had with the Perrégaux bankers were seized.

At the Emperor's request, the two agents were brought before a special military commission set up by decree on 6 July 1804.[84] They were shot on 31 May 1805. The press carried the details. For example, the *Moniteur Universel* of 2 June 1805[85] reported the accusation made by the Commissaire-Rapporteur:

> And these culprits are not of the kind of obscure spies that the subaltern agents of the English governments send from time to time to our coasts, to find out about the state of our armaments, to spy on the departure of a convoy, or to go by night and avoid the police, from farm to farm to gather the musings of some rebellious Chouans, who are delirious because of poverty and fear. [...] The spies whose fate you are about to decide are of a different quality. The Toulon refugees, whose number of officers and sailors is estimated at around 500, remain, while waiting to 'throw them into the South' via Spain, as an available fund, and since the destruction or submission of a large number of the Chouans leaders, Baron d'Imbert, with his Toulon refugees, is, for the English police, what Georges [Cadoudal] was with his Breton sailors and peasants.

The treatment meted out to d'Imbert's agents was particularly harsh, especially as the French police were convinced that the mission had achieved nothing.[86] D'Imbert even reproached his agents in letters dated 31 March and 2 April 1805 for their lack of progress. Rossolin confessed only to having warned Dubuc of the fleet's departure from Toulon, thus showing that he had a correspondent in that port, whom he refused to name.

D'Imbert's agents were caught when naval espionage was of particular concern to Napoleon, who felt on 6 May 1805 that 'at a time when [he] was moving so many squadrons, it [was] necessary to crack down on spies'.[87]

D'Imbert, unaware of the fate of his agents, continued to send them letters,

A page of the letter from d'Imbert to Dubuc mentioned in the *Bulletin*, Saturday, 25 May 1805: Fouché revealed to the security magistrate that the letter contained a secret message from d'Imbert to Dubuc in invisible ink: 'I have finally received, my dear Dubuc, your letter of 10 February …' The letter is signed 'David'; d'Imbert's pseudonym. (French National Archives, Paris)

one of which, seized the day after Dubuc's execution,

had undergone various chemical tests, carried out with all the precaution required not to alter the handwriting. The sympathetic ink is of a particular composition and absolutely different from the previous one. We finally managed to decipher it in its entirety. It is dated 14 May and signed in full (in white) by Imbert.[88]

This letter announced the arrival of a new agent called 'Michel' with 'liqueurs' for sympathetic inks.

Fouché was convinced that d'Imbert had a regular correspondence via Calais: d'Imbert had given Rossolin an itinerary entitled 'Diverses routes de Paris à Rotterdam' (Various routes from Paris to Rotterdam), which the police had seized from his papers. In it he indicated 'all the places where you can ask for passports, those where they are not required, the inns where you should stay, etc.'. Furthermore, the *Bulletin* reported:

> Finally, we note that d'Imbert wanted Dubuc to establish a coastal connection between Calais and Dunkirk. The iron box is the method that has always been used on the coast of Normandy and Saint-Malo: it is deposited in an agreed place where it is picked up, either from the land or from the sea. When the place cannot be determined with sufficient precision, a man stands on the shore and beats a lighter to signal to the rowboat. Baron d'Imbert's correspondence via Calais (as it seems certain that he has had one there for a long time) is very well followed.[89]

A page of a letter from d'Imbert to Dubuc, showing the tests to detect invisible ink carried out by agents of Fouché's police force. (French National Archives, Paris)

D'Imbert sent a new agent; another naval officer evacuated from Toulon in 1793, André Laa.[90] In 1804, he had already been sent to France[91] in his native region to try to break out another royalist agent, whose career was just as incredible as d'Imbert's, Chevalier de Rivoire St-Hyppolite, a prisoner of Bonaparte in the Château de Pau. When he arrived in Paris on 1 June 1805, Laa learned of the execution of Dubuc and Rossolin and left hastily for Bordeaux, where he was subsequently arrested.[92] The *Bulletin* of 6 July 1805 confirmed: 'We have finally acquired positive proof that Laa is indeed the emissary sent from London on 14 May by Baron d'Imbert to Dubuc, to bring him the sympathetic inks and a memorandum on the operations to be followed.' André Laa was executed on 24 July.

In London, d'Imbert was admitted to the table of Comte d'Artois, and one of Fouché's agents reported in August 1805:

All this society dreams of is an attempt on the Emperor's life, and discusses nothing but ways of achieving it, especially the Prince [d'Artois], the Baron de Roll, Dutheil, Butler and d'Imbert. All are generally despised in London, both at court and in private societies.

The English government was very suspicious – even reproachful – of these 'ultra royalists' maintained by Comte d'Artois.

D'Imbert's activity in England came to an end with his deportation, the arbitrary nature of which[93] was to fuel the parliamentary debates on the Aliens Act[94] in 1816. He was never informed of the charges against him and all his papers were seized.

A double agent? Prison, trial and a vain attempt at recognition 1807–44
As both Fouché's *Bulletin*s and Bourrienne's *Memoirs*[95] show, d'Imbert was not deported from England because he was suspected of 'being an agent of Bonaparte' but for the reasons he has always put forward: he was annoying the English Ministry by demanding payment from Edward Cooke for the costs he had incurred in financing his network of agents. He even claimed that Cooke had been involved in embezzlement. He left a detailed account of his arrest and arrival in Altona on 1 May 1807. The English newspapers had published the list of deportees, and Louis Antoine Fauvelet de Bourrienne, the French ambassador to Lower Saxony, was waiting for him when he arrived. Baron Hue and General Danican[96] escaped him, but he had d'Imbert, his sixteen-year-old nephew, his secretary and his cronies arrested.[97] Bourrienne proposed to d'Imbert that he be struck off as an emigrant in exchange for information. He agreed to collaborate but pointed out that, 'I had only served the old dynasty

and never the English; my refusal to march against Spain [when asked by the English] proves this sufficiently.'[98] D'Imbert's weariness was understandable. Worn out and disillusioned by more than fourteen years in exile, he resolved to provide the notes and information that Bourrienne requested; in particular the names of *émigrés* employed by England. Ironically, d'Imbert then denounced Du Bouchet,[99] whom he did not know was the double agent behind the failure of his network.

At Fouché's request, d'Imbert travelled to Paris, arriving on 27 January 1808, where he thought he would begin a new career as a conspirator. He was even working 'with as much zeal as pleasure'[100] on a new plan for the navy when he was arrested on 7 April 1808 and taken to La Force prison. Once again, he was denied the right to know the reasons for his arrest.

D'Imbert had arrived in France at the wrong time. Fouché implicated Bourrienne, who had 'recruited' d'Imbert, because a quantity of English goods arrived in Hamburg and Antwerp, where the blockade was ineffective. Moreover, d'Imbert was no longer of any use: as his interrogations and those of Plagnes show, Fouché was only interested in Général Dumouriez and the famous agent Puisaye, and d'Imbert had no information on them. In addition, the principal network of espionage, that of Jersey, had just been decapitated and the royalist opposition, reduced to the brigandage of some Chouans, did not frighten Napoleon any more.

D'Imbert was refused removal from the list of *émigrés* and was sent under house arrest to Dijon, without any means of support. After four years, the mayor of the town took pity on him and begged the minister to authorise him to go to Marseille where he could find some help and acquire the inheritance left by his mother, which was enjoyed by his sister-in-law, who refused to communicate with him for fear of being compromised. D'Imbert argued that he had always put his zeal and devotion solely at the service of his country and hoped to make amends for 'his political faults. Happy is the man who has not committed them during ten years of unrest and misfortune! […] A Frenchman may go astray but he always remains French.'[101] Finally, in April 1813, he was authorised to go to Marseille, still under house arrest.

La Restauration
Once the monarchy was restored in 1814, d'Imbert thought his misfortunes would come to an end. But the counter-revolutionary activism he naively boasted about in his memoirs and the *factums* he tirelessly published during this period were to do him a disservice. Like many agents suspected – rightly or wrongly – of having been double agents, he struggled to be rehabilitated after 1814 and went through a series of trials and imprisonments. For, as Kant pointed

out, once peace was restored, the deception that spies inevitably use to achieve their ends made 'mutual trust impossible'. The means employed were contrary to the chivalric spirit of the French noble ideal and to military honour.

After Napoleon's abdication, the difficult restoration of the monarchy – in a constitutional form – after twenty-five years of conflict, meant that all French people had to be accommodated, including those who had served the Empire. The return of the *émigrés* after twenty-five years of exile was not without its problems. They were vindictive against those who had served the Revolution and the Empire, and their return even upset the royalists in the 'interior'. King Louis XVIII, in a bid to appease them, granted the Charter of 1814, which established a constitutional monarchy and granted democratic freedoms to citizens.

Adding to the complexity was the question of the return of officers from the *Ancienne Marine*, most of whom had not sailed for twenty-five years. Even though Louis XVIII, in an order dated 25 May 1814, decided to reward 'the loyalty and devotion of former officers of the Navy', commissions examined each request and the terms of return were strict. The episode of the Hundred Days and Napoleon's short-lived return in 1815 caused confusion in the army and navy, and the first purge followed.[102] The Radeau de la Méduse affair in 1817 implicated an officer of the *Ancienne Marine*, captured the imagination of public opinion and served as a pretext for discrediting the former officers, who were accused of incompetence. The many letters and petitions kept in their files show how difficult it was for them to obtain justice, if only to have their record of service recognised and to maintain their retirement pensions, which were reduced by their years of exile without the possibility of serving.

In this poisonous climate, d'Imbert, who had initially been included in the Ordinance of 1814, which elevated him to the rank of rear-admiral, was soon disillusioned. Someone conveniently put the letters sent by d'Imbert to Fouché in the hands of Viscount Dubouchage, Minister of the Navy. The Minister then proposed to the King that d'Imbert be dismissed from office. D'Imbert then embarked on a series of legal actions. When he was finally reinstated in 1819, the debts he had incurred led to his imprisonment. He claimed that he was being 'spied on' and 'pursued' by ill-intentioned people. He was attacked, injured and robbed. If all this is proven by the lawsuits he won, it is difficult to say whether they were reprisals for his former activities as a spy or intimidation by his creditors.

Even though he fought hard to have his rank of rear-admiral restored and to receive a decent retirement pension, he died alone and destitute in 1844 and the State paid for his funeral. Although d'Imbert's network was less prestigious than that of others (d'Antraigues, Fauche-Borel, Philippe d'Auvergne), the fate of his agents shows that he succeeded in creating a climate of fear for Napoleon, destabilising him at a time when he was still hoping to 'land in England'.

These 'conspiratorial' *émigrés* were deliberately fostered by England in order to destabilise the enemy. Like d'Imbert, they were often former officers who had already faced danger. These officers, who had embraced the career of arms to cover themselves with glory and honours in battle, were forced to bribe their former comrades or deliver tactical information to the enemy of yesterday, in order to ensure the triumph of the noble cause that they put above all else. D'Imbert, in the midst of his setbacks in 1822, exclaimed:

> Ah! If, fulfilling the wishes of the agents of the Convention, I had followed the instructions they forced me to receive, if, gorged with gold and clothed with power, I had entered the path they wanted to mark out for me, where would I be now? Would a voice be raised to accuse me? Would my rights, my honours and my prerogatives have been disputed for a moment, and would the gates of a debtor's prison have opened to swallow me up? And where would the continuation of my military career not have led me naturally? But I regret nothing; isn't a Frenchman too happy to be able to say: I have constantly served my country and my King?[103]

The Storming of the Bastille, 1789, see colour plate 5

The Evolution of British Naval Leadership and Decision-Making in the Face of Sickness

David Rothwell

Operating successfully in the West Indies was one of the greatest challenges for European navies in the Age of Sail. It was a region that tested every aspect of a navy, from its leadership to its logistics. Also, because they were far away (about six weeks' sail from Europe, on average), operating in the West Indies forced naval officers to make decisions with limited or imperfect information about the situation in Europe. Seasonal hurricanes also forced naval officers to plan operations around nature's timeline rather than a war's. The possibility of fabulous wealth also provided countless temptations for officers to prioritise personal aggrandisement over the mission. Most of all, because of endemic tropical diseases, the West Indies exerted enormous pressure on a navy's ability to keep its men healthy.

When we study naval operations in the West Indies in the Age of Sail, we need to understand the unique pressures that these conditions put on officers' decision-making. This essay identifies three pressures that rose above the rest. First, naturally, was the mission. Officers had to consider their orders and their relationship to the strategic and operational situation. But that was not an officer's only concern. Officers also had to consider the health of their men. Sometimes officers chose to prioritise their men's health over the mission; sometimes they made the opposite choice. A third major pressure was the temptation of prize money. Because the West Indies formed the financial foundation of three major European empires, there was money to be seized and ships conducting commerce always seemed to be targets ripe for attack. Sometimes officers chose to sacrifice their orders and their men's health on the altar of glory or in the pursuit of wealth; sometimes officers chose the opposite.

We need to deepen our understanding of these pressures because there is some disagreement in the existing literature about how navies dealt with the challenges of operating in the face of endemic tropical diseases. J R McNeill and Michael Duffy have argued that naval officers prioritised mission, then glory or riches, and then health. Duffy, author of the definitive history of the British expeditions to the West Indies in the 1790s, asserts that while many naval officers avoided the West Indies, those who did go were attracted by prize money, rapid promotion and glory. Duffy notes that the common rank and file had far fewer chances of reward and thereby had far less enthusiasm. As a result, one may conclude that many naval officers, especially those who willingly elected to go to the West Indies, saw their men's lives in purely mission-driven, practical terms. The measures of protection that naval officers took to control morbidity and mortality were merely designed to increase the probability of naval effectiveness and victory.[1]

The examples of Admiral Edward Vernon,[2] Admiral George Rodney,[3] and Admiral John Jervis[4] lend support to McNeill and Duffy's argument that naval officers cared about mission and glory more than men's health. Callous and self-interested, Vernon bullied his subordinate general, Major General Thomas Wentworth.[5] Wentworth served as a replacement for two of his recently deceased superior generals and, according to Vernon, he was largely incompetent. Vernon forced Wentworth into an extended attempt to capture Cartagena de Indias (now Cartagena, Columbia) in 1741 despite layered defences and the mounting casualties posed by the rains of sickly season. Although hundreds died of fever, Vernon pushed Wentworth's forces until they were hopeless and near annihilation, finally reembarking them on 28 April. More than eight thousand men died between both army and navy. By June 1741, 77 per cent of the original nine thousand of General Cathcart's[6] force were no longer fit for service. In this, he was, like many other admirals and generals, representative of a self-interested, uncaring social structure that was devoid of sympathy and thought only of honour, glory and riches.[7]

Admiral Rodney at the Battle of the Saintes, 1783; oil painting by Thomas Gainsborough (1727–88). Behind is the French *fleur de lys* naval ensign from the captured *Ville de Paris*. (Unidentified location, Wikimedia, public domain).

Portrait of John Jervis. The inscription reads: Knight of the Bath, Admiral of the White, Commander in Chief of his Majesty's ships at the reduction of the islands of Martinque, St Lucia, Guadaloupe, Marie-Galante, … From a Capital Picture in the Possession of Francis Stephens, Esq. To whom this Plate is most Respectfully Dedicated, by his Obliged Humble Servants Laurie … Published 14th August 1794 by Robt Laurie and Ja^s Whittle, N° 53, Fleet Street, London. (Naval History and Heritage Command, Washington, DC)

George Rodney also typified this pattern of self-interest. On 16 November 1780, Rodney sailed for the West Indies without explicit orders and contrary to the will of the First Lord of the Admiralty, the Earl of Sandwich. Rodney landed in Jamaica, even though sickly season had not yet come to an end. Rodney seized St Eustatius in February 1781, and then looted and pillaged whatever he could on the island, relaxing his defences and leaving himself vulnerable to the French. Rodney's pillaging kept at least some of his force land-based through the onset of sickly season. Rodney finally exited St Eustatius for England in August 1781, having ignored both mission orders and his men's health in favour of maximising his personal gain.[8]

Finally, Duffy describes the Grey–Jervis expedition of 1794 in similar terms. John Jervis with General Charles Grey[9] took Martinique, St Lucia, and Guadeloupe by late April 1794. Jervis continued in the region, acting beyond his orders, with Grey stretching the interpretation of an order of council. Pursuing sheer avarice, Jervis stayed on or close to land after rain had begun and into sickly season, seizing American merchant vessels, and plundering as many ships and goods on the islands as possible, in part through extra-legal Admiralty prize courts. Jervis' actions resulted in the deaths of 1,225 British men from 1 April to 1 June 1794, and about two thousand sick recorded per month. Jervis' behaviour seems to confirm Rodger's description of him as a 'violent' practitioner of 'unbridled megalomania'.[10]

Erica Charters sees the hierarchy of officers' motivations differently, arguing that they did care for their men's health, and not just because doing so helped them complete their missions and win glory.[11] Cori Convertito provides data to support Charters' claims. In her study of the Leeward Islands and Jamaica Stations during the years 1773–1803, Convertito records a modest seaman sickness rate of 1 to 3 per cent for those on-board ship. Convertito calculates the overall mortality rate at these islands of 1 to 4 per cent annually, with spikes in the rate of mortality to 6 to 9 per cent in the epidemic years of 1793–98.[12] These low rates demonstrate naval officers' resolve and consistency in the protection of their seamen and soldiers.

Sir John Thomas Duckworth: mission, health and glory
One naval officer who can assist in this quest to illuminate the decision-making process is Sir John Thomas Duckworth, whose newly published papers form the heart of this project. Duckworth was a British naval officer who first entered the West Indies as a lieutenant in 1779. He served in the theatre multiple times as a captain, in 1780, 1781, and then from May 1795 to February 1797. He was made a commodore at Santo Domingo in March 1796 when Rear-Admiral William Parker[13] got sick. After a brief respite from duty, Duckworth became commodore again in 1798, and then Rear-Admiral of the White in 1799. He became Commander-in-Chief of the Leeward Islands Station in 1801 and then the Jamaica Station in 1803. He was promoted to vice-admiral in 1804. Examining how a veteran West Indies campaigner like Duckworth understood the threat of disease and tracing the steps he took to mitigate its effects will provide concrete evidence of the decision-making hierarchy – mission, health, glory – in action.

Sir John Thomas Duckworth as an Admiral, c1809–10, by William Beechey (1753–1839). (© National Maritime Museum, Greenwich, London)

The results of this research suggest that Duckworth often prioritised his duty and mission, which sometimes included obedience to an order to preserve his men's health. Next in the hierarchy, he prioritised his men's health, and finally he prioritised his own self-interest – glory or wealth – only when duty and mission and health aligned. Duckworth therefore exemplifies the shift in officer motivations identified by N A M Rodger. An older generation of naval officers, exemplified by Vernon, Rodney, and Jervis, joined the navy 'to make their fortunes'. By the 1790s, however, a new generation of officers came to see their service in different terms. Avarice and self-aggrandising glory seeking were replaced by humble and almost unwavering obedience to duty and patriotic heroism. The new naval officer and gentleman valued 'duty, self-discipline, and piety', and he achieved glory through obedience to duty, not through maximising his chances of making a lot of money. The British naval officer-gentleman now served God, king and Royal Navy.[14]

Yet, when Duckworth perceived some freedom of action within a given order, he would seize whatever chances were possible for prize money and glory (within the mission parameters) but only if he could do so and still preserve his men's health. In other words, all aspects of the hierarchy are visible in Duckworth's career, but he consistently put his men's health second and glory or wealth third.

This essay illustrates Duckworth's decision-making by examining two episodes from his career. The first describes the challenges of the summer of 1796 amid an outbreak of disease during operations around Jamaica and Haiti. The second examines Duckworth's return to the West Indies as he set up at Martinique and campaigned in the Leeward Islands in 1801.

The summer of the 1796 tropical disease outbreak: Jamaica and Haiti
The French revolutionaries had overthrown the French monarchy and taken over France in 1792. The French were seeking to topple monarchies in favour of republics around the world, leading to declarations of war by Prussia and Austria. In February 1793 France declared war on Britain. Britain's main objective in the war was to keep France from entering or occupying the European Low Countries of the modern-day Netherlands, Belgium and Luxembourg. Although contributing ground forces in Europe, Britain knew that she could defeat France more easily in other ways. Home Secretary Henry Dundas[15] sought to cut off French power at its origin; the French colonies. French economic and naval strength was rooted in its colonies in the West Indies, and Britain would use her most powerful military weapon, the Royal Navy, to defeat the French there. Dundas believed that by isolating the French West Indian colonies from succour and then systematically taking these islands,

Britain could achieve an enduring peace.[16]

By April 1796, after the ultimate failure of the Jervis–Grey expedition, Rear-Admiral Hugh Christian[17] and General Sir Ralph Abercromby had reclaimed many of the Leeward Islands at great cost.[18] Despite fastidious preparations and far more medical doctors than before, their large British force of thirty-five thousand campaigned into sickly season in the Caribbean and was reduced by fourteen thousand men, largely due to yellow fever and malaria. Abercromby and Christian failed to remove the French from some of their large colonies in the region; Guadeloupe and Saint-Domingue (a major French colony spanning the western region of what is now modern Haiti). The British held only a few towns in the latter colony, even though it was clearly a priority, responsible as it was for 40 per cent of French foreign trade and 66 per cent of their seaborne shipping. Crafty politician Victor Hughes[19] remained governor of Guadeloupe. Having already inspired and assisted pro-republican slave rebellions in Grenada, St Vincent and St Lucia, the maroons were now revolting, threatening control of Britain's most valuable Caribbean colony, Jamaica.[20]

As a result of a severe sickness to Rear-Admiral William Parker, Captain Duckworth took command of the Jamaica-based squadron, becoming commodore in late June 1796. Western Saint-Domingue was amid a bloody civil war between the freed slaves of 1791 and the French. Factions of French loyalists and republicans further complicated matters. The civil war brought many French army and naval forces to the area, threatening British holdings on Saint-Domingue and Jamaica. Defensively, Duckworth's operational objective

View of Port Royal and Kingston Harbour in the Island of Jamaica, 1782, an engraving by F Cary. (Library of Congress, Washington, DC)

was to protect British colonies and commerce in the region, including assisting Jamaica to suppress the maroon rebellion there. Offensively he was to wrest Saint-Domingue from the French and, if possible, deliver it unto the British.

As was often the case in the West Indies, though, Duckworth's real enemy was disease. Outbreaks of yellow fever and malaria in the summer of 1796 prevented him from deploying enough ships to accomplish his mission. As a result, he asked the Admiralty to send more ships and men to the region, even though it was still the height of the sickly season, demonstrating the pre-eminence of mission in his mind. In August 1796 Duckworth sought permission from Jamaica's governor Lord Balcarres (General Alexander Lindsay)[21] to impress one thousand five hundred men to replace those he had lost.[22] Lord Balcarres declined to help him, as he had lost three quarters of his white militia after just two years in Jamaica, while the army on station was already reduced significantly.[23] There simply were not enough healthy soldiers and sailors to go around.

That is not to say that Duckworth was indifferent to the risks of service in the region in sickly season. In his 1 June 1796 letter to his patron (and the father of one of his midshipmen) Edward Baker, Duckworth described his sorrow over the deaths of many men he knew well from his ship, the third-rate HMS *Leviathan* (74). These men died because *Leviathan*, in need of extensive repairs, required an extended stay at the unusually sickly, low-lying Port Royal, Jamaica, shipyard at the onset of sickly season.[24] He seemed to express true, heart-felt compassion:

> I am told I am fortunate in the way I have escaped, as they call it. But from such an escape, good God defend me in the future! As I have lost 40, and alas! Those I most love, viz. dear, dear Edward Baker, and my first lieutenant Mr Scott besides ... my boatswain, gunner, a soldier officer, and one of the mates. But as the *Africa*, who lay near me and had not half the damages to repair I had, has lost upward of 70 in five weeks, it is by comparison I am deemed fortunate ... I doubt not we shall soon return to our pristine state of health. But what availeth that to me now? I hope you will be able to read this scrawl, but there is no accounting for nerves.[25]

While Rear-Admiral William Parker was apparently content to keep his squadron anchored at ports near mosquito-infested areas during sickly season, Duckworth sought a modification of behaviour. On many occasions, Commodore Duckworth gave his officers orders to prevent their landing in regions he and his medical officers deemed as having bad climate and bad air.

He regularly ordered officers under his command to spend minimal time at the sickliest port, Port Royal, and instead return quickly to the Mole St Nicholas, Saint-Domingue (now Haiti) when their ships needed repair, as evidenced in letters to John Fishley,[26] Captain Drury,[27] Captain Pigot,[28] Captain Tripp,[29] Captain Winthrop[30] and Lieutenant Bennett.[31,32]

Often, Duckworth's orders helped him keep his men healthy, as they required him to remain at sea even in hurricane season. On 15 September Lord George Spencer[33] expressed remorse on the great loss of life reported by Duckworth due to the ravages of disease but commended him for 'keeping as much as possible at sea and on the least unhealthy stations to preserve the remainder of your officers and men'.[34] Therefore, Duckworth's acts of compassion may have been duty-driven as much as originating in a true concern for his men. However, many officers had relatives in the services, including such powerful men as Dundas, and later Duckworth's own son joined the army. Despite practical concerns, a true concern for preservation of life might have also been present, as Charters argues.

Nevertheless, what emerges from a close reading of Duckworth's correspondence in 1796 is that he prioritised his mission above all else. Despite his squadron being degraded by disease, damage and convoy duty, Duckworth vowed to persevere. He reported the debilitated condition of his squadron to the Admiralty on 25 July upon assuming day-to-day command while Rear-Admiral Parker awaited the return of the July convoy to England from the safety of the Jamaican mountains. He expressed his misgivings about his ability to accomplish his mission without additional ships. The French at Saint-Domingue received three convoys of supplies and reinforcements protected by two ships of the line, and four frigates and corvettes. Shortly thereafter, Parker took the third-rate HMS *Swiftsure* (74) with her crew on his return to England, further reducing his force. Duckworth explained to the Admiralty that his whole squadron was very weak because of 'the ravages of the plague', which is 'a destructive process that is beyond belief'.[35] He had tried to make do, but his ships were damaged and undersupplied. The ships Duckworth named with sickly crews included his own ship, *Leviathan*, as well as the third-rates *Alfred* (74) ('very sickly'), *Canada* (74), *Hannibal* (74), *Argonaut* (64), and *Dictator* (64); the fourth-rates *Abergavenny* (54), *Hindostan* (54), and *Malabar* (54); the fifth-rates *Ceres* (32), and *Hermione* (32), and the brig sloops *Albacore* (16), *Marie Antionette* (10) and *Drake* (16). Captain Drury of *Alfred* captured the French *Renommee* on 17 July 1796, but soon after reported to Duckworth that his crew was very sickly by 26 July. Duckworth advised him to drop off his damaged ship at sickly Port Royal and return to Duckworth at Mole St Nicholas as soon as possible. Drury had suffered so many losses that both his 'men and officers are dropping off daily'.[36] In spite of so many setbacks and regardless of so much death all around him, Duckworth vowed to do all that he could to accomplish the mission through the exertion of his full effort with spirit and enthusiasm to accomplish the Admiralty's orders.

Leeward Islands, 1800–01
With victories in Italy and against Austria (which would withdraw from the war in February 1801), Bonaparte had again turned the tide of the war in favour of the French in 1800. France and Spain had forced Portugal to abandon its alliance with Britain. In July 1800 the Danish tried to push their shipping through a British blockade without being searched. As a result, England responded aggressively, and by the end of 1800 the country entered into conflict with the Armed Neutrality alliance of Denmark, Sweden, Prussia, and Russia, significantly improving Duckworth's prospect for prize money. By the end of Duckworth's time in the Leeward Islands, Britain and France had agreed to the Peace of Amiens, drawn up in October 1801 and ratified in March 1802.[37]

Britain's remaining possessions at Saint-Domingue were by this time given to Toussaint L'Ouverture[38] in exchange for his promising not to attack Jamaica. British colonies remained in the area, however, with those of five other nations. Britain sought to control her own islands in the region, and to deter adversaries from attacking them. Britain also sought to deter uprisings and rebellions within her islands and to suppress the influence of other nations, such as France, which were helping to foment disorder. Many privateers infested the local seas, and Britain sought protection for her own and allied trade.[39]

By the time of his arrival in the Leeward Islands in 1800 Duckworth was a Rear-Admiral of the White, having been promoted in 1799 shortly after his capture of Minorca. His letters leave it uncertain as to why he was ordered to the region, although his prior experience, seasoning and his special relationship with Lord Spencer (who gave him special honours in promotion to rear-admiral) and his clear and continued desire for prize money and honours probably played a role. He was placed loosely under Jamaican Commander-in-Chief Vice-Admiral Lord Hugh Seymour.[40] Aside from not having to contest for Saint-Domingue any longer, Duckworth's duty remained privateer suppression and convoy and colony protection. To protect the British colonies in the area, Duckworth's strategy included reconnaissance, surveillance and intelligence gathering on Guadeloupe and Porto Rico (now Puerto Rico), since these islands were the adversaries' regional hubs of power. To accomplish his objectives Duckworth had only one line of battle ship, his own *Leviathan*, and frigates and smaller ships in varying quantities and qualities.[41]

Here again, we can see Duckworth prioritising mission yet remaining aware of health concerns. In a late July 1800 letter to Lord Spencer, Duckworth betrayed his worry over having adequate strength to prosecute his mission in the Leeward Islands because of reduced numbers of men and ships. Two of his ships were damaged, and he did not have enough ships or ships of the line to begin with. An outbreak of sickness at Antigua significantly reduced the numbers and vitality of men on one ship. Duckworth questioned every aspect of his mission: the ability to provide adequate protection to convoys and suppress privateers and the ability to adequately protect British colonial possessions, especially Surinam. Nevertheless, Duckworth promised Spencer to give his 'utmost exertions'.[42]

As Duckworth's worried letter to Spencer illustrates, Duckworth also had his crews' health at the forefront of his mind, even as he promised to complete the mission. Additional threats to his forces appeared as the rains of sickly season began at Martinique, his main station in the region. Duckworth felt that his squadron would certainly meet its destruction if he kept them at Martinique during that period. To mitigate the threat of disease, Duckworth thus again decided to take his chances on the open seas during hurricane season and sent his squadron out to sea.[43]

Duckworth sought to avoid landing at both Martinique and Port Royal during sickly season, but many officers and men still became sick, further diminishing his capacity to complete his mission. The low position of the hospital at Port Royal led to recurrent and unremitted occurrences of malaria. By late July 1800 it became necessary to replace many officers as they were moved to healthier climates or died. Two ships were rendered ineffective due to sickness; the fourth-rate HMS *Amphitrite* (40) and the sloop HMS *Gaiete* (20). Combined with the loss of ships sent to escort three convoys since April, Duckworth could only promise Lord Spencer his best effort to ameliorate his squadron's weakness.[44]

Another source of sickness came from French prisoners, so Duckworth asked Lord Spencer's permission to establish the sloop HMS *Frederick* (20) as a receiving ship for them. Duckworth believed that the men were spreading sickness because they were received onto his own squadron's ships without purification. He also requested that the ship be permitted to receive his own convalescents because the low position of the Port Royal hospital had been producing a great deal of malarial fevers.[45]

Occasionally, there was nothing to be done but to send a weakened ship back to Britain. Duckworth initially hoped that he could replace the losses in his marine regiment using men from the fifth-rate HMS *Hydra* (38). However, he later learned that the weak *Hydra* crew was 'diabolical', and so he could not use these men as replacements. Duckworth thus asked the Admiralty to send replacement marines instead and he sent *Hydra* back to Britain on 31 October.[46]

In 1796 Duckworth had been frustrated in his attempts to win glory. His weak squadron, overextended responsibilities and concerns about his men's health had prevented him from following in the footsteps of Vernon, Rodney and Jervis. But in 1801, Duckworth was luckier. Following the outbreak of war with the Armed Neutrality, Duckworth and Lieutenant-General Sir Thomas Trigge[47] took advantage of the opportunity to attack vulnerable Danish and Swedish possessions. A new opportunity for prize money and glory had arisen, even available to Duckworth's weak, small force. Duckworth planned with Trigge to attack St Bartholomew (now known as the French Saint Barthélemy), and then proceed to other islands 'in pursuit of the Admiralty's intentions'.[48] Note here the contrast, especially with Rodney: Duckworth nestled his avarice under the Admiralty's mission.

Beginning on 14 March 1801, Duckworth and Trigge, in a well-coordinated joint action, rapidly achieved success in taking multiple, lightly defended Danish and Swedish islands with few losses. They took St Bartholomew, St John, St Thomas, St Croix and St Martin with one thousand five hundred troops from Martinique, St Kitts, and Antigua. Duckworth's squadron proved vital to stymie enemy relief to the assaulted islands while protecting disembarking troops. The amphibious campaign was not only a self-interested action; the Danish and Swedish islands were specified targets in their orders.[49] Duckworth and Trigge rapidly took advantage of the opportunity to serve both interests.

Mission: the priority

For Duckworth, whenever mission conflicted with glory, riches or health protection, the mission invariably won. Yet whenever possible, Duckworth sought the protection of his own and his men's health. Unfortunately for him, the mission was not his to determine nor his to control. For an admiral with substantial political capital, refusing orders may have been an

Fort Willoughby, Charlotte Amalie, St Thomas, Virgin Islands; Duckworth and Trigge conquered this fort in 1801. Shown in the present day.
Contributor/photographer not listed.
(Library of Congress, Washington, DC)

option, but Duckworth did not have that kind of influence. He could not expect the same treatment as Lord Nelson[50] when Nelson refused Lord Keith's[51] three orders to join him off Brest and, instead, continued his pursuit of Lady Hamilton.[52] Nor was it likely that Duckworth would want to refuse his operational duty. He was a patriot with a deep-seated hatred of the French and little respect for the Spanish. Duckworth also had a family to feed, and his concerns showed in his frequently received updates from Marmaduke Peacock on the well-being and status of his son and daughter in England. It was for his family, after all, that Duckworth seemed to be fighting. Duckworth pointed to his son as the source of his joy when he gained far less wealth than expected from a captured convoy.[53] That is not to say that Duckworth did not care about money: like all admirals, he continued to fight for it with other admirals and made use of chances that duty afforded him.

It is hard to know the source of Duckworth's compassionate actions toward his men. The Sick and Hurt Board exercised increasingly centralised power, authority and legitimacy during the period considered here, 1796–1802. Furthermore, Duckworth considered himself personally beholden to Earl St Vincent (John Jervis), his Commander-in-Chief and then First Lord of the Admiralty, and he took it upon himself to follow all his orders. Also, St Vincent was an admiral who, in addition to the strict rules of conduct and discipline he imposed on the Channel Fleet, also imposed strict rules meant to increase the health protection of British naval men. Significant failure in paternalistic and compassionate behaviour was unacceptable as it would place overseeing politicians in hot water. New health regulations were introduced after the Grey–Jervis disaster, regulating diet, hygiene, clothing, exercise and location for sheltering. Failures in health protection could lead to the decreased status of an officer, disdain from other officers, insufficient troops for mission, blame and low morale and capability. Thus, the degree to which compassion represented Duckworth's motivation to protect his men's health remains an open question. However, in his letter to Edward Baker, Duckworth certainly showed a wellspring of emotion about the dead and dying of his own flagship. Given that Duckworth spent a considerable amount of time on administrative actions to acquire goods and resources to improve his men's health and that he obtained a reputation as an admiral who took care of his men, his interest in his men's health and well-being was probably genuine. Thus, Duckworth likely epitomises Charters' popular, paternalistic British military officer of the eighteenth century.[54]

Duckworth had many reasons to pay careful attention to orders. He was court-martialed three times. He had been criticised by other naval officers, army officers, marine officers, contractors and governors, and repeatedly he had to defend himself before the Admiralty. Men from his own flagship mutinied against him in 1797.[55] Even a French naval officer accused him of prisoner mistreatment, and again Duckworth had to defend his conduct. In all these trials and tribulations Duckworth must have learned the value of keeping within the boundaries of defensible conduct.

The specific challenge for Duckworth in the West Indies was that prioritising his men's health over the mission would almost certainly have forced him to abandon his station. Miasma, or air pollution, was perceived to be the cause of his men's fevers and there was no cure for miasma except to avoid it. To do so, Duckworth could have gone to the mountains in Jamaica or sailed north, but either action would have compromised his mission. All Duckworth could do was to follow the advice of his doctor and that of the Sick and Hurt Board. If Duckworth fully pursued gold and glory he would have also failed in his duty, immediately alienating himself from the Admiralty. The result would have most likely been court martial and dismissal. Since he neither owned the mission nor the ship, Duckworth could not freely pursue glory or riches like a privateer or pirate. Although the hope for riches was the most common inspiration for seamen, including naval officers, he could not freely pursue that hope.[56]

In sum, Duckworth emerges from his letters as a duty-driven, health-conscious officer, in sharp contrast with the earlier generation of glory-seeking, callous officers like Vernon and Rodney.

The author wishes to thank Dr Evan Wilson, Dr Ross Dancy, Dr John Hattendorf (all affiliated with the US Naval War College, Newport, Rhode Island), and Mr Tom Walich (retired magazine editor of Lake Forest, Illinois) who advised on the draft.

North East View of Fort Louis in the Island of Martinique, see colour plate 6

The Seafaring Saga of Joshua Penny, 1788–1815

William S Dudley

In the Atlantic maritime world of the eighteenth and early nineteenth centuries, warfare at sea was endemic between the European colonial empires of Great Britain, France and Spain. As seen from the perspective of British colonists, these contests were embodied in Queen Anne's War, King George's War, the Seven Years' War (French and Indian War), the American War of Independence and the War of 1812. These three nations battled each other on the European Continent, on the Atlantic Ocean, the Caribbean and the North American mainland. This was an age of economic exploitation. With the twin goals of dominating trade and expanding their mercantile empires, they sought to overwhelm their seemingly perpetual adversaries. They captured each other's treasure ships, warships, trading vessels, plantation islands, slaves and mainland settlements; all was fair game in the competition for wealth and power.

Europe's largest navy, the Royal Navy, struggled to sustain its fleets with seamen, often at the expense of merchants as well as the sailors themselves. Americans who went to sea to work in trade did so because there was a better chance of financial gain in commerce rather than the Royal Navy's ships.[1] The risks of seafaring were many in which the prevalence of diseases would ruin a man's health, accidents at sea could cause permanent injury or death and ship-to-ship battles could take a terrible toll. From the viewpoint of a navy's commanders, there was always a need for more manpower to work a warship and its guns. If men did not volunteer for sea service, they had to be found and compelled to serve at sea, often for years at a time, under swift and harsh discipline.

Since Elizabethan times, Parliament had enacted laws that established and reiterated the legality of pressing individuals to man royal naval vessels in times of need.[2] Thousands of American seamen's accounts of their impressment by the Royal Navy are held in the US and British National Archives and other repositories. American ship captains were required to file a report at US consulates when sailors were impressed from their ships so that the federal government had a record of these events for diplomatic purposes. Many such reports have been published or excerpted for publication in maritime histories about the age of democratic revolutions that took place from 1775 to 1815.

In 1776, with the Declaration of Independence, the US Second Continental Congress condemned this practice as one of twenty-seven outrageous acts inflicted on American colonists, as follows: 'He [King George] has constrained our fellow Citizens taken Captive on the High Seas to bear Arms against their Country, to become the executioners of their friends and Brethren, or to fall themselves by their Hands.'

Difficulties for Americans arose because of the United States' insistence that when British immigrants became naturalised citizens they were no longer considered British subjects and were, therefore, no longer liable for disregarding and disobeying English laws concerning its subjects. British authorities disagreed, insisting that a subject born under English sovereignty never lost his identity as British no matter where he was living, under any circumstances.[3] Although many examples of impressment have been studied and accounted for, there is one recently rediscovered that deserves singular attention.

This involved Joshua Penny, the son of an American farmer living in Southold, Long Island, New York, who went to sea in 1788 at fifteen years old and remained a sailor for the rest of his life. He was originally employed in coastal merchant shipping, but he was impressed many times, and as often escaped. Yet, an escapade that took place in South Africa in the late 1790s makes his narrative unique.[4]

Joshua Penny goes to sea

Joshua Penny was born in 1773. His father was Edward Penny, whose wife had nine children, of which Joshua was one of the youngest. His father wanted him to become a doctor and indentured him to a local physician when he was fourteen. Yet at age fifteen, Joshua told his father he wanted to go to sea. His father cancelled the indenture and arranged for his son to join a merchant vessel heading to Guadeloupe, French West Indies.

Joshua reported he did not like the ship for some unstated reason. He signed off the vessel and next shipped out on the brig *Perseverance* under Captain George Lippincott. Joshua was paid $2.50 per month for his menial duties (probably as cabin boy). As it turned out, he did not get along with the first mate and complained to the captain about his mistreatment. Joshua jumped ship when they arrived at Port Royal, Virginia. He met two kindly men who listened to his story and brought him back to the ship. There he again complained to the captain, who became angry and threatened the mate for mistreating the boy.

Joshua, mollified, stayed with the brig as it voyaged to Oporto, Portugal. On the way, the captain discovered that most of his cargo of corn had been damaged by dampness and had to be heaved overboard. The crew exchanged what was left of the corn for a return cargo of salt to Norfolk, Virginia, and then returned to New York. The captain paid Joshua off, with a bonus. Joshua continued to sail in another ship on trading voyages between New York, Charleston and the West Indies. At Charleston, he met two Irish merchants, brothers, who persuaded him to travel with them to Georgia to trade with the Indians. Although his narrative does not identify the particular tribes, they probably were Creek, Cherokee or both. Joshua and his two Irish friends traded with these tribes for more than a year, travelling back and forth between Atlanta and Augusta.

At length, the two brothers decided to return to Ireland and invited Joshua to accompany them. After arriving, Joshua wanted to travel alone, and soon enough he was picked up by a press gang from a Royal Navy 74-gun ship. After an interview, the captain ordered him off the ship, perhaps because he was lacking in experience. Making his way to Liverpool, he visited the American consul, where he obtained a 'Protection' document, stating he was an American-born citizen of the United States, including his physical description. Signed and sealed by the consul, it supposedly kept the bearer from impressment into British service; however, the press gangs and ship captains often ignored these documents or destroyed them, saying they were fraudulent or had been stolen from another person.

Having thus protected himself, Penny signed on as a crew member of the slaver *Budd*, outward bound from Liverpool to Annamaboe (Anomabu) on the African Gold Coast (Ghana). Then, with 382 slaves in her hold, *Budd* sailed for Jamaica. There, Penny was seized from the slaver by a press gang from the sixth-rate HM frigate *Alligator* (28), which then sailed to Havana. When he refused the captain's offer to sign-on (volunteer to be a paid member of ship's crew), he was transferred to the third-rate HMS *America* (64). In her, Penny sailed to Portsmouth, England, where he was transferred to another third-rate, HMS *Stately* (64), commanded by Captain Douglass.

Stately soon sailed for the Cape of Good Hope in 1795, as part of a squadron comprising *America*, the third-rate *Ruby* (64), and HM Sloop *Rattlesnake* under Commodore Blankett. They set sail for Simon's Town (Simonstown), South Africa, on a bay near the foot of Table Mountain. There they were joined by a squadron under Vice-Admiral Lord Keith, commander of the British naval expedition of 1795, sent to seize the Dutch colony, then under French dominion. Penny and his shipmates were sent ashore with weapons, to drill before going into action.

After five weeks of drill with British Army troops and Royal Marines commanded by Major General James Craig, under the overall command of Major General Sir Alured Clark, Joshua's comments make clear he and his

Cape of Good Hope, an engraving showing Table Mountain and Bay with a Royal Navy squadron at anchor, Cape Town, South Africa, c1796. English School. An illustration from *The Life and Adventures of Joshua Penny*, by Joshua Penny (1815).

messmates made a poor impression as the sailors were unfamiliar with marching and close-order drill. They were repulsed in the first skirmish against the Dutch at Muizenberg, which the British eventually captured; however, the defenders retreated to Constantia plantation on the outskirts of Cape Town. This desultory warfare continued for two months.

Joshua Penny: deserter
At this point, Penny became disenchanted with military life and deserted with other shipmates. To their surprise, the Dutch farmers they met were hospitable, giving them food, drink and shelter. After Lord Keith and General Craig received reinforcements, the Dutch governor surrendered the Cape Colony, bringing it under British rule. This meant life became much more difficult for the deserters, as the British demanded the Dutch populace give up any deserters they harboured under the threat of being transported to Australia. The Dutch farmer told Penny and his messmates they had to leave. At first, they walked several miles toward the sea on the possibility they might find an American ship. Luck was with them, as they met two deserters on the beach from a whaling ship. Penny and friends continued on until they met a watering party from the British ship *John*, commanded by a captain from Nantucket. They went out to the ship, met the captain and soon signed on for a whaling voyage.

It did not take long for Joshua to develop a dislike of the captain because of his harsh treatment of the crew. When *John* next returned to Simon's Town, he volunteered to go ashore to find more water and vegetables. He was allowed to go and did not return, jumping ship once again. He returned to the Dutch farm where he had been a guest. The farmer said he could not stay long because the press gangs were nearby, hunting for deserters, and that he should travel to the interior where he would encounter the 'Hottentot' (now known as Khoikhoi) people who had befriended, worked for and intermingled with some of the Dutch for well over a century.

Penny followed this advice. He and another deserter by the name of Vanderveit walked north toward mountainous 'Cold Bockveld' (Koue Bokkeveld) where they found a camp of Dutch and their Hottentot allies. They welcomed them to strengthen their number as they were under assault by a band of hostile Bushmen. Penny and his friend witnessed a successful surprise attack by the Dutchmen and Hottentots against the Bushmen, involving firearms and poisoned spears. Following this event, Joshua remained with the Dutch and Hottentots for six months, learning a good deal from the Hottentots on how they subsisted in the wild; a lesson he would need before long.

As of August 1796, a year had passed since Penny had arrived at Simon's Town as an impressed sailor with the Royal Navy, and since the battle of Muizenberg he had been on the run. He seemed unafraid to take on new experiences and challenges, as though his few years at sea as a deckhand had toughened him. He wrote that he now felt ready to rejoin civilisation and was curious as to whether any American ships had arrived.

On his long walk toward Cape Town, he met a farmer who mentioned that he had hired an American sailor in circumstances similar to his own. Joshua wanted to meet him so he accompanied the farmer to his property, where he was introduced to John Johnston of Bristol, Rhode Island. The two men had much in common and agreed that they would leave the farm and travel together. They finally arrived at Cape Town and stopped at the home of one John van Reinesburgh, who invited them to stay a few days after warning that police patrols were visiting homes, asking for news of any vagrants or deserters.

When the police did arrive, they examined the two and took them to a jail, where they joined others who were incarcerated for the same reason. Lieutenants from the British warships at anchor visited the jail to question the prisoners. Penny recognised one of those as Lieutenant Pingally, for whom he had worked. This officer had him released and brought him back to the *Stately*, the same ship that brought him to the Cape. From there, he was ordered to the third-rate HMS *Tormentor* (74) and from there to the third-rate HMS *Sceptre* (64), remaining in her while she lay at anchor in Table Bay. At that time, the

Royal Navy was also blockading Port Louis at Isle de France (Mauritius). The sloop *Rattlesnake* was assigned to the blockading force and needed men; so Joshua was drafted to join her crew. When *Rattlesnake* captured a Danish cutter, Penny was put on board as one of the prize crew that was ordered to return to Table Bay, where he rejoined *Sceptre*'s crew. Soon enough, he was drafted to serve in the sixth-rate HM Sloop *Sphinx* (20), to cruise off St Helena. One night when *Sphinx* was at anchor, Penny and his American messmates, having bribed the sentry, lowered themselves overboard to swim to an American whaling ship that lay nearby. His messmates made their escape, but he could not, being a poor swimmer. He returned to *Sphinx* by climbing the anchor cable. When the captain investigated the absence of the missing sailors, he interrogated and caught Penny in a lie when he claimed not to know they had escaped. The captain responded, 'You are a Yankee, sir, and have been seven years without ever being flogged, and now I'll flog you [even] if you are God's first lieutenant.' So saying, he called for the ship's company to witness punishment, along with the surgeon. Penny was drawn up, tied by his wrists on a grating, and as the boatswain flogged him, Penny fainted. When the surgeon intervened, the captain exclaimed, 'He shall take his dozen, dead or alive.'[5] When *Sphinx* returned to Table Bay, the captain sent Penny back to *Sceptre*.

It is no wonder that Penny had had enough of seafaring. So after a deliberate drunken fight with a British sailor, he feigned illness so well that the ship's surgeon ordered him to a shore hospital. While in transit, he bribed the two guards escorting him and escaped. Then and there, he decided to ascend the 3,800ft to the top of Table Mountain and remain there until the British fleet left Table Bay, regardless of how long it would take, and that he would 'rather become a lion's breakfast than be taken to another floating dungeon'.[6] He went back into the town, purchased as much food as he could carry in a knapsack, and hiked to the mountain. He also carried a knife and a calabash full of brandy.

Life on Table Mountain
There was no path to follow. It was a matter of climbing from rock to rock, pulling himself up by the stems of plants, and traversing when there was no way upward. It took him four days to climb to where he could take shelter and be out of sight. Penny eventually found a ledge that led into a cave with access to a nearby spring. With the flints he carried, Penny could cook and keep himself relatively warm, though he realised he should not light a fire at night that could be spotted from the sea. The animals he saw included goats, antelopes, wolves and lions. Only the wolves threatened him, but his aggressive behaviour deterred them, so they never bothered him again.

Penny did find other caves, where he moved to escape annoying insects, but

Entrance to Joshua Penny's cave, Table Mountain, South Africa. Access is nearly inaccessible now except from above, using a rope to rappel the cliff.
(Photo courtesy Mountain Club of South Africa, Sheldon Dudley, Cape Town, South Africa)

the first cavern he returned to many times. It was located at about 3,000ft above ground level and afforded a broad view of the sea unless fog or low-level clouds intervened. He was able to survive, as he had learned to live off the land while dwelling among the Hottentots and observing their ways of gathering wild honey, nuts and berries, and when living among American natives in Georgia, how to kill, skin and preserve the meat and skins of animals that might cross his path. He could even ferment honey by mixing it with crushed root flour, that when mixed with water, became mead; a homely, slightly alcoholic brew.

Every few weeks he ventured out to where he could view the shipping on Table Bay, hoping the navy would be gone and the merchant ships had returned. In this he was often disappointed, until after eighteen months as a caveman, he saw only one vessel. With some relief, Penny discovered this was a formerly Danish brig that had been taken as a prize, sold and was under the command of a civilian captain. Joshua, now bearded and hirsute and dressed in animal skins, hesitantly approached the captain as he landed at the beach. The captain exclaimed, 'What in the name of God are you? Man or beast?' Joshua responded, asking the captain if he needed a deckhand. The captain said that he did and sent him to the ship. Joshua cleaned up, trimmed his hair, shaved his beard and was given some clothes.

Penny returns to the sea

Learning that Penny had deserted from the *Sceptre*, the captain informed him that she had sunk in Table Bay after dragging her anchors in a wicked storm and went down with all hands in November 1797. The brig soon sailed for St Helena, bound for London; however, she would have to wait four months for the homeward-bound East India Company fleet to arrive.

Eventually, another ship arrived and anchored nearby. She was an American Calcutta-built ship named *Indian Chief*. On discovering she was American, Penny went on board and with tears in his eyes met the first Americans he had seen in two years. He asked whether the ship had lost any hands and found that, indeed, they had lost a young man named John Porter who looked a good deal like Penny. Penny asked if he might have the man's protection paper and received it without any objections. When he returned to the brig, Penny

Wreck of the *Sceptre* (1781) of 64 guns, in a tremendous Hurricane off the Cape of Good Hope 1809. Plate 32 from *The Mariner's Marvellous Magazine, or Wonders of the Ocean; Containing the Most Remarkable Adventures and Relations of Mariners in Various Parts of the Globe. In Four Volumes, Embellished with Forty Engravings*, published by Thomas Tegg, Cheapside, J and A Duncan, Glasgow; J Sutherland, Edinburgh; and J McClery, (© National Maritime Museum, Greenwich, London)

produced the document and asked the captain to sign him on board as John Porter. The captain liked the idea and agreed.

When the India fleet arrived at St Helena, a boarding officer came to the Danish brig and took Penny to the Indiaman *Admiral Hughes* for the voyage to England. As Penny clambered aboard, who should he meet but Lieutenant Pingally, who immediately recognised him. Pingally remarked that fate had been kind to both of them, as he had been sent ashore just two hours before the storm arrived that wrecked the *Sceptre*. From then on, the officer and the American seaman got along quite well during the blustery voyage to the Downs.

As for the Danish prize brig, she barely made it to London and had to be towed because of her leaking condition. When the Port Regulating Officer interviewed Penny, Lieutenant Pingally was standing alongside and, though smiling, made no remark when Penny gave his false name and showed his protection paper; with a nod from the officer, Penny was then allowed to leave. Pingally later mentioned that he would soon take command of a 20-gun sloop of war and, if Penny were willing to come with him, the lieutenant would give him 'any office he should merit'. When Penny refused, Pingally remarked, 'Well, I wish you safe home. If I could not man a ship without impressment, I should never wish her to be manned.' Then he added, 'I knew you to be American or perhaps I should not have suffered you to get off as you have.' In his narrative, Penny remarked, 'This was a good Englishman. Anyone else who was acquainted with him would gladly leave another ship and run to him.'[7]

Penny returned to the Danish brig to say farewell to the captain and collect what was due him. The captain gave him his earnings plus a bonus of two dollars. With that, Penny left the Downs with a shipmate, heading for London. Anxious for home, he worked his passage on *Dauphin*, under Captain Wallace, bound for Charleston. Once there, he chanced to meet a Long Island man, Enoch Rider of Sag Harbor, who took him to an official to obtain a proper 'protection' to replace the one he 'borrowed' from the ship at St Helena. At this time, in early 1799, Penny did the unexpected. Instead of finding a ship bound for New York to visit his family, he shipped out on *Dauphin* again as a deckhand to return to London with Captain Wallace, who offered him a fair wage.

After a stormy passage, having discovered that Wallace would not soon return to the United States, Penny went to Wapping on Thames, where he found a former American privateer schooner (name not given) advertising for American seamen. She was bound for Brest, France, then possible because of the Peace of Amiens, heralding a temporary end of the long war and an improvement of Franco–British relations.[8] The schooner delivered him and other American sailors to Brest, where they boarded an armed sloop of war, *Le Diable en Quatres* (The Devil on All Fours), which had been purchased by the

American consul in Brest to convey homeward-bound American citizens. Yet, once at sea, she was commandeered by French naval authorities to escort General Le Clerc's expedition to Saint-Dominque. They arrived at Cap François in late December 1801, where Penny witnessed the destruction and mayhem of the slave revolution that Le Clerc and his army had been sent to suppress.

Penny luckily found the American sloop *Hero*, whose captain, Nathan Fellows, was recruiting deckhands and about to depart for Stonington, Connecticut. After twenty-one days at sea, they sighted Montauk Point, Long Island; a few hours later, the sloop entered Stonington Harbour. From Stonington to Long Island, Penny crossed the turbulent Sound in a small craft. He was injured when she capsized on landing and the cargo barrels fell on him, fracturing his leg. He recovered in the sea captain's home for several weeks. Penny sent word to his Southold home, and his sister came to meet him. Before long he arrived home to be with his family in 1803, after a nine-year absence. His parents had assumed he was lost at sea.

This ended the first phase of Penny's life in the war-torn maritime world, as fraught as it was with the uncertain twists of fate that he had so far survived.

Artefacts found in Joshua Penny's cave: fragments of a Guernsey frock, shift, and blanket; clay pipe bowls, bracelets of woven twine or marlin and other items. (Photo courtesy of Mountain Club of South Africa; Tracks4Africa; Sheldon Dudley, Cape Town, South Africa)

More fragments from Joshua Penny's cave life, including a rusty knife blade, a portion of a sack he created, the shard of a broken bottle and animal bones. (Photo courtesy of Mountain Club of South Africa; Tracks4Africa; Sheldon Dudley, Cape Town, South Africa)

For those who may be sceptical about Penny's caveman existence on Table Mountain, South Africans years ago uncovered material evidence in a cave of his eighteen months-long stay in that mountain vastness. The Mountain Club of South Africa's clubhouse (mcsa.org.za) has on display recovered artefacts from Penny's cave.[9]

Penny's life in the US during the War of 1812
When Joshua Penny returned to the United States, he was thirty years of age, in the prime of life, and had spent half his life at sea, most of it as an impressed seaman on British warships. He had been an unwilling participant in the war against the South African Dutch, had deserted, escaped, camped with Hottentots and lived a solitary caveman's life for more than a year on the formidable Table Mountain. He had survived for fifteen years by his wits and courage, taking the risks as they came. Then, with his nation at peace, he married, settled down at Three Mile Harbor near the farming and fishing village of Easthampton, Long Island, bought a trading vessel and went to sea once again. For the next nine years, he was in the coastal trade and often visited the West Indies. During this

period, however, diplomatic relations between the United States and Great Britain deteriorated, with the US declaring war on 18 June 1812.

With the War of 1812, the Royal Navy blockaded the New York and New England coasts. With several enemy 74-gun ships, numerous frigates, smaller sloops and brigs of war standing offshore, few American vessels could venture out of New York Harbour and Long Island Sound without risking capture. Penny, based at Three Mile Harbor, sold his ship, swearing, 'I resolved to put myself in an attitude to annoy the enemy of my country [and] determined to avail myself of the first opportunity of doing mischief to those who had so long tortured me.'[10]

By July 1813, it was commonly known that Commodore Stephen Decatur Jr and his squadron (*United States*, *Macedonian* and *Hornet*) had attempted to escape the Sound by the Montauk route on 1 June though forced to turn back to New London, Connecticut, by a stronger blockading squadron.[11] Penny was well aware of Decatur's presence at New London; he was also aware, through close observation, that the Sound in that area was watched closely by Vice-Admiral Sir Thomas M Hardy, commanding the British squadron, whose flagship, the third-rate HMS *Ramillies* (74), with the fifth-rate frigate HMS *Orpheus* (36), kept a close blockade of Decatur's ships at New London.

Near Penny's home, Three Mile Harbor lies in the bight between Orient Point and Montauk Point on the South Fork at the eastern end of Long Island. So too does the large, privately owned Gardiner's Island dominated by an English-styled manor house, owned by the wealthy Lion Gardner, a descendant of the original owner of the same name who had come from Connecticut to purchase the island from the Wyandanch Indians in 1639. Admiral Hardy occasionally visited Lion Gardiner with Captain Hugh Pigot of *Orpheus*, to enjoy his hospitality of an evening and no doubt to remind Gardiner of who was really in charge in the Sound. He persuaded this American 'lord of the manor' that his flagship would enjoy the fresh fruit, vegetables, beef, and pork raised on Gardiner's farm. Gardiner had little choice but to offer hospitality to his enemy, lest he lose everything. There was no force at his

Admiral Sir Thomas Masterman Hardy, oil painting by Richard Evans (1784–1871). (© National Maritime Museum, Greenwich, London)

ready disposal to resist the admiral's blandishments.

Penny, having observed the admiral and members of his crew visiting the island, determined to visit Decatur's ship at New London, to inform him of the British behaviour at Gardiner's Island and to suggest this might provide an opportunity of capturing some enemy officers and men or even Admiral Hardy himself and Captain Pigot of *Orpheus*. Decatur, excited by the idea, agreed and asked Penny to pilot a small expedition from his squadron. Decatur provided four boats, manned and armed from the squadron, under a Lieutenant Gallagher, and promised to pay Penny to conduct them to the island. They set out from New London on the night of 26–27 July 1813 and on arriving hid themselves in the marshes, although one boat was missing. This boat, under the command of Midshipman Ten Eyck, became separated, and landed in a different location. Ten Eyck and his crew left the boat on the beach and hid in a thick grove of trees.

At dawn, Gallagher and Penny observed a squadron of nine boats getting under way from *Ramillies* and *Orpheus*: a gig with Captain Pigot, four cutters, two barges and two launches, carrying 160 Royal Marines and a carriage gun. This made it clear to Penny that he had been betrayed. He, Gallagher and their men returned to their boats and pulled to Fire Place Point, a high bluff above Gardiner's Bay.[12] They made good their escape, but were closely pursued by the British boats, firing with their carriage gun. When two officers and four seamen from *Ramillies* arrived the next day, Ten Eyck and his men surprised, captured and conveyed them, with Penny and Decatur's other boats, to Sag Harbor to notify the local militia, which had already been alerted by the gunfire offshore.

From this point on, things did not go well for Joshua Penny. He and Decatur's men waited five days, then recrossed the Sound to return to New London and brought the prisoners to Decatur. He gave the prisoners the choice of parole or of joining the US Navy. The officers and men chose parole and returned to *Ramillies* to report to Admiral Hardy. He told them to disregard their parole, to which they had agreed under duress. Penny received his pay from Decatur, sailed his skiff back to Three Mile Harbor, and rejoined his wife and family.

He enjoyed a few days of local fame and obtained a certificate from local officials attesting to his good character. He planned to return to Decatur and to enlist in his ship. In the meantime, and before he could return to see Decatur, a 'gentleman' (unnamed) came to his house saying he had come from New York on the recommendation that Penny was a man who could assist in a torpedo attack on Hardy's ships. Penny agreed to help, but the weather was not propitious. Perhaps, this was just as well, for Hardy was no stranger to torpedo attacks in the Sound and moved his squadron frequently to throw off would-be attackers. One day in late August, Penny and a neighbour spotted a boat offshore sounding the depths of the bay near his house. He suspected this was the forerunner of an attack on his house and had already asked the militia to post guards nearby, although they had not arrived.

Had Penny acted on this instinct immediately, he might have put himself out of harm's way. Instead, he went to bed as usual only to be awakened by rude raps on his door coming from a man who claimed to be sent by Decatur. From the voice, Penny recognised the deception and ran for his gun, but was too late. As the door broke in, he was told not to resist – there were 500 armed Royal Marines and sailors from Hardy's squadron and he was now their prisoner. He and an elderly friend, Robert Gray, soon found themselves in shackles on board Hardy's flagship, undergoing an interrogation by the admiral himself. On 23 August, Major Benjamin Case, commander of the Easthampton militia, addressed a letter to Hardy, as follows:

> Sir: The inhabitants of the town of East Hampton have requested of me a flag [of truce] which I now authorize, for the purpose of demanding Joshua Penny, natural-born citizen of the township of Southold on this island, and a resident of the town of East Hampton. He is demanded as a non-combatant, being attached to no vessel as a mariner or corps of military whatever but was taken from his own house unarmed. The bearer of this flag is Lieut. Hodges, an officer of my command, in government service. You will have the goodness to deliver Mr. Penny to Lieut. Hodges, as he cannot consistently be retained as a prisoner of war by any article in the cartel agreed on, ratified, and confirmed by the agents of each of our governments for the exchange of prisoners.
>
> Given under my hand, at the garrison of Sag Harbor, the 23d day of August 1813.
>
> Benjamin Case, Major commanding the troops of the U.S. service at Sag Harbor.[13]

To this demand, Hardy replied the next day, rejecting the claim that Penny was a non-combatant and insisting he was a hostile civilian and a notorious character, having led a group of Decatur's sailors to capture British seamen, as a paid pilot of the enemy, that he planned to destroy the British squadron with a torpedo, and that he had acted as a spy while visiting *Ramillies* to sell fruit and clams, in preparation for these nefarious actions. In closing, Hardy wrote, 'I cannot think of permitting such an avowed enemy to be out of my power when I know so much of him as I do. He will therefore be detained as a prisoner of war until the pleasure of the commander in chief is known.'[14]

While Penny stayed confined and in irons in *Ramillies*, he was approached by the ship's master-at-arms to try to pry information from him. He said to Penny, 'Should I have to hang you, I should be sorry to have you suspect an innocent person of having betrayed you. Whom do you suspect is your betrayer?' Penny answered that he did not know, remarking that he had seen a number of boats trading with *Ramillies* in the daytime and the betrayer might be one of these traders. Then the master-at-arms told him a name, saying that no one in the ship except Hardy knew. He asked Penny if he would be willing to obtain a torpedo for Hardy, and that if he did Hardy would release him with a reward of $3,000. Penny refused to answer. He was then informed that he would be sent to Halifax and confined at the notorious Melville Island prison, where thousands of other American sailors were confined, many from captured privateers.[15]

Many months later, when Penny was severely ill with a high fever in the prison, he learned that he would be released because he had been captured contrary to the stipulations in Major Case's letter to Hardy. Yet, this may well have been the result of interventions on his behalf by Secretary of the Navy William Jones, and subsequently President Madison. Jones had urged Madison to use the existing system for exchange of prisoners in Penny's case, saying that the US should retaliate by treating select British prisoners in the same way that Penny was being abused and in this way gain reciprocity.[16] Madison followed up by writing to John Mason, the US Commissary of Prisoners, stating, 'The peculiarity of the case of Mr. Penny marks it for a distinct notice and vindication. You will meet it by putting into the same state of degradation and suffering a British prisoner at least equivalent in estimation ...' In closing, the president remarked that British commanders of privateers would be appropriate as subjects for this treatment.[17]

Penny was finally released in May 1814, having been incarcerated for nine months and nine days in Melville Island prison. A cartel delivered him to Salem, Massachusetts, where sympathetic citizens donated clothing and cash enough to see him leave in a carriage for New London, and from there he found a vessel to take him to Long Island. He rejoined his family, who were in good health, and moved them all to Sag Harbor to escape the scene of his kidnapping. There, the saga of seaman Joshua Penny ends, but with what we know of him it is not unlikely he was soon again looking for a ship. The long-ago memories of the brutality thrust upon Penny and other impressed American sailors in Royal Navy ships and naval prisons such as Melville Island and England's Dartmoor still resonate in the United States today whenever the War of 1812 is discussed.

Trafalgar's Last Survivors

Hilary L Rubinstein

The masts that once were clad with sails –
The hulls instinct with life –
The lads who braved a thousand gales,
And twenty years of strife –
The trophied stern – the gilded prow –
What have they done? Where are they now?

Thus wondered Napoleonic Wars veteran Lieutenant Alexander D Fordyce RN in the opening stanza of a poem published in 1839.[1] Naturally, he was not alone in his curiosity, especially as the Victorian era progressed, with various candidates suggested in the press as the 'last survivor of Trafalgar'. This article examines claims and reports of Trafalgar's final survivors, many of whom lived to an advanced age in the second half of the nineteenth century.

Greenwich pensioners commemorating the Battle of Trafalgar. Scottish artist John Burnet's engraving of his own oil painting, Greenwich Hospital and Naval Heroes (exhibited in 1837) showing a zestful commemoration of Trafalgar, with 'Nelson' inscribed on the picnic basket.
(Library of Congress, Washington, DC)

French and Spanish survivors
When the second-rate French ship *Formidable*'s (80) surgeon died in 1866, it was suggested that he was the last survivor of France's Trafalgar fleet.[2] However, in 1874 the death of a Monsieur Plihon, who taught English in Nantes, prompted a suggestion that he was the battle's last survivor: he had reportedly been a cabin boy on *Berwick* at the battle and until 1814 was a prisoner of war in England, where, the story went, no less a personage than the Archbishop of Canterbury saw his academic potential and funded his English lessons. Later, in 1880, ninety-four-year-old Henri Blanc of Paris was touted as the last survivor.

In fact, Louis André Manuel (aka Emmanuel-Louis) Cartigny (1 September 1791 to 21 March 1892), from Hyères, in coastal southern France, a powder monkey on *Redoubtable* at the battle, was the last French survivor, often referred to as the last Trafalgar one of all. Slightly wounded, he had become a prisoner of war in England for some years, before being exchanged, thereafter resuming his naval career. Following the war, he returned to Hyères, supplementing his small pension by running the Grand Café de Quatre Saisons there. 'He may be seen on fine days taking his promenade unaided ... and is still able to describe his recollections of the memorable battle,' reported British clergyman Reverend Mortimer Kennedy when Cartigny was ninety-eight, two years before his death.[5] Frail, gaunt, but still capable of cogent reminiscence at his life's end, Cartigny was a proud recipient of the Legion d'Honneur and much fêted by his compatriots.[6]

The year before he died, he had sent Tsar Alexander III his salutations on 'the dawn of an eternal friendship' between their two countries.[7] To her regret, Queen Victoria arrived in the district for a stay just too late to meet him or be officially represented at his funeral. But shortly afterwards she had a pleasant formal meeting with his grandson. A painting of Cartigny by British

A portrait of Louis Cartigny in *The Graphic*, 16 November 1889.

artist Milly Childers (whose Liberal Party politician father Hugh had been First Lord of the Admiralty, 1868–71) was shown at the Chicago Exhibition in 1893.[8]

The Spanish fleet's last Trafalgar survivor was early suggested as Don Xavier Ulloa, who died in 1856 aged eighty-four.[9] But that fleet's apparent, and certainly consensual, last survivor was Don Gaspar Costela y Vasquez, who had been a seaman on *Santa Ana*. Born in 1787, he had entered his 105th year when he died in 1892 at the convalescent home for naval pensioners at San Fernando, Cadiz, having outlived Cartigny by about a week. Like the Frenchman, he was in full possession of his faculties, was proud of his presence at Trafalgar, and had enjoyed sharing his memories with many appreciative listeners. He was laid to rest on 8 April with full naval pomp.[10] (There seems to be no trace in official records of the death at Dallas, Texas, in 1898 of a supposed cabin boy at Trafalgar on Spain's, *San Juan Nepomuceno*, Pedro Antonio Zia Martinez.[11])

With the deaths of Cartigny and Costela, 'the veterans of Trafalgar, unless any remain in England, have entirely disappeared', declared a press report in 1892. And, as a military publication observed around the same time, the 'mania' for 'last survivors' of the great land and sea battles of the Napoleonic Wars had by then been extended to encompass veterans of Admiral Lord Exmouth's victory over the Barbary states at Algiers in 1816 and Admiral Sir Edward Codrington's defeat of the Turks at Navarino in 1827. (Cynics and misanthropes were alert for yarn-spinning beggars falsely depicting themselves as battle survivors in the hope of receiving alms.[12])

UK veterans

'It is not very easy to say who the last [British Trafalgar] survivor is,' stated naval affairs journalist and historian (Sir) William Laird Clowes in 1895.[13] Several persons had been suggested as such, with much inevitable gun-jumping to premature conclusions. William Saunders (real surname Sandilands), a feeble resident of Tewkesbury, Gloucestershire, dependent on paltry parish relief, was suggested in mid-1858 as 'one of the last' if not 'the very last' of the survivors of *Victory* at Trafalgar.[14] An able seaman, he had been a maintopman on *Victory*, and at the battle was captain of a gun. Having helped to carry badly wounded midshipman William Rivers (1788–1856; lieutenant, 1806) to the cockpit, he was, the article claimed, sent by the dying Nelson to enquire of Hardy how many enemy ships had struck. (That question and its answer are, of course, usually depicted as part of a direct conversation between the admiral and captain themselves.) As William Sandilands, 'Saunders' died and was buried at Tewkesbury in April 1867 aged eighty-nine, his presence at Trafalgar widely noted in newspapers.[15]

The last surviving participant in Nelson's 'death scene at Trafalgar' was, according to a press report late in 1869, William Turner, who had recently died (aged eighty-eight, the official record shows) at Warrington, Lancashire, where he seems to have been a whitesmith, a trade he perhaps learned in a ship's armoury.[16] Newspaper, genealogical, and official archival records indicate that *Victory*'s last Trafalgar survivor was Scottish seaman James Chapman, who died at Dundee in 1876 aged ninety-two.[17] At the battle there were two Scots of that name, both landsmen: our man was the volunteer from Edinburgh who, by the time of his discharge from the Navy in 1814, was rated able seaman.

So much for the supposition that James Sharman from East Anglia – not to be confused with Thomas Sharman of the third-rate HMS *Polyphemus* (64) – who had helped to carry the mortally wounded Nelson to the cockpit, was the sole member of *Victory*'s company still alive. ('He is now looking hale and hearty as ever, taking great delight in reciting to any passing stranger the incidents of that engagement.'[18]) According to a press report early in 1879, a Henry Morrissey, recently deceased at Halifax, Nova Scotia, had seen Nelson fall on *Victory*, where he himself was wounded. A William Morrissey from Newfoundland had served on the second-rate HMS *Prince* (98) at Trafalgar, but this Henry is mysterious. Also hard to track down is a seaman surnamed McHardy who reportedly died in Edinburgh in June 1879 aged ninety-five, and was also said to have seen the stricken admiral in the cockpit.[19]

John Haswell, whose mother is known to have been living in London's Lambeth district in 1808 when he made his will in her favour, was a sixteen-year-old 'boy third class' at Trafalgar. His naval service, but not his occupational connection with the sea, ended in 1817, and it was as a retired boatman in the Coastguard that he died at Ballyheigue, County Kerry, Ireland on 15 September 1877. Apparently he failed to receive the Trafalgar medal in 1847, having missed the deadline for applications.[20] A report in a Melbourne, Australia, paper that a man named George Hippwood (Hipwood according to www.ancestry.com) who had died at that city's Benevolent Asylum three weeks earlier aged ninety-five was a Trafalgar survivor is unconfirmed by available evidence.[21]

A singularly curious claim circulating in 1872 concerned Canon Andrew Knox, vicar of Birkenhead, Lancashire (who died aged eighty-four on 12 October 1881). This was that at Trafalgar he 'received a shot in his neck, which prevents his turning his head either to the right or left' although otherwise fine, and that he often told of how he had been with Nelson in the latter's 'last moments'. There is no record of Knox having been at the battle, nor does this strange anecdote seem to have been repeated upon or after his death.[22]

'When an old salt very long in receipt of a naval pension', named as John

Crawford, his birth year given as 1787, died in Forfarshire in 1882, it was suggested in the press that *he* was the last British survivor.[23] Unlike two namesakes also from north of the border, he seems to be unlisted in key online databases regarding Trafalgar participants.[24] In any case, the suggestion, as we shall see, was incorrect. Nor does there appear to be any plausible confirmation of a report that an Irish-born powder monkey at Trafalgar named John O'Brien had died in Illinois aged 108.[25]

George Browne, born about 1784 in or near Bridgwater, Somerset, where he died on 22 April 1856, had been a lieutenant on *Victory* and was made commander in 1810 after serving on Lord Collingwood's first-rate *Ville de Paris* (110). Called to the bar in 1821, he became a retired captain in 1840. In the temperance movement's *Christian News*, soon after his death, this dedicated teetotaller was mistakenly described as the last of the country's Trafalgar captains. The British Trafalgar captain who outlived the rest was the Earl of Northesk's flag-captain on the first-rate HMS *Britannia* (100), Charles Bullen, who died on 2 July 1853 aged eighty-three.

The fifth-rate frigate *Phoebe*'s Thomas Bladen Capel was runner-up, dying on 4 March 1853 aged eighty-one. Then came the third-rate *Orion*'s Edward Codrington, who died on 28 April 1851, having turned eighty-one the previous day.[26] Other examples of relative longevity included the third-rate *Revenge*'s first lieutenant at Trafalgar, Admiral (retired) Lewis Hole, who upon his demise at Barnstaple on 16 July 1870 aged ninety-one was described as the battle's 'senior surviving officer'; William Mannell, a quartermaster on *Victory* at Trafalgar, who died at Greenwich on 9 March 1871 aged ninety-four; Commander (retired) Stephen Hilton from Kent (lieutenant 1806), master's mate on the third-rate *Minotaur*, who died in 1872 aged eighty-six; his shipmate Commander (retired) Charles Wolrige from Devon (lieutenant 1808), a midshipman at the battle who died in 1874 aged eighty-five; Vice-Admiral (retired) Joseph Gape, died 12 March 1876 aged eighty-two, who had been a volunteer first class on the third-rate *Ajax*; and third-rate *Swiftsure*'s acting surgeon at the battle, Scots-born Peter Suther, who ended his career as deputy inspector of hospitals and fleets, dying at Southsea on 21 March 1877 aged eighty-two.[27]

John Mills was allegedly a young seaman on the third-rate *Defence* at Trafalgar, who died aged ninety in January 1879 at Portsmouth, where each Trafalgar Day a boat from *Victory* rowed him to her harbour mooring so that he – Trafalgar medal on his chest and a store of memories in his heart – could join the commemoration on board her. Perhaps his name was garbled in the telling, for he is missing from the official list of those who in 1847 received the Trafalgar medal and clasp.[28] In any case, as candidates

A portrait of James Fynmore in *The Graphic*, 30 April 1887.

for Britain's 'last survivor' these men, like other veterans dying in the 1870s, were mere also-rans. Unquestionably, the very last Trafalgar survivor among British officers was Lieutenant Colonel James Fynmore of the Royal Marines Light Infantry. His father and namesake was captain of marines on the third-rate *Africa* at Trafalgar, sustaining a slight wound, and he himself was a volunteer first class on her. Born at Exeter on 9 August 1793, he ultimately joined the marines, becoming captain in 1826, major in 1846 and lieutenant colonel in 1854.

An engraving of James Fynmore's watercolour of the dismasted and drifting *Africa* (insert: Fynmore himself). *The Graphic*, 24 October 1886.

When he was eighty-two he depicted, in watercolour, *Africa*, battered and dismasted by the enemy and blown off course during the gale that set in on the evening of Trafalgar, rejoining Collingwood's fleet next day with assistance from the third-rate *Conqueror* (Captain Israel Pellew), which had suffered relatively lightly. Fynmore died on 15 August 1887.[29]

Under the name H J Blyth, a relative of Fynmore by marriage – probably Chatham-born Henry James Blyth, whose death aged seventy-seven at Woolwich was registered early in 1925 – composed well-intentioned doggerel in honour of the old man ('To the Last Surviving Officer of the Battle of Trafalgar'). Sons of the latter had settled in Australia, and the lines appeared in a Sydney paper during 1923:

> When, on that fateful morn the drummers beat
> To quarters, and the gallant British line
> Rush'd like sea-lions o'er the foaming brine,
> All hearts on fire the ancient foe to meet:
> What were thy thoughts as 'mid the roar and heat –
> Sails rent, masts reeling, death-bolts crashing broke
> The lofty sides, and through the flash and smoke –
> Thou saw'st men gasping at thy childish feet?
> A child thou wert, fresh from the fair green soil
> Of Britain; yet undaunted, proud and high,
> Thy young heart beat beneath the father's eye;
> And when, at last, call'd from thy bloody toil,
> The heroes sprang to hail the victory dear,
> 'Twas thy small voice that led the singing cheer![30]

Of some interest is the fact that James Hughes-Collingwood (1872–1963), a lieutenant commander in the Royal Naval Reserve who served as Conservative Member of Parliament for Peckham (1922–24) was Lieutenant Colonel Fynmore's grandson. His father was Cornish-born Chatham Dockyard clerk William Collingwood Hughes (1831–89), through whom he claimed (how accurately is uncertain) to be related to Nelson's second-in-command at Trafalgar and adjusted his birth name to emphasise the kinship. He believed he may well have been the last living person who had heard anecdotes of Trafalgar from an actual participant – his mother's father.[31]

Runners-up to James Fynmore among officers for recognition as 'Trafalgar's last British survivor' were Vice-Admiral Spencer Smyth (died 3 April 1879 aged eighty-seven), a midshipman on *Defiance*; Admiral William Ward Percival Johnson (died 26 December 1880 aged ninety), a midshipman of the brig-sloop

Childers (14), who was reputedly a guest aboard *Victory* at the battle; Commander William Vicary (died 21 March 1882 aged eighty-nine), a volunteer, first class[32] on *Achilles*; Commander Francis Harris (died 9 July 1883 aged eighty-seven), a volunteer, first class, on the second-rate *Téméraire*; Admiral Robert Patton (died 30 August 1883 aged ninety-two), a midshipman on the third-rate *Bellérophon*; and Admiral of the Fleet Sir George Rose Sartorius (died 13 April 1885 aged ninety-four), midshipman on the second-rate *Tonnant*. Like Fynmore, they had regularly attended the Royal Navy Club of 1765's annual Trafalgar Day dinner at Willis's Rooms off London's St James's Square.[33] The *Illustrated London News* (1 March 1879) carried an engraving, based on previous individual portraits, of all seven venerable warriors seated together.

The *Naval and Military Gazette* of 11 October 1876 noted that the recently deceased Commander Masters Norman (born 1784), whose lieutenant brother William was killed aboard the third-rate *Thunderer* at Trafalgar, had been the

A composite engraving of 'The Surviving Officers of the Battle of Trafalgar', in *Harper's Bazaar*, 12 April 1879, p.237. Left to Right: Smyth, Vicary, Johnson, Sartorius, Harris, Fynmore, and Patten.

oldest officer in the Royal Navy as well as the final survivor of the 1801 expedition to Egypt under General Sir Ralph Abercrombie and Admiral Lord Keith, Commander-in-Chief, Mediterranean. He was, however – reflected the *Gazette* – 'by no means the last of the gallant officers' who fought in 'great naval engagements', as in addition to 'the handful of naval veterans who are about to witness the seventy-first anniversary of Nelson's immortal victory' the Canadian Admiral Philip Westphal and Commander James Fitzmaurice, who had fought at Copenhagen (2 April 1801), were at that time still alive. So, indeed, were veterans of other naval actions during the century's infancy. Westphal died at Ryde on 18 March 1880 aged ninety-eight, the oldest commissioned officer in the service: he had been made lieutenant directly after Copenhagen.[34] Admiral Charles Bethune (né Drinkwater; 1802–84), was the last surviving officer, and possibly the last surviving crew member, of the third-rate *Northumberland*, which took Napoleon from Torbay to St Helena in 1815.[35]

Admiral Sir Erasmus Ommanney, who died aged seventy on 21 December 1884, was widely considered the last survivor of Navarino, where he served aboard the third-rate *Albion* under his paternal uncle, Sir John. However, Commander John Cawley, born at Plymouth in February 1810, whose father and namesake was at Trafalgar, was arguably Navarino's last survivor. A midshipman on the third-rate *Genoa* who passed for lieutenant in 1829, he appears in the 1901 Census living in Lambeth with his niece and nephew, and died there in 1904 aged ninety-six.[36]

Along with 'Who was the last survivor of Trafalgar?' were subsidiary queries: 'Who was the last person alive who actually spoke to Nelson? Who was the last living person who had at least set eyes on him?' When Commander Henry Augustus Fawcett (1791–1882; lieutenant, 1811) was a midshipman on the American Captain (Admiral) Benjamin Hallowell's (Carew's) third-rate *Tigre*, Nelson, piped aboard some months before Trafalgar, asked his name. On receiving his answer, the great man teasingly continued, 'Well, little fellow, and can you tell me the whereabouts of the French fleet?' Overawed and flabbergasted, the boy merely shook his head. But he never forgot that brief encounter, and surmised in old age that he might be the last man alive to whom Nelson had spoken.[37]

Fraudulent claims
Who was the last living person who saw Nelson? That honour, readers of London's *Daily Telegraph* (19 March 1907) learned, belonged to Joseph Stuckey, whom the paper's reporter had briefly interviewed the previous day. Born in Newport, Monmouthshire, on Christmas Eve 1799, Stuckey was a former sailmaker turned ship's stoker who served on the sloop *Miranda* during

the Crimean War. He had more recently been working as a crossing sweeper in London's Kentish Town (removing dung and detritus from the roadway), but a work-related accident had taken him from his lodgings to St Pancras Infirmary. 'Propped up in bed with a red shawl round his shoulders, in a comfortable little room to himself,' Stuckey, his previously unkempt locks freshly trimmed, looked remarkably fit. 'With his neat, grey beard, keen eyes, clear-cut features, and face but slightly lined, his appearance is such as to make it seem almost incredible that he should have looked upon Nelson in the flesh,' ran the report, which included a photograph. 'Yet, as a child, he says he remembers seeing him at Portsmouth in the year of Trafalgar. He is proud of the memory.'

The report, and subsequent features in various newspapers, caused something of a sensation across Britain, eccentric but popular novelist Marie Corelli being so entranced that she sent the ancient mariner £5 (about £500 in today's currency). But certain natives of Newport smelled a rat. One of them, seventy-one-year-old retired sailmaker Edwin Trew, living in London's Tottenham, paid an unheralded visit to Stuckey's bedside and (to the patient's unconcealed dismay) not only bluntly announced that he recognised him, since they had once both been apprenticed to the same master in Newport, but disclosed that to his certain knowledge Stuckey was just a few years older than himself.[38] That, and testimony from several current Newport residents also in a position to know, scuppered Stuckey's star status, one wag observing that the only Nelson the seventy-nine-year-old – existing records show he was baptised at Newport on 25 February 1827 – might truthfully have glimpsed was James Nelson Knapp, Newport's mayor during 1855–56.[39]

Newsprint was scarcely dry regarding Stuckey when a remarkable Trafalgar veteran called William Kingsley living in Missouri came to public attention. According to some accounts, this instant celebrity was a native of Cork; according to others a native of Limerick. 'He bears many scars, but is proudest of the one which marks the wound he received at Trafalgar, within a few hours of the time when Lord Nelson was killed,' a report in a Sydney paper said of this man, whose most recent occupation was digging wells.[40] An entry for Kingsley on www.ancestry.com has him born in Ireland on 11 June 1781 and dying at Bloomfield, Stoddart County, Missouri, on 18 December 1906. No plausible match is found in the United Kingdom's National Archives list of Trafalgar participants, although there is a namesake (a seaman on the third-rate *Spartiate*) listed on battle-related databases.[41]

If claims of Kingsley's longevity were true he would have beaten the record of the longest-lived human being authenticated with an official birth record – Frenchwoman Jeanne Calment (1875–1997), who died aged 122 years, 164 days, let alone the longest-living known male, Jiroemon Kimura of Japan

The Day after Trafalgar; the *Victory* trying to clear the land with *Royal Sovereign* in tow to the *Euryalus* by Nicholas Pocock, 1810. The view is towards the coast near Cadiz, with the lighthouse at Rota in the centre left distance. (© National Maritime Museum, Greenwich, London)

(1897–2013) who reached 116 years, 54 days[42] – and we would find him in *The Guinness Book of Records*. Kingsley lived his first sixty-five years before anaesthetics, died before antibiotics or other aspects of modern medicine and allegedly lived through active participation in the Napoleonic Wars, the American Civil War (as a private in the 8th Regiment, Missouri Cavalry, aged at least seventy-nine when that conflict began and eighty-four when it ended); thus his candidature for the description 'Trafalgar's longest survivor' must have been based on either fraud or fantasy.

Whether James Fynmore was in fact literally the last British survivor of Trafalgar or merely the last of officer status will probably never be known for certain. There may well have been a 'common sailor' at the battle who merits that title but has escaped history's gaze owing to incomplete extant records. On 3 April 1889, Joseph Sutherland, a powder monkey from Sheerness on the fifth-rate frigate *Beaulieu*, which had been ordered to join Nelson's fleet but could not fall in with it until the day after the battle, celebrated his 100th birthday at Sittingbourne, in his native county of Kent. Sometimes wrongly described as Trafalgar's last survivor – by people who assumed that *Beaulieu* had been in the actual fight – he died in March 1890. A large crowd, including 200 mariners, attended his funeral.[43] He may not have fought at Britain's greatest naval triumph. But he symbolised those who did, and indeed all who had gone down to the sea in wooden ships to brave the 'thousand gales' and 'twenty years of strife' that would secure British naval supremacy for over 100 years.

145

The War of 1812 in Parliament: Britain's Naval Operations and the Political Discourse, 1812–15

Kevin D McCranie

The 16-gun *Julia* reached Spithead in the dying hours of 29 July 1812, mooring about midnight. The Royal Navy brig carried important dispatches that went off post-haste to London, communicating the official account of the 18 June American declaration of war against Britain. *Julia*'s news confirmed unofficial reports that had circulated for at least ten days.[1]

The day after *Julia*'s arrival, the Prince Regent, the future King George IV, spoke before the combined houses of Parliament, closing the session. After mentioning the outbreak of hostilities, the Prince Regent noted, 'His Royal Highness is nevertheless willing to hope, that the accustomed relations of peace and amity between the two countries may yet be restored.'[2] British leaders did not want war with America in the midst of their ongoing war in Europe that included continued operations by Wellington's army in the Iberian Peninsula and Napoleon's invasion of Russia. As a result, British leaders sought to end the war with the United States quickly by resetting relations. They confidently thought this would occur when the Americans learned that British leaders had provided a pathway to ease tensions through an offer to suspend the Orders in Council that had placed restrictions on commerce with Napoleonic France and provided the British with justification to seize trade destined for French-controlled ports.[3] These trade restrictions had significantly impacted US commerce and contributed to the breakdown of relations with Britain.

At the end of the Prince Regent's speech, Parliament adjourned until 2 October. Just three days before it was scheduled to reconvene, the Prince Regent, at the behest of the ministerial leadership, dissolved Parliament. The resulting election delayed the official opening of Parliament until 24 November 1812.[4] Throughout the four months when Parliament was first in recess and later dissolved awaiting the new elections, negotiations based on the suspension of the Orders in Council went nowhere; instead, the War of 1812 intensified.

It should be noted that neither the Napoleonic Wars nor the War of 1812 resulted in British political leaders modifying the parliamentary calendar. This should not be surprising, however. Members of Parliament did not vote on operational decisions or discuss issues regarding the day-to-day fighting of the war. For the Royal Navy, such decision-making was in the hands of the Admiralty and its naval officers. Parliament served as the law-making body as well as what could be called the political conscience of the state. In this regard, Parliament provided funding and oversight. Moreover, the speeches and other actions by its members tended to be influenced by political and sometimes even personal agendas.

The conduct of the War of 1812 at sea was no exception. Members of Parliament found the naval war – especially the early war defeats in single-ship actions – to be quite valuable as political munitions to attack the ministerial leadership and further their own agendas. How this occurred allows for a more complete understanding of how Georgian parliamentary politics interacted with naval operations.

The War of 1812 begins

When the Prince Regent opened the new Parliament on 30 November 1812, he admitted the failure of peace attempts. Though he extolled British success along America's border with Canada including the capture of a large American force at Detroit, his comments were muted regarding the naval war, including the defeat of the frigate HMS *Guerriere* by the frigate USS *Constitution*.[5]

USS *Constitution* v HMS *Guerriere*, by Anton Otto Fischer.
(Naval History and Heritage Command, Washington, DC)

Following the speech, members of Parliament had an opportunity to respond: several addressed the naval war. George Canning in the Commons asserted:

It never entered into my mind that the mighty naval power of England would be allowed to sleep while our commerce was swept from the surface of the Atlantic; and that at the end of six months war it would be proclaimed in a speech from the throne, that the time was now at length come, when the long-withheld thunder of Britain must be launched against an implacable foe, and the fulness of her power at length drawn forth.[6]

Government leaders faced accusations of highlighting success along the border with Canada rather than providing a balanced appraisal of the war including the loss of *Guerriere*.[7]

The very start of the session found the Liverpool ministry then governing Britain backed into a corner respecting the naval war. As Britain's most powerful and flexible instrument of war, the Royal Navy had a tradition of victory, idolised in the personage of Nelson. The Americans did not seem to read the script that called for them to bow before Britain's naval supremacy. The Americans had not only fought well at sea, they had surprising successes, including the capture of a frigate and a large number of British merchant vessels.

Parliament's responses to American successes

The last days of December brought news of the capture of a second British frigate. This time it was HMS *Macedonian* by the frigate USS *United States*.[8] Like reports detailing the loss of *Guerriere*, this information arrived with Parliament in recess. The day after Parliament reconvened on 2 February, discontent boiled over.

The Right Honourable Robert Banks Jenkinson, Second Earl of Liverpool (1770–1828). Mezzotint by Charles Turner (1774–1857) 1827; based on a painting by Sir Thomas Lawrence (1769–1830). (Yale Center for British Art)

Britain's ministerial leadership defended itself against the handling of the crisis that led to war with America. This included making available to members of Parliament official papers outlining British actions prior to the war.[9]

Two weeks later, on 18 February, when Parliament again discussed the war, debate in both houses turned to the navy. In the Lords, Henry Petty-Fitzmaurice, third Marquess of Lansdowne, beseeched, 'If anyone were asked, what had been the success of our navy in this war, he would unfortunately find some difficulty in giving an answer.' He continued:

> Yet, if ever there was a contest where we ought to have been well prepared, where we had every advantage in regard to naval means, it was this contest with America, – a contest commencing at a time when our navy was almost liberated from every other occupation – when there could have been no difficulty, surely, in sending out a force capable of coping with the American squadron – a navy so inferior, so inexperienced, and so perfectly known in all its parts.[10]

The response highlighted a great deal of truth. The US Navy was small, possessing not even 3 per cent the operational hulls and less than 2 per cent the tonnage of Britain's navy.[11] It did have a short history, but the few years of its existence had brought it into contact with the British, making the Americans well-known. However, Lansdowne's statement also demonstrated considerable ignorance. Though the US Navy had a short history, it had been an active one given its actions in the Quasi War (1798–1800) against France and later in the Mediterranean to protect American trade against attacks by the North African powers often referred to as the 'Barbary Pirates'. Moreover, Lansdowne failed to recognise the difficulties of the operating environment including the sheer size of the Atlantic, the distance between Britain and America, or that the Americans declared war at the moment the Napoleonic Wars had escalated with the 1812 invasion of Russia. Finally, after twenty years of near constant war, the British navy sat on the edge of material and personnel exhaustion.[12]

The First Lord of the Admiralty, Robert Dundas, the second Viscount Melville, a sitting member of the Lords countered, 'Every exertion had been made by the Admiralty of which the force of the country was capable.'[13] The rejoinder from Richard, first Marquis Wellesley, announced, 'A time would come, and that very shortly, for an enquiry into the mode of conducting this war.'[14] Robert Banks Jenkinson, second Earl of Liverpool, the head of the ministry and another member of the Lords, came to Melville's defence, even using the example of Nelson to defuse the attack.[15]

On the same day, a similar debate occurred in the Commons. Ostensibly, this was a discussion about the reasons for the war, including Britain's efforts to avert hostilities. Debate, as in the House of Lords, drifted on to the naval war. The reason was simple, as Robert Stewart, Viscount Castlereagh, noted, 'The House must be sensible that no question could be more closely interesting to the country, touching as it did upon one of the main features of our security, the support of our naval power.'[16] This statement clearly identified the principal reason for the recurring nature of arguments addressing the naval war: Britain's navy was the superior instrument of national power and critical to British security, yet it could not destroy a vastly inferior opponent. One member questioned why the 'government were not able to afford such a force from the British navy, as might not only cope with, but sweep the petty fleet of America from the ocean?'[17] The fog of war, friction, the extensive area of operations, and advantages the Americans possessed in ships and personnel conspired to create conditions to make this naval war more difficult than anticipated. The loss of warships – especially *Guerriere* and *Macedonian* – were major points of concern. Sir Thomas Baring, another member of the Commons, ignorant of the state of the Royal Navy, claimed that it was land, not naval forces, that were overtaxed yet the navy had suffered defeat. 'For these things he censured ministers.'[18]

George Canning then stepped forward to make the day's most eloquent and impassioned speech that attacked the Liverpool ministry's handling of the naval war:

> I complain not of the naval department, but of the policy which controlled its operations. I complain that the arm which should have launched the thunderbolt, was occupied in guiding the pen: that admiral Warren [the commander-in-chief on the American station] was busied in negotiating, when he ought to have been sinking, burning, and destroying.[19]

The Right Honourable George Canning, MP (1770–1827) Shown here as Prime Minister. Engraving after Thomas Lawrence, c1822. (Wikipedia, public domain)

The conduct of the naval war served as a pawn in larger political struggles. Since the navy played an essential role in Britain's security, naval failure became a means of attacking Liverpool's leadership since no Briton could sit idly while the navy appeared ineffective. Some like Canning and Wellesley wished to challenge Liverpool and his colleagues' hold on parliamentary leadership. It could even be argued that there had been something of a power vacuum in Britain since the death of William Pitt the Younger in early 1806, and Canning and Wellesley continued to hold interest in filling this perceived void. Others were members of the more regular opposition.[20]

In hindsight, the naval defeats did little to shift the actual naval balance. The British eventually lost three frigates out of more than a hundred that were operational: the dominance of the Royal Navy was never in doubt. The moral effect was significant, however. The losses provided an issue for those seeking to stir the pot. Moreover, it was a topic that the ministry could not repudiate without providing confidential information about the state of the Royal Navy, to include its deployments and its manning. This was, in effect, a perfect means of challenging the Liverpool ministry.

The effects of the 18 February discussions were significant. A month later, when debate in the Commons occurred over Navy Estimates, William Dundas, a member of the Commons, one of the Lords Commissioners of the Admiralty as well as cousin to the First Lord, explained, 'If there appeared an excess over those of last year on the face of the present Estimates, it was to be remembered, that the number of our enemies had increased.'[21] John Wilson Croker, the Secretary of the Admiralty and another member of the Commons, provided a gloomy prediction:

> He was sensible that since the commencement of the French war, we had not had so formidable an enemy to cope with as we had at this moment. If the enemy went on increasing his means, we must do so too; and we must not forget that our navy must be the first object of our anxiety, as it was of our security.[22]

Though the previous statement aimed at French naval expansion, the war with America exacerbated the navy's overextension. The discussion over Navy Estimates allowed the ministers to create a narrative illustrating the stresses faced by the Royal Navy. On the one hand, it admitted some of the navy's problems; on the other, it worked to defuse accusations about the navy's response to America.

Debates in the House of Lords
In the Lords meanwhile, John Bligh, fourth Earl of Darnley, launched what would become a multi-year campaign to demand 'an enquiry into the naval administration of the country'.[23] His plea became more vociferous when news of a third British frigate defeat (the 38-gun *Java*) broke in England. One newspaper linked the loss to the 'the most culpable folly and neglect on the part of Ministers'.[24] Darnley pounced, calling the defeats a 'succession of disasters', and it 'only confirmed him in the propriety of bringing forward the subject for inquiry'.[25] Darnley appealed for the release of naval documents necessary to start the inquest, and the First Lord answered that 'no public inconvenience would arise from communicating these documents'.[26]

A month later, the discussion resumed with the Earl of Darnley arguing that he found 'himself compelled, from a sense of his public duty, to call their lordships' attention to our naval disasters'.[27] He blamed the ministers for 'the late disasters; of the officers and men who so gallantly, but unsuccessfully fought, nothing could be uttered but unqualified applause'.[28] From this and earlier statements, it is clear that members of both houses felt compelled to defend the officers and men of the navy. If service members were not at fault, the next most likely targets were the Admiralty and more specifically Liverpool's hold on power.

The partisan nature of the dispute is clear in Darnley's explanation: 'He trusted that the naval glory of Great Britain was not on its decline, although ministers appeared to exert themselves to the utmost to hasten its fall.'[29] The response from the First Lord of the Admiralty was quick. Whereas Darnley argued with passion and generalities, Melville responded with specifics.[30] Another member of

John Bligh, Fourth Earl of Darnley (1767–1831).
Attributed to artist Thomas Philips (1770–1845).
(National Trust, Addingham Park)

the ministry, Henry, third Earl of Bathurst, Secretary of State for War and the Colonies, came to Melville's support, observing:

... with regard to the capture of the three frigates, he would put it to the candour of the House, whether any certain arrangements could have been made to prevent these losses happening, as they had done, in very distant parts? One was taken off the Western Isles; another in the Brazils; and the third had been separated from a line of battle ship, when they were both on a cruize. There was in reality no foresight, no precaution, which could prevent such losses.[31]

Another supporter of the ministry noted the superiority of the American frigates in terms of size and manning.[32] Darnley also had advocates within the Lords. The two sides of the argument were clear. The ministry claimed that war is uncertain; the Americans were enterprising; and they eked out inconsequential tactical success in widely separated regions. Those in opposition linked the losses to negligence and mismanagement in the highest levels of leadership. The vote on the grounds for inquiry saw the ministry triumph 125 to 59.[33]

Though the Liverpool ministry weathered this attack, it affected the Admiralty's relationship with its commander-in-chief in American waters. Soon after the American declaration of war, the Admiralty had combined the North American Station with the Leeward Islands and Jamaica Stations and had selected Admiral Sir John Borlase Warren as commander-in-chief to oversee this extensive area of operations. Unprecedented in size, Warren neither got this unwieldy command

Admiral Sir John Borlase Warren (1753–1822), 1799 line engraving by James Fittler (1758–1835) after Mark Oates (c1750–1821).
(Yale Center for British Art)

fully under his control nor established a good working relationship with the Admiralty. Setbacks, including the frigate losses and the inability to demonstrate substantial progress against the American naval threat, soured the Admiralty's relationship with Warren. Discussions in Parliament did not help his cause. This led the Admiralty to begin considering his replacement, for Warren had become a political liability and the perfect scapegoat for Liverpool and his associates.[34]

It took until November 1813 for the Admiralty to break Warren's command apart, restoring independence to the Leeward Islands and Jamaica Stations, but news of this decision needed to cross the Atlantic. In fact, Warren did not learn about the break-up of his command until February 1814. The Admiralty eventually replaced Warren with Vice-Admiral Sir Alexander Cochrane. The First Lord justified this decision to Warren by claiming that he was too senior to command merely the North American Station. Continued delays meant that Cochrane did not fully assume command until 1 April 1814.[35]

In the meantime, the Admiralty needed in the short term a solution to the American naval threat. The expedient settled upon entailed the issuing of an Admiralty circular that restricted rules of engagement. The document asserted 'that they do not conceive that any of His Majesty's Frigates should attempt to engage, single handed, the larger Class of American Ships, which though they may be called Frigates, are of a size, Complement and weight of Metal much beyond that Class, and more resembling line of Battle Ships'.[36] Though the American frigates were not ships of the line in disguise, they were an overmatch for the standard British frigate, and this circular altered the rules of engagement to provide an effective means for diminishing the possibility of additional frigate losses until the sheer size of the Royal Navy could exert its influence on the naval war.

Debates in the House of Commons
Meanwhile, in the Commons, a new line of attack developed, spearheaded by Captain Thomas, Lord Cochrane. A courageous but controversial naval officer, he also served as a Member of Parliament for the constituency of Westminster. Though the electorate for most seats in the Commons comprised but a small number of privileged individuals, Westminster had a relatively large electorate. Cochrane was both popular and, at least on the surface, a reformist who sought to right abuses within the navy. However, deeper consideration indicates that Cochrane used arguments for reform to criticise his enemies among Britain's naval leadership.[37] In this context, he made a speech in the Commons on 5 July 1813: 'During the present war with the United States of America, his Majesty's naval service has, in several instances, experienced defeat, in a manner and to a degree, unexpected by the House, by this Admiralty, and by the country at

large.' Cochrane continued, 'That the cause of this lamentable effect is not any superiority possessed by the enemy, either in skill or valour, nor the well-known difference in weight of metal, which, heretofore, has been deemed unimportant.'[38]

In each of the three frigate losses, the Americans had in fact possessed the larger ship and its broadside threw a heavier weight of metal; however, the

Captain Thomas, Lord Cochrane (1775–1860), 10th Earl of Dundonald. Engraving by John Cook based on a painting by James Ramsay (1786–1854), originally published in 1866 by Richard Bentley, London. (Dibner Library of the History of Science and Technology, 2003, Smithsonian Libraries, Washington, DC)

Admiralty had not clearly addressed these factors. Cochrane exploited the uncertainty about the nature of the American frigates to make his argument stronger, arguing that the problem 'arises chiefly from the decayed and heartless state of the crews of his Majesty's ships of war, compared with their former energy and zeal, and compared, on the other hand, with the freshness and vigour of the crews of the enemy'.[39] This was a serious attack since one newspaper described Cochrane as 'an intrepid officer, and is as distinguished for the earnest benevolence with which he enquires into the wants and comforts of his seamen'.[40] Cochrane exploited the fact that service aboard warships was difficult, and as long as the Napoleonic Wars continued, little relief could be expected. Even in hindsight, it is difficult to determine what Cochrane sought. The session of Parliament was nearly over, and by Cochrane's own admission, he did not expect immediate action.[41]

Cochrane's accusations demanded a response. Croker, as Secretary of the Admiralty, defended the Royal Navy and the Liverpool ministry. He claimed:

> The statements those Resolutions contained were so astonishing, true it was less astonishing, when coming from the noble lord, than from any other person; – but still even from him they were so astonishing, that surely they ought not to have been so suddenly, and with so little preparation, brought under the consideration of the House. There was no one but the noble lord who conceived that the disasters, which we had experienced in the course of the present war with the United States, were not to be attributed to a superior force on the part of the enemy, but to a decay of spirit and ardour in our seamen in the defence of their country.[42]

Several days later, the debate resumed. When Croker again spoke, he announced:

> The communication which he was about to make to the House had not been sought for or prepared by him. It had presented itself to him, as if from a divinity, to confute and confound the noble lord's misrepresentations and libels, to rescue the honour of the British navy from unfounded aspersions, and raise the glory of the British flag still higher than ever.

On his way to Parliament, Croker had received reports that the British frigate HMS *Shannon* had captured the American frigate USS *Chesapeake* on 1 June 1813.[43] Though *Chesapeake* was not one of the three large American frigates, she was at least a frigate, American, and on the losing side. *The Edinburgh*

Advertiser declared, 'This most gallant and brilliant action is a fine *Commentary* upon the Extraordinary speeches of Lord Cochrane.'[44]

In this debate, both Croker and Cochrane pointed to singular examples to support their arguments. Croker roused the members with news of a long hoped for victory, while Cochrane provided individual examples of seamen who had suffered grievously. In the end, victory triumphed over hardship.

The War of 1812 comes to a close

Within days, Parliament adjourned, only returning for the new session in late 1813. Throughout the session spanning the winter of 1813–14, the naval war with America proved a less contentious topic of discussion because of the ever-increasing minimisation of the American naval threat. Other issues took over the discourse. If anything, statements in Parliament respecting the war with America became even less common over the summer of 1814.[45] Victory in the Napoleonic Wars did much to sooth any discontent.

During the early months of 1815, an old nemesis, the Earl of Darnley, used news of the capture of the United States frigate *President* as a platform to extol the valour of British seamen on the one hand and attack 'the proverbial misconduct of our naval government' on the other.[46] Victory against one of the three large American frigates signalled that the British navy might have finally turned the corner, but it had taken too long, and Darnley wanted to know why. He sought a comprehensive inquiry, 'for he thought it highly material to ascertain the general state of our navy, in order to see how our naval administration had throughout performed its functions, and in what condition that force was left'.[47] The Admiralty provided the requested documents.

Over the next weeks, news arrived in Britain that the United States had ratified the Treaty of Ghent, officially bringing the war to an end, but if anything, this only encouraged Darnley. In June 1815, he again broached the subject as part of his continued effort to learn why the British navy proved unable to rapidly eliminate the American naval threat. It is difficult to determine how much external events skewed the debate, for Darnley orchestrated this latest attack on 12 June, just six days before the Battle of Waterloo. Needless to say, members of the Lords had more immediate considerations occupying their thoughts.

Darnley recounted, 'It appears to me, that however you may be disposed to forget the late war with America, and to think all retrospective inquiry inexpedient and unavailing, you cannot shut your eyes to the importance of considering whether the naval service of the country is well or ill conducted.'[48] After significant debate, one member of the Lords noted: 'a weaker case had never been brought before the House, particularly as contrasted with the voluminous mass of papers that had been moved for in support of it'. Sarcastically, he ribbed: 'He could assure the noble mover, that he would never vote for his being made first Lord of the Admiralty.'[49] Darnley's motion died with that rebuke and along with it Parliament's interest in the War of 1812 on the oceans.

Parliamentary attacks on ministers
Too often histories of the War of 1812 are confined to North America or the oceans. Less often does the impact of the war travel to Britain. This is made all the more complex because political leaders in London tended to view the War of 1812 within the broader Napoleonic struggle, making it difficult to disentangle the two. This is especially true when discussions turned to priorities, force allocations, or even budgetary issues for land and naval forces. Parliamentary discussions were influenced by the war with America, no more so than during the critical opening months of the war and to refute Lord Cochrane's contentions. It is important, however, to consider the nature of how naval events from the War of 1812 influenced the parliamentary discourse. Members in both houses used the war to attack the ministers. Some attacks came from outright members of the opposition while those who held more narrow grievances against the current leadership orchestrated other critiques.

The naval war was low-hanging fruit, especially in light of the frigate defeats during the first half-year of the war. Only Cochrane questioned the zeal of Royal Navy personnel. Though he did this to highlight how long and gruelling the Napoleonic Wars had been: this line of argument backfired. It proved more effective to directly criticise how the ministers had handled the war. Attacks on Liverpool and his associates in early 1813 are especially significant because a better appreciation of these attacks makes the actions of the Admiralty, as well as its strained relationship with their naval leader in North America, much more understandable.

Facts and Firsts for The United States Navy: Remembering the Cruise of the USS *Essex*, 1812–14

Brenden L Bliss

The date 28 March 2024 marked 210 years since the ignominious end of the USS *Essex*'s voyage, one that had started with great promise. Outside of historians and naval experts, few today remember what should have been a momentous accomplishment for the young United States Navy. This article will look back on the voyage, what it accomplished, and how the memory of those events changed with time.

The Enos Briggs company built *Essex* in 1799 in Salem, Massachusetts. At the gun deck she was 141ft long and 118ft on the keel, with a 37ft beam and a draft of just over 12ft. She displaced 850 tons and was rated for 32 guns.[1] *Essex*

The Frigate '*Essex*', 32 Guns, built in Salem 1799. Unknown artist, unknown year. (Naval History and Heritage Command, Washington, DC)

was categorised as a frigate, being larger than a sloop or brig, but was at a disadvantage in her weight class against America's most likely opponent since the British had 'not sent to sea a frigate of less than thirty-eight guns since 1784'.[2] *Essex* served her country well over the next decade, including participation in the conflicts with the Barbary States.

Captain David Porter took command in 1811 and he took her on her first war cruise in July of 1812. On 13 August, *Essex* captured HMS *Alert*, the first British warship that America captured in the war. It might be worth noting, however, that *Alert* carried only 16 guns compared to the 46 that *Essex* had been modified to carry during the war. This paper will discuss the nature of those guns in more detail later.

In the autumn, *Essex* returned to sea to join Commodore Bainbridge's squadron with USS *Constitution* (44) as the flagship. However, Porter was delayed in sailing and was not able to find Bainbridge at several pre-designated rendezvouses. In January 1813 Porter learned that Bainbridge had defeated the fifth-rate HMS *Java* (38) off the coast of Brazil on 29 December 1812. With *Essex* cruising off South America, Porter realised it was too dangerous to continue looking for Bainbridge, so he decided to take *Essex* around Cape Horn and attack British merchant shipping, specifically Britain's whaling fleet.

This was not the first time *Essex* had entered distant seas. On her shakedown cruise in 1800, she had in fact become the first American warship to round the Cape of Good Hope and enter the Indian Ocean. Under Porter's leadership, *Essex* was the first US warship to round Cape Horn and the first to enter the port of Valparaiso, Chile. Porter took a broad view towards his mission of hurting Great Britain, which is perhaps why he then supported US Consul General Poinsett's efforts in aiding the

Portrait of David Porter. Oil on Canvas by Orlando S Lagman, c1965. (Naval History and Heritage Command, Washington, DC)

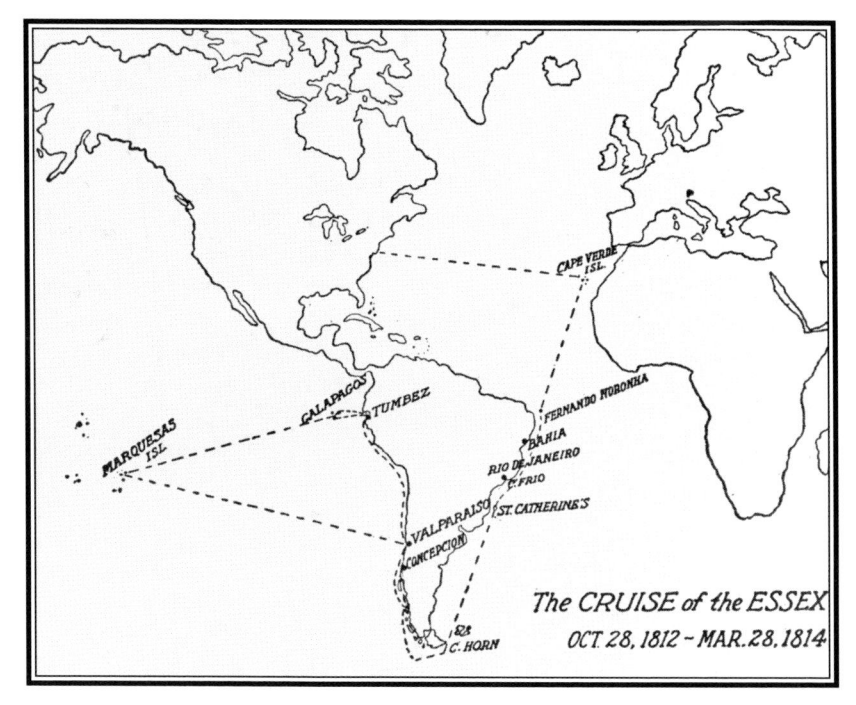

The Cruise of the *Essex*, October 28, 1812 to March 28, 1814. Unknown artist, unknown date. (Naval History and Heritage Command, Washington, DC)

dictatorship of Jose Miguel Carrera, who was leading one of the Chilean factions actively rebelling against Spain. While Poinsett went so far as to lead troops in battle as an officer in Carrera's army, Porter mainly provided moral support on the diplomatic front while intentionally not correcting the Chilean misconception that the presence of *Essex* indicated that the United States was officially supporting their fight for independence.

That relationship would have long-ranging results for the United States, as Porter would later advocate supporting Carrera in his revolutionary efforts against Spain into the 1820s. This put him in conflict with Henry Clay, speaker of the House of Representatives, who supported the rival factions led by O'Higgins (pro-British) and San Martin. The squabble between Porter and Clay actually weakened the overall US support for South American freedom fighters and allowed President Madison and Secretary of State Adams to promote a policy of neutrality. They feared that US intervention would prompt France to send its fleet in support of Spain's effort to retain control of her colonies. This argument ensured that Congress would delay any recognition and support to the region until after the signing of the Adams-Onis Transcontinental Treaty of 1819, which ensured the transfer of the Floridas to the United States and stabilised the Spanish–American border from Louisiana to the Oregon Territory. Only after that did the US recognise the independent nations of Chile and Argentina.[3] Therefore, the cruise of *Essex* indirectly influenced American foreign policy towards South America and perhaps facilitated the acquisition of Florida.

Essex in the Pacific
Setting aside that diplomatic mess, *Essex* also made history when Porter sailed to the Marquesas Islands to rest and refit his command, which by that point included several captured British whaling vessels. While there, he renamed the island of Nuku Hiva, Madison Island and claimed the group on behalf of the United States. This would be the first time an official representative of the American government demonstrated imperial ambitions by officially claiming land beyond North America. Although it may seem a bit humorous now, Porter did his best to expand US influence and trade into the Pacific. However, Congress had other things to worry about in 1814 such as avoiding the British Army as it set fire to Washington, DC. Thus, Porter's actions in the Pacific were never officially recognised nor ratified by the nation.

Essex's voyage is also noteworthy as it facilitated the first instance in which

Essex Rounding Cape Horn in 1813. Painting by unknown artist, unknown date. (Naval History and Heritage Command, Washington, DC)

a US Marine Corps officer took command of a naval vessel. Marine Lieutenant John M Gamble was placed in command of *Greenwich*, with which he captured a British vessel. Gamble later had the distinction of sailing the converted whaler *Sir Andrew Hammond* into Honolulu harbour, making it the first American naval vessel to fly her flag in that port. Gamble impressively sailed a leaking ship more than 2,400 miles from the Marquesas Islands to Hawaii with a crew of seven, only two of whom were completely healthy and uninjured, all without the aid of anchors, boats, charts or instruments of any kind. *Sir Andrew Hammond* was also the first American naval vessel likely to have Hawaiians in her crew as she sailed between the islands of Oahu and Hawaii in June 1814, before HM Sloop *Cherub* (18) interrupted the voyage by capturing the converted whaler.

With so many noteworthy accomplishments, one wonders why the ship and her voyage are not remembered more widely in American culture, in a manner like that of the USS *Constitution* or USS *Monitor*. Recounting the records and momentous events of these warships began almost as soon as they were christened. *Essex* is no exception. In fact, Porter himself started the ball rolling when he published information about his cruise in 1815, a revised edition in 1822, and a further account in 1823. Expanded accounts were published after the US Civil War, some of which included information provided by Admiral David Farragut, who had served as a midshipman aboard *Essex*, as well as by Porter's son, Admiral David Dixon Porter. The story was often repeated and analysed every few decades by individuals such as William James, Edward Pelham Brenton, Theodore Roosevelt, Alfred Thayer Mahan, Ralph Paine, C S Forester, Harry L Coles, Francis F Bierne, Betty Shepard, Frances Robotti and James Vescovi, Stephen Budiansky, George C Daughan, Donald R Hickey and Andrew Lambert. And yet, with so many historians having written on the subject, it is surprising how much room remains for controversy and debate. In fact, one could suggest that several of the above authors' works contain errors if not blatant inaccuracies and biased accounts. The majority of those listed above who wrote prior to the twenty-first century seem to have not relied to any great extent on anything other than Porter's account of the cruise and his ensuing defeat at the Battle of Valparaiso. A notable exception was British author William James, who in 1817 wrote a direct rebuttal of American (mainly David Porter's) accounts of the War of 1812. With that in mind, it is useful to compare Porter's version of events with those recorded by later historians. These works have shaped the story of *Essex*.

Once he had crossed into the Pacific in early 1813, Porter sailed to Valparaiso to resupply and gauge the atmosphere. He was surprised to find the Chilean people in rebellion against Spain. Chilean authorities willingly accommodated his needs since they hoped that the lone American warship's presence signalled the United States' support for their war of independence. Porter then sailed to the Galapagos Islands; the centre of the whaling trade during that period. He quickly captured nine British ships, recaptured one American ship taken earlier by the British and disarmed a Peruvian vessel that was attacking American shipping. He converted one of his prizes into an armed auxiliary, which then captured three additional British ships for a total of thirteen. The most seaworthy of the captured ships was converted to a war sloop and renamed USS *Essex Junior* (20).

After several months of stalking the whaling grounds, Porter took his fleet of remaining ships (several had been sent back to America to be sold in prize courts, and some as transports for the prisoners he could not take care of) to the Marquesas Islands. He felt this was an isolated spot where he could careen and refit his ships in peace. While doing this he claimed the island chain for the United States. Porter subsequently became involved in local affairs in order to maintain his crew's safety and secure a source of supplies. These actions resulted in the marines and crew of the *Essex* engaging in three significant battles with the local inhabitants, one of which the Americans lost.

C S Forester pointed out that 'the visit of the *Essex* to the Marquesas was a romantic episode with its feasts among the coconut palms and its little native wars and its Polynesian beauties, but it was nothing more'.[4] In relation to the War of 1812 he was certainly correct, but perhaps not when considering the impact on the Marquesas Islands. Porter arrived only a few weeks after several American sandalwood merchants left the islands. Historians now see these two arrivals as the start of an increase in bloodshed between islanders and visiting mariners, due, in part, to the violence Porter's men perpetrated. His defeat also demonstrated to the islanders that white men were vulnerable and could be beaten in battle.

Essex in Valparaiso

After departing the Marquesas, Porrter took *Essex* and *Essex Junior* back to Valparaiso to continue his mission. However, HMS *Phoebe* and HMS *Cherub*, under the command of Captain James Hillyar, caught up with him and blockaded the American ships. It is only at this point that any significant differences start to appear between Porter's account and those of later historians. This is perhaps natural as the final capture of *Essex* is the most controversial aspect of the cruise. The question must be asked, why did Porter return to Valparaiso when he knew that was where the British would likely be searching for him? By going there Porter was essentially placing himself in the lion's mouth and daring it to bite. In attempting to paint Porter in the best light possible, Ralph Paine said that it was only after *Essex* returned from her refit in the Marquesas Islands that Porter was informed of *Phoebe*'s search for him. Paine also stated that Porter 'assumed that the *Phoebe* was alone'.[5] This is clearly not true since Porter himself stated that he had received letters from the American consul in Buenos Aires before he retired to the Marquesas Islands which informed him that *Phoebe*, *Raccoon* and *Cherub* 'had sailed from Rio de Janeiro for the Pacific Ocean in pursuit of the *Essex*'.[6]

Forester is one of the few writers who criticise Porter's decision to return to Chile. It is clear that Porter did so looking for a fight. He had gathered more than six months' provisions during his stay in Marquesan waters. He also knew that a British fleet was actively looking for him along the South American coast. If he had wanted to remain a strategic threat and continue executing the mission objectives behind his sailing to the Pacific in the first place, then prudence would have dictated his avoiding Valparaiso. Even if he was motivated only by earning prize money, as his decisions to send the captured whalers back to Chile and then America for sale suggests, then he would have avoided battle. He could have gone back to the South Atlantic, further into the Central or North Pacific, down towards Australia or even over into the Indian Ocean. All options would have greatly increased British fears and anxiety regarding the threat to commerce and security *Essex* posed.

Being unable to easily identify Porter's next target would most certainly have tied down additional British resources that otherwise were being used to great effect in blockading the American coastline. As Forester stated, 'his cruise might have continued in glory instead of ending in glorious disaster'.[7] However, Porter

USS *Essex* and USS *Essex Junior* Pursued in Valparaiso Harbour. Watercolour on paper, artist unknown, date unknown. (Naval History and Heritage Command, Washington, DC)

chose none of these options. Instead, he anchored in Valparaiso and waited five days until James Hillyar's force arrived. There was no real strategic reason for this delay even assuming that Porter's decision to entertain the leading people of the town aboard the *Essex* was for diplomatic leverage and not simply an 'opportunity to return their civilities' as he claimed.[8] His delay must be seen as a desire to bring the British to battle in the hopes of winning glory and honour.

Setting aside Porter's motivation for returning to Valparaiso, it is worth remembering his statement, echoed by Paine, that *Phoebe* had been sent after *Essex*. Harry Coles also supported this idea when he wrote that 'it was not to be expected that the British government would permit this marauding to go on indefinitely'.[9] As a result the Admiralty sent *Phoebe* and *Cherub* to track Porter down. However, this was only a partially true statement.

Captain Hillyar, in command of *Phoebe*, was ordered to proceed from England to the Columbia River in Oregon territory in March 1813, the same month, incidentally, that Porter arrived in Valparaiso.[10] The British were annoyed with American fur traders, working for John Jacob Astor, who were encroaching on land claimed by Great Britain. Once Hillyar arrived in Brazil he learned of *Essex*'s presence in the Pacific. Rear-Admiral Sir Manley Dixon modified Hillyar's orders to include keeping an eye out for *Essex*. It was out of concern for this unexpected American military threat that the admiral added HMS *Cherub* and HMS *Raccoon* to Hillyar's command.[11] It was only after Hillyar rounded Cape Horn and reached Valparaiso that he became aware of the extent of Porter's attack on British commerce. Hillyar, like Porter, decided to take the widest possible view of his orders and sent *Raccoon* alone to the Columbia region while he remained with *Phoebe* and *Cherub* to seek out and stop Porter's depredation of British whalers.

Coles was, however, entirely mistaken when he wrote that after disposing of *Essex*, 'Hillyar proceeded northward to destroy the American fur posts on the Columbia River.'[12] In fact Astor's men heard that the Royal Navy was on its way north and sold the operations at Fort Astoria to the British-owned North West Company before *Raccoon* arrived. Thus, Hillyar only indirectly had anything to do with hindering the American fur trade.[13] Such an oversight does call into question the accuracy of Coles' account in general.

The historical commentary begins to blur again when addressing the eventual meeting between Porter and Hillyar. Porter spent several pages describing Hillyar's aggressive entry into Valparaiso harbour and an ensuing near collision between *Essex* and *Phoebe*. It is interesting that Hillyar made no mention of this event in his accounts. Ralph Paine took the position that Hillyar knew that the *Essex* was unprepared for action, Porter having just hosted a party on board the night before. It was out of a desire to take advantage of this opportunity that

Hillyar brought his ship so close to *Essex* when entering Valparaiso.[14] That is certainly possible but other possibilities seem just as likely, such as the unpredictable nature of the winds in the region. If that was the case then Hillyar simply lost control of his vessel and naturally would not want to report the incident to his superiors. It is also possible that he never had any intention of engaging the Americans, so the entire affair was trivial in his eyes. Only Porter, who may be trying to put a positive spin on losing his command, highlights the event. David Farragut (a midshipman at the time and David Porter's foster son) also recounted the event in his memoirs, suggesting that the ships did in fact come close to each other, but perhaps it was not as exciting or pivotal an event as Porter claimed. Francis F Bierne accepted with some hesitancy that Hillyar accidentally bore down on *Essex* and luffed his sails so that the jib boom crossed over *Essex*'s forecastle. He also claimed that, 'Porter, against his better judgment but out of respect for Chilean neutrality, accepted the apology.'[15]

The issue of neutrality will be revisited shortly but apparently the two commanders reached an agreement of some kind regarding the safety of Valparaiso. This is likely why Hillyar, even though he had the advantage in weaponry, did not attempt to engage Porter but instead instituted a close blockade of the harbour. Many writers do not spend much time on this point other than to emphasise that the blockade was a recognition of Chilean neutrality. Forester, on the other hand, clearly had a keener understanding of seamanship than many of the earlier authors who wrote on the encounter between *Essex* and *Phoebe*. He pointed out that:

> Hillyar kept the roadstead closely blockaded – no easy feat on that precipitous coast with the treacherous winds blowing down savagely over the hills above the town. To have maintained station for three weeks without once being taken unawares was a remarkable achievement on Hillyar's part.[16]

Forester also defended British actions when he discussed why Theodore Roosevelt's accusation of Hillyar's conduct was 'to cast the wildest and most vicious aspersion without any justification at all'.[17]

The vicious aspersion Forester referred to was Hillyar's decision to engage *Essex* in what Porter claimed were neutral Chilean waters, which the British should have respected as such. This point has been one of the more hotly debated aspects of *Essex*'s last cruise. In order to fully understand the issue of neutrality it is necessary to review the final steps leading to that last engagement.

The encounter between *Essex* and *Phoebe*
While being blockaded, Porter claimed to have attempted several times to bring *Essex* into single action against *Phoebe*. He apparently wanted to keep *Essex Junior* out of the fray but also knew he would be badly outgunned if both the *Cherub* and *Phoebe* were to engage him. Porter's efforts included flying provocative flags and allowing the crew to sing taunting songs at the British. Porter also took two of his prize ships with their valuable cargo out into the bay and burned them in the hopes that Hillyar would attempt to stop the destruction of British property.[18] These two prizes were the ships Porter had earlier sent to Valparaiso to be sold. It would seem that he had convinced the Chilean leaders to give him 'permission to sell his captured whalers and their cargo on Chilean soil'.[19] Apparently however, no one was either willing to or still had the money on hand to purchase the cargo and vessels.

It would seem that Hillyar's steadfast refusal to be baited into an engagement when he clearly knew his duty was to protect British interests and not take unnecessary risks by duelling with *Essex* prompted Porter's decision to flee. It is interesting that once again many American historians have written greater glory into the account than seems to have been historically the case. Bierne stated that Porter 'weighed anchor and sailed proudly out with the intention of running the blockade. Scarcely had the *Essex* reached open water with all sails set when a squall struck her.'[20] The implication was that Porter was tired of waiting and boldly wanted to engage in a fight or thumb his nose at the British by escaping. This seems at odds with Porter's own account that during a stiff breeze one of *Essex*'s anchor cables parted and she then began to drag her anchor. This situation prompted Porter to cut the remaining cable and attempt an escape. The full spread of canvas was not a proud display but a simple attempt to maximise the wind in order to gain all possible speed in outrunning *Phoebe* and *Cherub*.

It was a risk to have a full spread of canvas in such stormy conditions, which the more cautious Hillyar was avoiding. Unfortunately for Porter, that risk did not pay off; instead as he rounded a headland out of the bay's protection, *Essex* encountered the storm's full fury and her main topmast snapped and fell, taking several men into the sea with it. Porter attempted to return to safety now that he knew there was no chance of outrunning *Phoebe*. He anchored close to shore in the hopes that Hillyar would avoid a conflict out of respect for Chilean neutrality; but as *Phoebe* and *Cherub* continued to bear down on *Essex*, Porter prepared his ship for battle. Bierne demonstrated his support of American honour when he wrote:

the *Essex*, badly crippled, endeavored to regain the safety of the neutral port. Porter made the shelter of the bay while the *Phoebe* bore down upon him, followed by the *Cherub*. It was apparent that, regardless of the respect owed the Chileans and of Porter's consideration previously shown him, Hillyar this time meant business.[21]

Bierne put Porter in the best possible light. Porter did try to get back into Chilean waters to claim the protection of neutrality, but he did not go back into Valparaiso bay; he went into a smaller bay 3 miles up the coast. Whether he was close enough to the Chilean shore to claim neutrality has been a debate ever since. Bierne accepted that he was, which other historians have agreed with, but he did not mention the dubious nature of Chile's neutrality as a balanced perspective should have. Chile was a colony of Spain. In 1813 Spain was an ally of Great Britain. So technically Chile, belonging to Spain, should not have claimed neutral status. However, the Chileans in control of Valparaiso were in rebellion against Spain with the goal of becoming an independent nation; thus, they hoped to remain neutral in the Anglo-American conflict. As an ally of Spain, Great Britain was in a difficult position and should have aided the loyalist faction in fighting against the rebellious Chileans, not negotiate the neutrality of their waters. On the international stage, no one had recognised Chile as an independent state, which meant legally there was no basis to claim neutrality.

Forester did deal with the issue of neutrality by considering that since the

Battle between the U.S. Frigate USS *Essex* and HMS *Phoebe* and HMS *Cherub*, March 28, 1814, off Valparaiso, Chile. Drawing by Captain David Porter, USN, engraved by W Strickland. From *Journal of a Cruise made to the Pacific Ocean in the U.S. Frigate ESSEX, 1812–1814*, Volume 2. (Naval History and Heritage Command, Washington, DC)

final battle was 3 miles distance from the town, there was no danger to the inhabitants. It is likely that was all Hillyar was worried about earlier when he repeatedly refused to engage *Essex* in battle. Forester also noted that, although it was likely a violation of neutrality, 'there is no record of any resentment being aroused [by Chile or Spain] – after the action Hillyar made use of the facilities at Valparaiso without opposition'.[22]

In one of his more recent works on the topic, Donald Hickey also commented on the neutral waters issue by noting that 'it is easy to argue that its [Chile's] waters deserved no special protection, and the United States conceded as much by never protesting the British violation'.[23] None of these writers takes the issue to the next step by considering whether the Americans had negated the right to neutrality by their own actions. In his unpublished master's thesis, Kenneth Michael Hillyard astutely pointed out that Captain Porter pushed the bounds of neutrality by trying to have his prize ships sold in Valparaiso. Porter then burned the prizes *Hector* and *Catherine*. However, a group of English merchants in town, and apparently the Chilean governor as well, felt that the 'burning of the English prize in the Port, [was] a complete violation of all law'.[24] Porter knew of the government's position in the matter, and feared that the governor of Valparaiso might remove any privileges or protections of neutrality that *Essex* had previously enjoyed. It is unclear if that happened, but if it did then it was likely not ordered by the Carrera government.[25]

Setting aside the issues of neutrality, the conduct of the battle itself was rather one-sided. *Essex* put up a game fight but was outmatched, outnumbered and outgunned from the beginning, especially since *Essex Junior* remained out of the battle (apparently on Porter's orders, although that is not entirely clear). A large factor in Porter's defeat was the fact that *Essex* was armed almost exclusively with carronades and not the traditional long guns that the Royal Navy had in much larger number. Historians who analysed the battle have addressed this issue of armament, even if not always accurately.

Paine stated that Porter 'had unluckily changed her [the *Essex*'s] battery from the long guns to the more numerous but shorter range carronades'.[26] This is simply not true. The United States Secretary of the Navy made that decision before Porter took command of *Essex*. In fact, Porter initially refused to take command and did so only when Secretary Hamilton agreed to remove four of the carronades and replace them with 18pdrs.[27] Sadly for Porter, that order was never carried out before *Essex* got under way on her final cruise.

According to Bierne's recounting of the battle, Porter was hampered by his damaged topmast and unable to easily bring his guns to bear. This, combined with bad luck, seemed to be why he lost the conflict. Bierne did not consider the qualities and short range of carronades compared to the long guns of the

British. He mentioned that *Essex* lost fifty-eight killed, sixty-six wounded and thirty-one missing, which meant only seventy-five men were left effective.[28] The British expressed some reservations regarding these figures, especially the number of missing, since *Essex*'s books and papers regarding the crew complement did not survive the engagement. Bierne summarised his account with this closing comment: 'Thus, disastrously but gloriously, ended the cruise of the *Essex*.'[29]

In comparison, Forester pointed out that, '*Phoebe*'s long guns, well served, caused frightful havoc in the *Essex* during half an hour's bombardment,'[30] which was due to good gunnery but also the inability of *Essex* to bring her shorter-ranged carronades into action.

Hickey also brought up the issue of carronades by stating that the United States Navy realised that *Essex*'s loss was due, in part, to exclusive reliance on short-range weapons. 'Taking this lesson to heart, the United States never again sent a frigate to sea without a substantial complement of long guns.'[31]

Retrospectives on the *Essex* cruise

The capture of *Essex* denied Porter the glory and fame he had hoped for. Perhaps as a consolation and an attempt to salvage his image, he wrote multiple editions of his journal and claimed that the cruise had inflicted on the British damages of $5 million. He also seemed to suggest that although the final battle was a loss, the cruise made up for it by its gloriously patriotic earlier accomplishments. Subsequent historians echoed these themes. For example, Paine mentioned that Porter was finding 'more British ships and sending them

Commodore David Porter, USN (1780–1843). Engraving after an original painting by Alonzo Chappell, published by Johnson, Fry & Company, New York, 1862. (Naval History and Heritage Command, Washington, DC)

into the neutral harbor of Valparaiso or home to the United States with precious cargoes of whale oil and bone'.[32] Also, he did not explain that there was no record to indicate whether any of those ships or cargos were transferred successfully to America since most of them were recaptured by the British or destroyed by Porter himself. Bierne also reiterated Porter's claims that *Essex* had 'captured 12 of the whalers, 360 seamen, whale oil and other property to the estimated value of $2,500,000'.[33] Closer examinations such as those by Robotti and Vescovi strongly suggest that this was a wildly overinflated estimate on Porter's part.

Half of Porter's claim was based on damages inflicted in direct action against British whalers and half was as a result of protecting American commerce from British interference. Hickey noted that there 'were no armed British ships cruising in the Pacific until Porter drew them there',[34] although this is not entirely accurate since at least two of the ships Porter captured were armed merchantmen with Letters of Marque. Also, Hillyar had arrived with *Phoebe* and an armed merchant vessel to resolve trade disputes on the Columbia River before the British Admiralty was aware of Porter's actions in the Pacific. Hickey's point remains, however, that *Essex* only concentrated British attention on the Pacific, which may have made trade issues worse for American vessels, not better.

The patriotic value of the cruise did not fade with time but was reinvigorated to fit the needs of each new generation. Ralph Paine infused his accounts of the War of 1812 as only someone writing directly after the close of the Great Patriotic War could have. He stated that *Essex*'s 'long and venturesome voyage is still regarded as one of the finest achievements of the navy'.[35] He also waxed poetic when he claimed that, 'the *Essex* has a peculiar right to be held in affectionate memory, apart from the very gallant manner of her ending, because into her very timbers were builded the faith and patriotism of the people'.[36]

Forester clearly had a more balanced perspective of the entire cruise than earlier writers. His comments, in some respects, were likely aimed to counter the patriotically biased accounts of the previous century. He did, however, point out something that previous writers had not: the cruise highlighted, 'Porter's ability as an administrator and leader'.[37] By recruiting from captured whalers he 'actually had more men under his command at the end of it than at the beginning – something unique in the naval history of the period'.[38] Porter was also able to keep his men as an effective fighting force 'for seventeen months continuously, his crew in health and discipline, without once calling at a home port. Drake and Anson could hardly boast of more in that regard.'[39]

Forester concluded his account by bringing a refreshing appraisal of the actual value of *Essex*'s cruise. He noted that 'so ended an episode in American naval history whose importance springs mainly from the romance that surrounds it'.[40] Forester also considered the British reaction in 1814 to the episode by noting 'nor did the press indulge in any extravagances. "An event," said the *Naval Chronicle,* "of comparative insignificance," in which "owing to our superiority of force we have nothing to boast."'[41]

Historian James Ripley Jacobs claimed:

> the *Essex*, before her cruise ended in magnificent defeat at the hands of the British squadron whose sole mission was to hunt her down [a claim this article has previously noted is not the whole truth], had wrecked Britain's large and very prosperous whaling industry in the eastern Pacific and sent all British merchant traffic along the west coast of South American scurrying out of the area from Cape Horn to Panama.[42]

The word choice highlights the patriotic spin put on the incident. It is not clear how allowing one's command to be trapped and outgunned, then shot to pieces with 67 per cent of the crew listed as casualties can really be 'magnificent', but the image of British ships scurrying like rodents to distant corners is certainly patriotically evocative.

In conclusion, the cruise of USS *Essex* was full of accomplishments and 'firsts' for the young United States Navy. She was the first American warship in the Pacific, she claimed the first overseas territory of the new nation, and she set the stage for important future diplomatic decisions. However, these accomplishments were, in large part, overshadowed by her use as a tool, first by Captain David Porter to redeem his reputation, and then by later American writers in efforts to develop national pride and patriotic jingoism. And yet today, perhaps one of her enduring legacies, which should not be forgotten, is the small cemetery in Valparaiso containing the last remains of the American sailors killed during the battle. They were laid to rest in an act of respect jointly by Captains Porter and Hillyar shortly after the decisive British victory. For the last 210 years, Chile has maintained this cemetery for those men who fought and died for their nation. Perhaps this should serve as a welcome reminder of how nations can come together to move past the physical and rhetorical conflicts of the past.

The Cost of Wartime Innovation: Copper Bottoms and British Naval Operations during the American Revolutionary Wars, 1779–83

S A Cavell

By the start of 1779, the Earl of Sandwich, First Lord of the Admiralty, faced grim prospects in Britain's war against the rebellious North American colonies. The internecine struggle was now a worldwide conflict involving France and Spain, whose combined force at sea ended Britain's naval superiority. The Royal Navy's ninety ships of the line had, to this point, maintained the advantage against sixty-six French line of battle ships, but the addition of fifty Spanish two and three-deckers changed the dynamic.[1] The threat of invasion from a combined fleet sailing up the Channel loomed large, while the outlook for the besieged British garrison at Gibraltar and for colonial possessions in the West Indies darkened. In addition, Sandwich's position at the Admiralty hung by a thread.

The navy's failure to destroy the French fleet at the Battle of Ushant in July 1778 led to a vicious fight between Admirals Keppel and Palliser, which became a proxy war for Whigs and Tories and further

John Montagu, 4th Earl of Sandwich, 1718–1792, 1st Lord of the Admiralty, 1783, by Thomas Gainsborough (1727–88). (© National Maritime Museum, Greenwich, London)

destabilised an already fractured Parliament.[2] Calls for the removal of Sandwich were only stayed by the arrogance of demands made by Admiral Lord Howe, the only man with the experience to replace him. The Prime Minister, Lord North, lacked the decisive leadership qualities needed to control both his War Cabinet and the military situation, and Sandwich languished in a 'palsied state' while his fate, and the progress of the war at sea, hung in the balance.[3]

At the heart of the problem was a lack of ships. Sandwich's weak political position at the start of the American war prevented a full naval mobilisation and implementation of a rapid shipbuilding programme. The government's focus on land campaigns in the American colonies and a desire to maintain peace with European powers by not overtly expanding British naval capacity contributed to the lack of preparedness.[4] In addition, Sandwich's relative poverty, 'a crippling practical defect in the expensive business of high politics', left him open to charges of bribery and corruption from political opponents and reduced the impact of his demands in Parliament.[5] Not until January 1778 did the Cabinet finally prioritise the need for naval reinforcement.[6] By this point, expansion of the war had shifted the focus away from the Thirteen Colonies and placed it on the West Indies, East Indies, the French Atlantic coast and the Channel, forcing the Royal Navy to play catch-up when it was almost too late. Immediate naval expansion was now an existential requirement for Great Britain.

Experiments with copper sheathing
For about twenty years, the Admiralty had experimented with copper sheathing placed on the hulls of warships.[7] In theory, copper would prevent the burrowing of shipworm or *teredo navalis*, a mollusc in the family of clams that can grow to more than an inch in diameter and over a foot in length and, in the process, devour a ship's planking to the point of disintegration.[8] The 'worm' was particularly active in the tropical

Historical illustration of the shipworm species Teredo Navalis from *Popular Science Monthly*, Vol 13, September 1878. (Wikipedia)

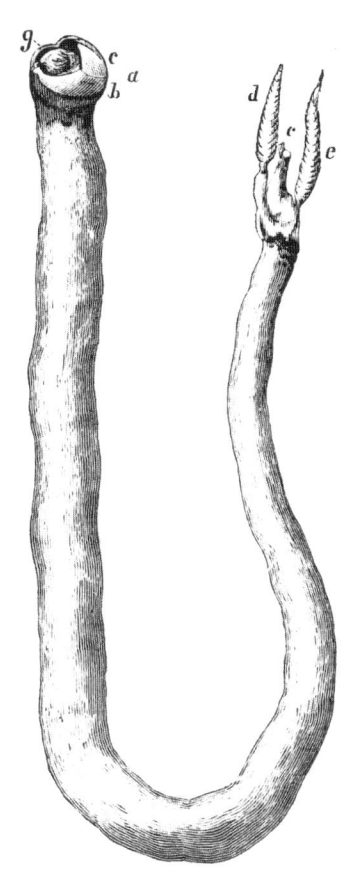

waters of the West and East Indies although, by mid-century, the harbours of southern England were equally infested.[9] Trials of the new technology were sparse and confined to small vessels like HMS *Alarm*, a 32-gun frigate that, in 1761, was the first Royal Navy vessel to receive a fully coppered hull.[10] Copper sheathing was seen as a more effective alternative to the existing method of wood sheathing, which attempted to provide a 'sacrificial' outer layer of planking.

The wood sheathing never lasted long, and vessels were forced to return to dock for new cladding every six to fourteen months to avoid damage to the hull.[11] The constant need to recall ships to dockyard facilities for refit took dozens of vessels off the line at any given time, severely reducing Britain's ability to exercise command of the seas. In wartime, the problem was crippling. Although copper was considerably more expensive and took longer to apply, the results were encouraging. Early tests showed that where the copper had not worn through, or had been scraped away by anchor chains, the planking beneath remained worm free. An added benefit was that the slow decay of copper in seawater dramatically reduced the growth of marine life, like barnacles and weed, which made the ship faster and more manoeuvrable than its fouled counterparts. The possibility of keeping coppered ships at sea for two to three *years* without the need for refit, and the fact that faster ships held significant

His Majesty's Ship the *Alarm*, a Fifth Rate … conducting a Spanish Prize into Gibraltar. Etching by unknown artist, 1781. (Wikipedia)

tactical advantages in battle, meant that the copper sheathing more than paid for itself and made both financial and strategic sense. By some estimates, a coppered fleet was effectively one third larger.[12] Captain Charles Middleton, Comptroller of the Navy (later first Baron Barham in 1781, Admiral and First Lord of the Navy in 1795), went so far as to suggest that, 'It is actually more than doubling our number of ships,' although this reflected his hyperbolic enthusiasm for the technology.[13] While the numbers were debatable, copper sheathing as a force multiplier was not, and it provided an immediate solution to the Admiralty's most pressing problems. In early 1779, Sandwich ordered the entire fleet to be coppered, committing vast financial and dockyard resources to the purpose.[14]

Commanders at sea were quick to sing the praises of their coppered ships. In July 1779 Captain Lord Mulgrave remarked that, '*Courageux*'s copper has answered beyond my hopes, as her superiority in sailing is hardly credible.'[15] By September, Admiral Sir Richard Kempenfelt was confident that 'twenty-five sail of the line, coppered, would be sufficient to hazard and tease this great unwieldy, combined [Franco-Spanish] armada, so as to prevent their effecting anything'.[16] Two years later, he noted the strategic possibilities of a coppered fleet 'always ready for service' in year-round campaigning; summer in home waters and winter in the West Indies, without cessation.[17] Admiral Sir George Rodney credited his victory over the Spanish at the 'Moonlight Battle' in January 1780 to the innovation, stating that, 'without the copper bottomed ships the Spanish fleet so lately defeated could not have been brought to action.'[18] His victory at The Saintes in 1782 was similarly attributed and Rodney held firm in his belief that 'copper bottom ships are an absolute necessity'.[19] Captain Walter Young, stationed in the West Indies in April 1780, begged Middleton, 'For God's sake and our country's, send out copper-bottomed ships to relieve the foul and crippled ones.'[20] Yet, despite the praise, both Sandwich and Middleton knew there were problems.

Chief among them was the matter of galvanic action and the deleterious effects of copper on the iron bolts and fittings that held ships together. One report detailed, 'an iron bolt of the diameter of an inch and a quarter has been reduced in a couple of years to a size of a quill'.[21] Similar results had been found over the previous decade of tests, and although the process of electrolytic degradation was not yet understood, the problem was clear. Experiments with various compounds, including tar and zinc solutions, and with copper bolts and rudder pintles failed to produce a solution.[22] One technique, which involved the application of thick brown paper to the hull before the copper, provided a barrier between the iron bolt heads and the sheathing, and where contact was prevented the deterioration of iron could be slowed. It could not, however, be stopped.

Moreover, Sandwich and Middleton also knew that where copper sheathing was torn off or worn through, a wooden hull was as susceptible to shipworm as it had ever been.[23] Once infested, the worm continued to burrow, even into planks that appeared to be protected by copper. As Roger Knight pointed out, 'copper sheathing, like the links of a chain, had to be completely effective to be effective at all'.[24] While Middleton refused to publicly acknowledge the limitations of the new technology, Sandwich was not so cavalier. But as the navy's strategic situation worsened, the advantages of copper sheathing could not be ignored. His solution was twofold – proceed with coppering the fleet and simultaneously develop a permanent remedy to the iron problem.

Disasters at sea
By 1781 many of the first ships to be outfitted had been sailing on coppered hulls for about three years. Their bottoms remained relatively clean, obviating the need for careening and scraping or refitting. By all appearances, copper sheathing had done its job, allowing vessels to stay at sea longer and remain fast and agile. Appearances though, were deceiving and captains began to report the leaky condition of their ships due to rotten timbers and the excessive opening of seams as their vessels worked at sea. Then, disasters began to accrue.

At the Battle of the Virginia Capes on 5 September 1781, the condition of Royal Navy ships mirrored the disastrous outcome for Britain's interests in North America. As the combined squadrons of Rear-Admiral Thomas Graves from New York, and Rear-Admiral Samuel Hood from Jamaica, came together to stop the French fleet under the Comte de Grasse from occupying the Chesapeake, the unseaworthiness of many British ships was evident. The third-rate HMS *Terrible* (74), notable for 'her exceeding bad state even before she left the West Indies', was flooding at a rate of 6ft per hour before the battle began.[25] The firing of her guns and the rigours of working the ship in heavy seas were too much for the hull, which had been weakened by shipworm and the erosion of her iron fittings. When the pumps could no longer keep up, *Terrible* was scuttled.

In the aftermath, much criticism was levelled at her captain for failing to do his utmost, but other senior officers in Hood's squadron were equally concerned for the viability of their ships. Captain Lord Robert Manners, aboard HMS *Resolution*, was a witness to *Terrible*'s fate and noted, 'We felt severely the danger of keeping coppered line of battle ships out long without looking at the bottoms.'[26] Six months later, his doubts about *Resolution*'s soundness were palpable, 'next month the ship will have been three years coppered and out of dock … copper-bottomed ships, when they once begin to show their defects, drop all at once'. Manners, like other captains in the squadron, feared their ships would not make it to England for refit: '*Invincible*, who is now in as bad a state as the *Terrible* was, and several others, which they are afraid even to trust home.'[27]

Such was the case for Graves' convoy of warships, prizes and ninety-two merchantmen that was struck by a storm on 17 September 1782 in route from Jamaica to England. His flagship, the third-rate HMS *Ramillies* (74), HMS *Centaur* (74), and some French prizes from the Battle of the Saintes, including the first-rate *Ville de Paris* (110), were lost in the onslaught of weather, along with three thousand five hundred lives. The sorry state of their worm-eaten timbers and withered iron fastenings were blamed for their loss. The subsequent courts martial acquitted the captains of any wrongdoing, but correspondence revealed that problems in the British ships had been evident long before the storm.[28] Within two weeks of the convoy's departure, Graves lost three of his nine escorting warships, which were forced back to port due to their excessive leaking and rotten timbers.[29] Such defects had been masked by copper sheathing and the faith placed in its ability to keep ships at sea for years without examining the hulls.

In August 1782 the spectacular loss of HMS *Royal George* stunned Britons and sent chills through the newly installed First Lord of the Admiralty, Augustus Keppel, who took over from Sandwich with the fall of the North ministry in March. The first-rate, 100-gun ship capsized at anchor in Spithead while being heeled over for repairs, drowning at least five hundred sailors and civilians,

The *Ville de Paris*, Foundering in the Middle of the Atlantic Ocean. A hand-coloured engraving of 1808 by E W (artist), Thomas Tegg (publisher). (© National Maritime Museum, Greenwich, London)

including Rear-Admiral Kempenfelt.[30] Despite the litany of errors that attended her 'heaving down', a court martial determined the reason for her loss was that 'some material part of her frame gave way, which can only be accounted for by the general state of the decay of her timbers'.[31] The testimony given by a gunner's mate who was in the gun room when he heard a 'great crack' added that, 'she gave a great jerk or crack at first, and – within a moment after – another and went down'.

These 'bodily cracks' were taken as evidence of the ship's structural unsoundness due to the shipworm damage covered up by copper sheathing and its electrolytic effects on her iron fittings.[32] It is possible that court martial president Vice-Admiral Samuel Barrington, a Whig and a vocal opponent of coppering, used the forum to level a professional and political indictment of Sandwich, Middleton and other administrators from the previous government.[33] Yet the presence of twelve other admirals and captains of various political stripes suggests a more balanced assessment in the court's decision and a broad acceptance of the problems associated with copper sheathing.[34]

Of the 217 vessels in commission during the American War, approximately sixty-five were lost to a variety of causes between 1775 and 1784.[35] Exactly how many of these were a direct result of copper sheathing is unknown, although the findings of various courts martial and the evidence from official correspondence suggest that coppering and the navy's overconfidence in its ability to keep ships at sea for years on end was a significant contributor to the losses. Admiral Hood, in early 1783, expressed a common fear: 'I dread what may happen to the King's ships if we have not peace to occasion their being called home to have their bottoms inspected; for on being obliged to unhang the Barfleur's rudder, her stern post and plank, for five feet under water was eaten by the worm in a manner not to be conceived ....'[36] Later that year even Middleton acknowledged the extent of the problem and that 'alterations ... in the manner of sheathing ships is of greatest importance'.[37] Keppel's Admiralty put a temporary stop to coppering until a solution could be found. He was fortunate that the war ended, as Hood hoped, in September, alleviating the need to keep vessels constantly at sea.

Historical views of copper sheathing
Historians have alternately criticised Sandwich – either for his overzealous use of a technology that was insufficiently tested and whose problems were well known, or for dragging his feet on the decision to copper, despite Middleton's insistence.[38] Whatever the angle, the condemnations only highlight the precarious nature of Sandwich's position during what Nicholas Rodger called 'the worst crisis in the Navy's history, when the country came nearest to a

complete defeat at sea'.[39] Such a desperate situation meant that no administrator could ignore the opportunities that copper sheathing afforded.

Unlike Middleton's overly optimistic claims, Sandwich's assessment of the short-term benefits and long-term costs revealed a pragmatic understanding of the operational and political stakes. As a result, he took a calculated risk, and committed the navy to a promising, if imperfect, technology. The magnitude of the decision to copper the fleet, both in terms of hard costs and opportunity costs for ships removed from service during the application process, necessitated the approval of George III, which he obtained before moving forward.[40] Even so, Sandwich was an experienced politician in a fiercely polarised Parliament, and understood that the decision, and whatever fallout came from it, would be his burden alone to bear. It was a bold choice in the face of dire circumstances. The cumulative results of naval action against France and her allies suggest that the risk paid off, albeit just in time, with a fortuitous end to hostilities preventing further catastrophes.

On a more positive note, Sandwich's grand experiment brought about some long-term benefits. The problems caused by copper sheathing sparked rapid innovation. When Sandwich ordered the fleet to be coppered in 1779, he also ordered the first trials of copper alloy bolts and fittings, as a way of eliminating the electrolytic effect on iron. While the process of creating an alloy that was both strong enough to replace iron and ductile enough to withstand the constant movement of a ship's timbers was far from simple, a suitable copper and zinc, i.e. a form of brass, compound was eventually found.[41] Middleton, who remained at the Navy Board despite the turnovers in government during 1783, adopted the brass alloy fittings in December of that year, completing Sandwich's vision.[42] The result was that before the start of the French Revolutionary War, all Royal Navy vessels were 'copper bottomed and copper [alloy] fastened', which provided Britain with significant advantages over her French and Spanish rivals, who were 'still struggling to overcome the technical problems of coppering'.[43]

Ultimately, Sandwich can be seen as the 'sacrificial innovator' whose controversial career ended, in part, under the weight of blame associated with the negative effects of copper sheathing.[44] His efforts, however, to find solutions to the various problems forced rapid progress in naval architecture that allowed the Royal Navy to exercise significant advantages in future conflicts. Sandwich's leadership at the Admiralty turned Britain's wartime desperation into an opportunity for technical development that produced a stronger and more advanced fleet that, by 1805, exercised true naval superiority over the world's oceans.

HMS *Formidable* careened in Malta Dockyard,, see colour plate 7

The Historical Significance Behind the Name of Villeneuve's *Bucentaure*

John Easton Law

On 21 October 1805, as HMS *Victory* slowly approached the sprawling, curved and uneven line of ships comprising the Franco-Spanish fleet, Nelson looked for the allied flagship, Admiral Villeneuve's *Bucentaure*. Once spotted, *Bucentaure* was Nelson's immediate target; Villeneuve's flagship was part of Nelson's battle plan to cut the allied fleet's line of battle in three.

Steering for *Bucentaure*, Nelson hoped to separate Villeneuve's flagship from his ships in the centre and in the vanguard of the line, while Nelson's second in command, Vice-Admiral Collingwood, led his column toward the rear of the enemy line. Nelson knew that breaking the enemy's line would have great tactical and psychological impact. But, there may have been more significance to Nelson's targeting *Bucentaure* than is normally acknowledged.

Earlier in his naval career, Villeneuve had been one of the few captains to escape from the Battle of the Nile, commanding the eighty-gun *Guillaume Tell*.[1] In the spirit of revolutionary France, that ship had been named after the legendary Swiss hero who, it was widely claimed, had sparked a popular rebellion against Austrian rule in the early fourteenth century. Villeneuve's flagship at Trafalgar was another well-designed ship of the line, carrying eighty guns and built at Toulon. Laid down in November in 1802, she was launched in July 1803 and fitted out by January 1804. Like *Guillaume Tell*, her name recalled another perceived defeat of an *ancien regime*. To appreciate that, a return to earlier 'Napoleonic' history is required.

The changing balance of power; the French invasion of Italy
On 19 August 1796, Spain allied with France, with the result that the British became anxious to prevent the assembly of a hostile naval force intent on invading British soil or making an expedition to the West Indies. Admiral Sir John Jervis defeated the allied fleet in the battle off Cape St Vincent of 14 February 1797. As decisive as it was, the battle's outcome could not prevent a major shift in the balance of power on the Continent, away from Austria and its allies, in favour of France. That country's invasion of Italy had begun in 1796, energised by Napoleon's appointment to command the Army of Italy on 1 March.

The reasons for the French invasion of the Italian peninsula were partly historic. From the late Middle Ages, France had seen northern Italy as an area of influence, if not an opportunity for direct rule. More immediately, the motives were ideological and strategic; to defend the Revolution and defeat *anciens regimes*. French motives were also economic, given the wealth of the region in terms of raw materials, developing industries and potential taxation. The area also had a rich cultural heritage, giving the revolutionary armies the opportunity to justify and celebrate their conquests with selective looting.[2] Napoleon Bonaparte's Corsican and Tuscan origins and connections could have added a personal incentive to political and military aims.

Military considerations also entered the picture. Success would deprive the Royal Navy of bases and sources of supply; Genoa and Livorno (Leghorn) for example. It would also deprive the British of much strategic and tactical 'intelligence' on the movement of troops and ships of war and supply, a subject well worth exploring further. A large population offered possibilities for recruitment, conscription and billeting. The region's Alpine passes were gates to central Europe. Its navigable rivers led to the Adriatic. Moreover, elements of the population, especially among discontented members of the urban bourgeoisie – even in Venice itself – could be persuaded to hope for the realisation of social, legal and political changes associated with the Revolutionary cause.

Many of France's key successive victories took place in territories ruled by the Venetian Republic, a long-acknowledged sovereign power. The confrontation between the two republics was unequal for various reasons. For centuries Venice had been ruled by a relatively large but virtually closed hereditary aristocracy, one easily perceived by its enemies as the negative epitome of an *ancien regime*, virtually a caricature.[3] Its subject territories on the Italian mainland and on the eastern shore of the Adriatic had once been protected by state-of-the-art fortifications and by effective armies and fleets. But by 1797 Venice and its dominions had become relatively under-defended. The Republic still had a functioning diplomatic service, but one reporting to an almost paralysed government. To make matters worse, while declaring neutrality, the Republic had harboured in Verona the Bourbon Comte de Lille, the brother of Louis XVI, and his royalist supporters. The Comte took the title of Louis XVIII.[4]

The Bourbon claimant was persuaded to leave, but that did not save the Republic's territories in Italy from being 'occupied'. This caused some acts of defiance, some violent, some more gestural. The aggression of the French occupation of Verona, for example, provoked a rebellion among the citizens in April 1797, resulting in France's further punishment of the civilian population and extensive looting.[5]

The final challenge to the Republic's survival came on 20 April when a lightly armed French vessel – provocatively named the *Liberateur d'Italie* – attempted to enter, by design or accident – the Venetian lagoons. The Venetians fired upon the invader, killed the captain and captured the vessel. For Napoleon this incident was the convenient last provocation. France issued an ultimatum, a call for surrender, to Venetian delegates on 25 April 1797. On 29 April, French land forces reached the lagoons, and on 9 May Napoleon – like Attila whose armies, in the mid-fifth century, had overrun most of north-eastern Italy if not the islands that later became Venice – issued a further demand for the Republic's surrender. On 12 May, the Venetian government dissolved itself, and its head of state, Doge Ludovico Manin, went into dignified retirement. French troops occupied the city and its fortifications.

The fall of the Venetian Republic
The first 'Napoleonic occupation' was brief. By the Treaty of Leoben of 18 April 1797 between France and Austria, Venice had been allowed a degree of autonomy. The subsequent Treaty of Campo Formio of 17 October 1797 gave Venice to Austria, but before the handover in January 1798 some significant changes took place in the city. The French had installed a new government of Venetians, though how far it was 'Vichy' in terms of initiative and compliance is unclear. There had been some protests at the fall of the Republic but no organised resistance. The new government adopted some demonstrations of revolutionary principles. A 'Tree of Liberty' was celebrated in the Piazza San Marco on 12 May and expressions of its previous government and social order in terms of monuments and coats of arms were slighted, though not always totally destroyed. Following the policy carried out in northern Italy, in Venice the French conducted a ruthless theft of significant works of art; the bronze horses from the façade of the Basilica of San Marco and Paolo Veronese's famous 'Marriage at the Feast of Cana' for example.[6]

But there were no tumbrils, and no guillotine, and that may have been – in part – because the French aims had become more naval than ideological. From as early as the Renaissance, France had appreciated the Republic's naval power on several levels. The state-run dockyard, the Arsenale, had employed the largest concentration of skilled workers before the modern era. It could sustain and build fleets that had long remained effective in the Mediterranean, moving from war galleys to sailing ships. The Arsenale had once impressed foreign visitors, but by the eighteenth century the dockyard and its fleets were in decline, though its traditions and potential in terms of skill and facilities remained.

The significance of the *Bucintoro*

Another inheritance from the Republic's past was the concept of sea power and territorial waters, expressed in the *Bucintoro*, the 'golden ship', the Republic's state barge. The first time the vessel was named as the 'Bucentaurum' was in 1253.[7] From that time it had featured prominently in the record as a major expression of the Venetian Republic and its head of state, the doge.

For centuries, this vessel was built and moored in the Arsenale, and kept in the oldest part of the dockyard, the Arsenale Vecchio, near its protected entrance to the lagoons. In the middle of the sixteenth century, a bespoke warehouse was built, probably by the leading, classically inspired, architect Michele Sanmichele.[8] In constructional terms, the vessel saw centuries of rebuildings involving skilled naval architects and craftsmen. When Venice fell the *Bucintoro* had been launched after around eight years of rebuilding and decoration from 1719 to 1727.[9]

In her history, the *Bucintoro* had never been perceived as a warship.[10] She was not a sailing ship, but a galley, towed and powered by oars, and steered by sailors, both being recruited from elite workers in the Arsenale. However, in 1381 the oars were worked by prisoners of war taken when Venice defeated one of its old rivals, Genoa, and the doge was carried in triumph on the *Bucintoro* from Chioggia – one of the entrances to Venice's lagoons – back to the city.

The 1727 vessel was manned by 168 oarsmen, four to an oar. Following tradition, she had two decks, the lower one for the oarsmen, while the upper deck carried resident and visiting dignitaries. The doge and his entourage rode on the raised stern deck. It was decorated by symbols expressing the Republic's devotion to its patron saint, St Mark, by depictions of Justice, symbolising the perceived quality of its government, and by symbols of its close relations to the sea.

The *Bucintoro* had never been designed for the open sea, but to negotiate the lagoons and the Grand Canal, receiving – to impress – important visitors from the East and from northern Italy and Europe. However, some grand tourists – as Venice declined as a naval power – were not impressed. Lady Anna Miller, who visited around 1770, recalled that one observer described it as 'the ugliest, most tawdry, worst contrived vessel he ever saw; loaded with ornaments and gilding, and totally void of grace'. In 1777, Dr John Moore, while impressed by the Arsenale, described the *Bucintoro* as highly decorated but unseaworthy, 'a heavy, broad-bottomed machine'.[11] However, in 1789, Goethe – perhaps as a landlocked observer – was impressed by the Arsenale and by the historical and contemporary significance of the *Bucintoro*, which he described as 'one single ornament'.[12]

However, the significance of the *Bucintoro* lies in more than her role to impress – or disappoint – visitors. As has been mentioned, she had a key role in Venice's perception of itself as a maritime power; this can be seen in her central role in an annual ceremony, 'La Sensa', also known as the 'Sposalizio' or 'Marriage of the Sea'.[13] This ceremony took place on Ascension Day (Ascension = Sensa), a moveable feast that followed Easter. Its origins probably lay in the commemoration of a war fleet sent from Venice on Ascension Day in the year 1000 to assert Venetian ascendancy over the coastal cities of the northeastern Adriatic. From that victory came a ceremony that was part secular and part religious. The doge rode on the state barge from Venice to the lagoons and then to the Adriatic to sprinkle holy water on the open sea, as an expression of thanksgiving.

From the Venetian point of view this ritual was enhanced by events – as perceived by the city's chroniclers – when in 1177 Pope Alexander III gave the doge symbols of sovereignty in acknowledgement of the doge facilitating a reconciliation between the pope and the emperor. These symbols included a

The *Bucintoro* moored in the Arsenal; details taken from a woodcut view of Venice by Jacopo de' Barbari found in *Planta di Venezia* (*Map of Venice*) published in 1500. The artist shows the vessel built in 1462. He has depicted the figure of Justice, crowned and carrying a sword, in the bow. Also shown are the structures on the upper deck designed to support embroidered drapery covering the doge, leading members of the government and distinguished visitors on ceremonial occasions. (Wikimedia Commons)

ring with which to wed the sea, not as a token of an equal marriage, but rather as one of lordship. This was how marriage was understood at the time. The ceremony was one of both the spiritual and the temporal – divine protection for mariners and Venice's lordship over the sea.

The extent of this lordship was unclear, but some maps describe the Adriatic as the 'Golfo di Venezia', and the Republic came to appoint a member of its nobility as 'capitano' with a squadron of galleys to patrol the sea.[14] For how long this remained effective in the face of aggressive piracy and the rise of the Ottoman Empire is unclear. However, the 'Sensa' remained a major annual event, itself attracting a great deal of Venetian and foreign participation and a major fair in the Piazza San Marco, even if some observers – as cited above - were unimpressed by the *Bucintoro*.

The recording of the event was encouraged by the fact that the festival came close to the 'sailing season' and the arrival of pilgrims seeking passage on Venetian galleys to the Holy Land. One of the earliest accounts in print, in English, is by Sir Richard Guylforde for 1506.[15] The vessel Sir Richard may have seen was built in 1462. It was depicted in the 'view' of Venice by Jacopo de' Barbari, the large woodcut being published, for sale, in the city in 1500.[16] This shows the vessel moored in the oldest basin in the Arsenale, nearest to the lagoons. Its mast is not

Giovanni-Battista Brustolini, (born c1726). The Doge in the Bucintoro departing from the Porto del Lido (the principal passage from the lagoons to the Adriatic). Date unknown. Etching and engraving on paper. This shows how the printing press came to circulate images of Venice.
(Scottish National Gallery of Modern Art, Edinburgh)

The Bucentaure. Anonymous watercolour made at the request of the warship's first captain, Jean-Jacques Magendie, 1803. The frigate further out to sea has been identified as the Africa. (Wikipedia)

raised and the structures covering its upper deck are not decorated. However, what is just discernible is the figure of Justice, sword in hand, on the bow. This woodcut, prepared in the 1490s, launched a long tradition of depicting the *Bucintoro*, helped by the fact that from the late fifteenth century Venice had a flourishing printing industry, allowing for the production of printed images of Venice for wide circulation. For example, an anonymous engraving in the British Museum (1502–08) shows the vessel in considerable detail proceeding up the Grand Canal, with her mast lowered towards the Rialto Bridge. This rich, unbroken visual tradition is perhaps best known from the work of Francesco Guardi (1712–93) and above all by Giovanni Antonio Canal, Canaletto (1697–1768).

Venice remembers the *Bucintoro*

The Treaty of Campo Formio handed Venice to Austria, then a naval power. Before complying with the transfer, the occupying French reduced the Arsenale by seizing some vessels. They took the *Bucintoro* from her moorings. They publicly destroyed her gilded decorations, ostensibly for their gold, but a political, naval statement was clearly behind this gesture. To underline the fall of Venice as a maritime power, the French flagship at Trafalgar, *Bucentaure*, carried no tribute to Venice on her prow, but a centaur, a classical pun on the *Bucintoro*'s name. In Venice, the French kept the hull of the *Bucintoro* on which to mount cannon to threaten the Piazza San Marco, the centre of Venice's political, social and religious life. *Bucintoro* later became a prison ship before being dismantled in the Arsenale under Austrian rule.

Nevertheless, *Bucintoro* had had a longer, if less dignified, life than *Bucentaure*. At Trafalgar, that ship was badly damaged, with great loss of life and the surrender of her admiral and her wounded captain. The Royal Navy probably planned to take it back in triumph as more than a prize, but the surviving members of its crew managed to retake the ship, only for it to be wrecked off Cadiz in the course of the violent storm that followed the battle.

When Napoleon entered Venice on 29 November 1807, the elaborate festivities did not include such expressions of Venetian independence and sea power as the *Bucintoro*. However, the fall of the Republic did not erase the vessel from memory. The Sensa is commemorated in a '*rio*' and a '*fondamenta*' – a canal and its quay – in the region of Cannaregio. The dock and the 'Casa' – the warehouse – associated with the *Bucintoro* survive in the Arsenale. The representation of Justice from the prow remains as a model in the Naval Museum adjacent to the Arsenale. Fragments from the vessel are displayed in the Museo Correr in the Piazza San Marco, for which a scale model of the eighteenth-century vessel has been constructed. Other fragments of the original vessel may be held elsewhere.

Combat Glorieux du Vaisseau le Bucentaure contre trois Vaisseaux Anglais (Trans: Glorious Combat of the *Bucentaure* against three English ships), 1836 oil on canvas by Auguste Étienne François Mayer (1805–90). In this painting of the Battle of Trafalgar, Mayer identified the English warships as HMS *Sandwich, Temeraire* and *Victory*. However, *Sandwich* was not at the battle.
(Musée National de la Marine, Paris)

Detail of Mayer showing the centaur figurehead of *Bucentaure*.

Following Venice's unification with the Kingdom of Italy, the city made lavish preparations for the triumphal arrival of Victor Emmanuel II on 7 November 1866. A replica *Bucintoro* rowed him down the Grand Canal amidst cheering crowds on land and water. It was very much a token state barge with relatively few crew and oarsmen, but it did carry gilded features recalling the original *Bucintoro*, with Justice in the stern and Venice celebrated in the Lion of St Mark on the bow.

The oldest rowing and sailing club in Venice is named after the *Bucintoro*. La Sensa has been revived as a tourist attraction, with the city's mayor 'doing the honours'. Early in this century, Venice launched plans to rebuild the vessel in the Arsenale. A proposed cross section of the hull was exhibited in the Piazza San Marco in 2007. The following year the Fondazione Bucintoro, with its office near the Arsenal, launched an appeal for 20 million euros.

This appeal may have inspired a letter to *The Times* (28 February 2008) arguing that the French government, then under the presidency of Nicholas Sarkozy, should contribute by way of reparations! This appeal probably reached deaf ears, but the 'memory' of the *Bucintoro* and La Sensa had considerable resonance in nineteenth-century Britain. An early and evocative reference comes in Canto IV of Lord Byron's *Childe Harold's Pilgrimage* (1818):

> The spouseless Adriatic mourns her lord
> And annual marriage, now no more renew'd,
> The Bucentaur lies rotting unrestored,
> Neglected garment of her widowhood

Robert Browning picked up the theme in his evocation of a lost eighteenth-century Venice, *A Toccata of Galuppi's*, first published in 1855. At the second stanza we read the poignant question: 'Where Saint Mark is, where the Doges used to wed the sea with rings?'

On 1 August 1873 John Ruskin, who had come to know Venice well, expressed regret at the demise of the *Bucentaur*[17] but in his *Stones of Venice* (1851–53) he may have suggested a reason for an abiding British interest in the city as pre-figuring the rise and decline of a great naval and imperial power.

However, in the contexts of naval power and an appreciation of the command of the sea, the link between Venice's *Bucintoro* and France's *Bucentaur* – as far as I am aware – has not been made.

Postscript

As La Sensa and the central involvement of the *Bucintoro* long attracted the presence, and could involve the participation, of distinguished foreigners, as well as being much covered by artists and printers, it is worth speculating on the effect these events had on other governments and rulers with river routes and coasts on which to stake claims, parade, celebrate and impress.

On 30 April 1515 a major Venetian embassy to the court of Henry VIII reported from London that before meeting the monarch they were conveyed on the Thames to Richmond palace on 'a large barge prepared, precisely like a bucintor, covered with royal colours in cloth, the cabin being hung with arras (tapestry)'.[18] On the Thames, royal barge masters have had a role and identity since the Middle Ages, most recently for the late Queen Elizabeth.[19] On 14 January, the Thames receives an annual Anglican 'blessing'; no ring is involved but a wooden cross is offered to the river.

Returning to Venice, one of the Republic's closer neighbours, the Este Lords of Ferrara, used *bucintori* on the river Po during the Renaissance. Members of the dynasty had seen and travelled on the Venetian vessel.[20]

The author wishes to thank his son, James, for encouragement.

Venice: the Basin of San Marco on Ascension Day, c1740, see colour plate 8

Who Will Rule? The Struggle for Power in Río de la Plata, 1808–10

Ricardo Caetano de Moraes

After the French defeat at Trafalgar in 1805, Napoleon Bonaparte changed his strategy and decided to establish a Continental System against Britain – that is, to close all ports to British ships, seeking to destroy their trade. By early 1807, only Sweden and Portugal remained outside the blockade, which Napoleon deemed unacceptable. Spain also drew Napoleon's attention, as he considered it a rich nation ruled by a decadent dynasty. Thus, Bonaparte decided to seize the Iberian nations, exploiting their rivalries.

After signing a treaty with King Carlos IV, in which Portugal was divided between France and Spain, Napoleon issued an ultimatum to Prince Regent Dom João, demanding that he declare war on Britain and surrender his fleet to the French, under the threat of invasion. Unable to resist Napoleon and incapable of breaking ties with Britain, the greatest maritime power of the time and Portugal's ally since the Middle Ages, Dom João tried to maintain his neutrality at all costs. While he delayed a decision, the British government ordered the dispatch of a naval squadron to either rescue the Portuguese court or capture its fleet, depending on the circumstances.[1]

Rear-Admiral of the Blue Sir William Sidney Smith took command of the squadron. Bold, ambitious and inclined to disregard orders, he was one of Britain's most popular officers, famous for his actions against the French in the Mediterranean and the Levant. His orders were to proceed urgently to Lisbon, where he arrived on 17 November 1807. After negotiations with Lord Strangford, the ambassador to Portugal, Dom João agreed to take refuge in Brazil, along with other members of the House of Bragança. The Portuguese fleet

Sir William Sidney Smith (1764–1840) by an unknown artist, nineteenth century. Originally in the estate of John Bedford (Sotheby's auction, November 2019).
(Wikimedia Commons)

set sail on 29 November, carrying one thousand five hundred people, narrowly escaping the invading French troops. Sir Sidney deployed HMS *Marlborough* (74), HMS *London* (74), HMS *Bedford* (74) and HMS *Monarch* (74) to escort the fleet across the Atlantic, while the rest of the squadron remained to block the port of Lisbon, reinforced by some Russian ships.[2]

Among the members of the royal family in flight was Dona Carlota Joaquina de Borbón, Infanta of Spain and wife of Dom João since 1785. Ambitious, dynamic and arrogant, Dona Carlota considered herself Spanish above all and despised her husband, whom she found weak and indecisive. She had a reputation for infidelity and intrigue, having unsuccessfully conspired to take over the regency of Portugal in place of Dom João. Her aggressive stance kept her isolated in the Portuguese court, aggravated by the fact that Portugal and Spain had been enemies for years.

Upon arriving safely in Brazil, a grateful Dom João signed a decree opening the country's ports to 'friendly nations', meaning Britain. In March 1808, already established in Rio de Janeiro, the Prince Regent organised his government in the new capital of the Portuguese Empire, appointing Dom Rodrigo de Sousa Coutinho (later Count of Linhares) as Minister of War and Foreign Affairs. Immediately, Dom Rodrigo began dealing with the expansion of Portuguese domains in America, especially in the Río de la Plata region, which had maintained a long-standing conflict with Spain. He sent a letter to the *Cabildo* (town hall) of Buenos Aires, offering Portuguese protection to the people of the Viceroyalty of the Río de la Plata who might have been abandoned by Spain, hinting at the possibility of forcibly occupying the region, as he was supported by the British. At the same time, he sent Brigadier Joaquim Xavier Curado on a mission to Montevideo and Buenos Aires, aiming to convince the rulers of the two cities to accept the Portuguese proposal, gauge public opinion on the matter, and assess the state of local military forces. The *Cabildo* rejected the offer. Curado's mission also failed; Viceroy Santiago de Liniers in Buenos Aires refused to receive him, and Governor Francisco Javier Elío in Montevideo ignored his proposal.[3]

In May 1808, Sir Sidney Smith arrived in Rio

Dona Carlota Joaquina de Borbón by Nicolas-Antoine Taunay (1755–1830), c1817.
(Palácio Nacional, Queluz, Portugal)

de Janeiro, taking command of the British naval forces in Brazil, which were reinforced with three more ships; HMS *Foudroyant* (80), HMS *Surveillance* (36) and HMS *Confiance* (24).[4] The Portuguese court received him with full honours, Dom João decorated him, he received a property in the city, and quickly gained the favour of Dona Carlota and the princesses.[5]

Spain's crisis
The French army had entered Spain with the authorisation of King Carlos IV but quickly began behaving like an occupying force in an invaded territory. Meanwhile, Prince Fernando planned a change in policy, not in opposition to the French alliance but due to the sinister influence of his favourite, Manuel de Godoy. When the Prince was discovered and punished, the Aranjuez mutiny erupted in March 1808, forcing Godoy to flee. Shortly afterward, Carlos IV abdicated in favour of his son, who was proclaimed King Fernando VII. But the former king soon changed his mind and claimed the lost throne, which Fernando refused. Carlos then sought Napoleon's help to reclaim it. Napoleon summoned Carlos and Fernando to a meeting in Bayonne, where he forced both to abdicate the Spanish throne in favour of his brother, Joseph Bonaparte. The two former Spanish kings were kept as prisoners in France.[6]

The departure of the Spanish royal family to France sparked a revolt against the French, starting on 2 May in Madrid. It was violently suppressed. The Spaniards refused to accept Joseph Bonaparte as king and organised various local *juntas*, ruling on behalf of Fernando VII. While Spanish patriots were fighting fiercely against the French, starting the Peninsular War, delegates from three *juntas* asked for help from Britain, which had been at war with Spain since 1796. In July 1808, the British government ordered the cessation of hostilities and sent envoys to Spain to provide financial support to the patriots and to negotiate an alliance. Later, a Supreme Central *Junta* established itself in Aranjuez, in central Spain, and attempted to act as a unified national government.[7]

On 5 August, news of the Spanish revolt against Napoleon reached Rio de Janeiro. This completely changed Dom Rodrigo's plans for the Río de la Plata region because Spain went from being an enemy to a potential ally of Portugal. He immediately informed Sir Sidney Smith about Curado's mission and Portuguese intent, requesting British naval support if needed. Sir Sidney agreed and began planning the occupation of the Río de la Plata by Portuguese and British forces.[8]

Upon learning of the misfortunes of her father and brother, Dona Carlota conceived a bold project. She and her cousin, Dom Pedro Carlos – the son of her uncle Dom Gabriel and nephew of Dom João – were the only members of the Spanish royal family who were not prisoners. As the eldest daughter of

Carlos IV, it seemed clear to her that she had the right to be the Regent of the Hispanic-American Empire. On 19 August, Dona Carlota sent a document to the Spanish colonies titled *Manifiesto dirigido a los fieles vasallos de Su Magestad Católica El Rey de las Españas e Indias por su Alteza Real Doña Carlota Juaquina Infanta de España, Princesa de Portugal y Brazil.* In this document, Dona Carlota, declaring the double abdication in Bayonne null, considered herself the legitimate successor in America to King Carlos IV, replacing him while he was imprisoned, and instructing the Spanish domains to maintain order and defence until she sent Dom Pedro Carlos, temporarily authorised to regulate the government affairs of these domains.

Along with the *Manifiesto*, she sent two other documents signed on the same date: the *Justa reclamación que los representantes de la Casa Real de España Doña Carlota Juaquina de Bourbon Princesa de Portugal y Brazil, y Don Pedro Carlos de Bourbon y Braganza, Infante de España, hacen a Su Alteza Real el Príncipe Regente de Portugal,* and the *Respuesta de S.A.R. el Príncipe Regente de Portugal, a la reclamación hecha por SS. AA. RR. la Princesa del Brazil, y el Infante de España Don Pedro Carlos*. In the first, Dona Carlota and Dom Pedro Carlos sought assistance from Dom João – and, therefore, from Britain – in the task of fighting the French invaders in Europe and maintaining the integrity of dynastic legitimacy principles threatened in America; in the second, Dom João acknowledged the justice of the request, committing to do his best to accept the proposed alliance.[9]

Sir Sidney Smith supported Dona Carlota's monarchical pretensions, convinced that her coronation would resolve conflicts in the region and open the doors of Río de la Plata's trade with Great Britain.[10] He transferred his private secretary, the Spaniard José Presas, to Dona Carlota's service. Sir Sidney also assisted her in drafting the documents sent to the Spanish domains and letters to the main colonial authorities, besides preparing plans for a naval expedition to Río de la Plata. As a reward in case of success, Dona Carlota promised to grant him a dukedom.[11]

However, the *Manifiesto* was largely ignored in most Spanish domains. In Río de la Plata, Dona Carlota's appeal was rejected in September by the *Cabildo* of Buenos Aires and Viceroy Liniers, who reaffirmed their

Manifesto to faithful vassals of King of Spain, 1808 imprint by Carlota Joaquina de Borbón (1775–1830). (Biblioteca Nacional, Lisbon, Portugal)

loyalty to Fernando VII, but it was accepted by some *criollos*, among whom Manuel Belgrano and the Rodriguez Peña brothers stood out, starting a political movement known as 'Carlotism'. Two local parties emerged, the *carlotistas*, in favour of Dona Carlota's regency, and the *juntistas*, advocating the creation of a governing *junta* similar to those established in Spain. Political debates intensified as news from Europe arrived, where Spanish resistance to Napoleon had turned into the Peninsular War. Tensions increased due to constant disputes with Montevideo over Río de la Plata trade and the growing clamour for the replacement of Liniers, who was seen as a potential traitor due to his French origin.

Dona Carlota insisted on her claims, maintaining intense correspondence with her supporters and other influential individuals in Spain and America. However, her interests did not align with those of her husband or Great Britain.

In July 1808, Lord Strangford arrived in Rio de Janeiro, appointed as the British minister to the Portuguese court. His instructions emphasised the importance of signing a new trade treaty with Portugal as soon as possible, aiming to turn Brazil into an emporium for British products to be consumed throughout South America.[12] At first, Lord Strangford supported Dom João's plans for Río de la Plata, but he soon received new instructions from London. There was fear that Portugal would become excessively powerful in America, affecting British interests. Regarding Dona Carlota's monarchical project, there was concern that it might give rise to a new Iberian Union, now under Portuguese rule, shaking the European political balance.[13] Therefore, Lord Strangford worked to prevent Dom João or Dona Carlota from controlling Río de la Plata while seeking favourable trade agreements for Britain in Rio de Janeiro and the Spanish domains.

This policy shift placed Lord Strangford and Sir Sidney Smith on opposite sides. The disagreements between the two British representatives in Brazil gradually escalated, generating mutual criticisms and complaints, often with unusual verbal violence, regularly reported to their respective superiors in London.

Meanwhile, agitation continued in Banda Oriental. Inspired by the creation of the Supreme Central *Junta* of Sevilla, Governor Elío declared war on the French, established a governing *Junta* in Montevideo, and sent messages to other cities in the Viceroyalty, recommending that they do the same.[14]

In November 1808, the Spanish frigate *Prueba* (44) arrived in Rio de Janeiro on her way to Buenos Aires. Commanded by Captain Somoza, she transported the new Governor of Montevideo, Pascual Ruiz Huidobro, appointed to the position by the *Junta* of Galicia, even though it did not have the competence to do so. Supported by Sir Sidney Smith, Dona Carlota decided to board *Prueba* and head to Buenos Aires, where she would assume the regency of the Spanish

Empire in America. She wrote to Dom João requesting his authorisation to depart. Initially, Dom João agreed, but he soon changed his mind and withdrew his permission, likely influenced by Dom Rodrigo and Lord Strangford.

Dona Carlota summoned Somoza and communicated her intention, but he refused to obey her and set sail the next day. However, Huidobro failed to assume his post due to the lack of authority of the *Junta* of Galicia to appoint him. Unable to land in Montevideo, he headed to Buenos Aires, where he was received by Liniers and appointed to a naval command.[15] In early 1809, Martin de Álzaga led a mutiny against Liniers to create a *Junta* in Buenos Aires. He was defeated and arrested by the military forces led by Cornelio Saavedra; Liniers remained in power.

In February 1809, Portugal and Spain, which had been without formal diplomatic relations for years, agreed to an exchange of ambassadors. Dom Pedro de Sousa e Holstein (later Duke of Palmela) headed to Spain, while the Marquis of Casa Irujo went to Rio de Janeiro, appointed by the Supreme Central *Junta* of Sevilla. Casa Irujo's instructions focused on closely monitoring the movements of Dona Carlota and undermining the legitimacy of the Princess's direct communication with the Spanish colonial domains.[16]

Despite that, Dona Carlota continued to correspond intensively with Spanish personalities, advocating her cause, while growing closer to Sir Sidney Smith. The two visited each other regularly, and the Princess had gifted him with a diamond ring and a jewel-encrusted sword as a token of her gratitude for the safe journey to Brazil. In turn, he was delighted with Dona Carlota, whose open admiration was likely sincere, as Sir Sidney was a charming and pleasant man. The increasing intimacy between them began to generate rumours at the Portuguese court, which were exploited by Dona Carlota's enemies and reported to London by Lord Strangford.[17]

In May 1809, Rear-Admiral the Honorable Michael de Courcy arrived in Rio de Janeiro aboard HMS *Diana* (38). Lord Strangford requested that he take command of the British naval squadron, replacing Sir Sidney. Additionally, Courcy was invited to the royal palace to be introduced to Dom João and participate in the celebrations of the Prince Regent's birthday. Courcy thanked the royal palace for the invitation but informed them that Sir Sidney should be present as he was senior on the Royal Navy's list. However, Sir Sidney did not authorise him to disembark or participate in the festivities, 'not judging it proper'.

Dom João was surprised by the absence of the newly arrived admiral and astonished by the explanation given by Sir Sidney. Courcy paid a visit later on the same day to greet the Prince Regent and repeated the explanation; Lord Strangford deemed this affair 'very singular'.[18] After returning to London, Sir

Sidney claimed that he was following secret instructions from the British government to keep the French out of South America,[19] which he could not share with Lord Strangford, a claim confirmed by George Canning, Secretary of Foreign Affairs.[20]

Crisis in Río de la Plata and the May Revolution

To resolve the crisis in Río de la Plata and prevent the French from seizing the region, the Supreme Central *Junta* of Sevilla appointed Baltasar Hidalgo de Cisneros as the new Viceroy. He arrived in Montevideo in June 1809. Despite Belgrano's insistence, Liniers did not resist and handed over the position to Cisneros. After Liniers's fall, Elío dissolved the *Junta* of Montevideo and resumed the role of governor. One of Cisneros's first decisions was to order the Viceroyal *Cabildos* to suspend all communication with the Portuguese court in Rio de Janeiro and warned that any contact should be made through the ambassador, Marquis of Casa Irujo, further limiting Dona Carlota's actions.[21]

In November 1809, Viceroy Cisneros signed a free trade treaty with allied and neutral nations, but the British deemed it insufficient. Faced with protests from Buenos Aires merchants, the following month he ordered all British subjects to leave the Viceroyalty. At the request of British merchants, Admiral Courcy sent warships to Buenos Aires, while Lord Strangford negotiated the revocation of the decision. The British remained in the city during the negotiations. Lord Strangford began to consider the *juntistas* as more favourable to British commercial interests than the Viceroy and the *Cabildo* of Buenos Aires.[22]

On 14 May 1810, British ships arrived in Buenos Aires with news from Europe, reporting the invasion of Andalucía by the French in February, the dissolution of the Supreme Central *Junta* of Sevilla, and the escape of its members to Cádiz, who resisted, thanks only to British naval support.[23] Everything indicated that the French would soon completely occupy Spain. The *carlotistas* abandoned their cause and joined the *juntistas*, who redoubled their efforts to create an autonomous government *Junta*. They pressured Viceroy Cisneros to resign, as the authority that appointed him had disappeared. After intense negotiations, an open *cabildo* (a gathering of Buenos Aires notables) was scheduled to make a decision about the political future of Río de la Plata. The *cabildo* met throughout the day on 22 May, with about 250 participants from Buenos Aires. After lengthy debates, the creation of a government *Junta* was decided, initially led by Cisneros, who declared sovereignty by popular will but still pledged allegiance to King Fernando VII.

On 25 May 1810, the newly created government officially proclaimed the establishment of the Provisional *Junta* of the United Provinces of the Río de la

Plata, called the 'First *Junta*', initially composed only of citizens of Buenos Aires. Strong protests from the population forced Cisneros to resign as the *Junta*'s president, and Saavedra took over. The autonomy process of May 1810 became known as the 'May Revolution'.[24]

Aftermath

The May Revolution marked the end of Dona Carlota's hopes to ascend to a throne in South America. Although Governor Elío resisted in Montevideo, remaining loyal to Spain and even being appointed Viceroy by the Supreme Central *Junta* of Cádiz in early 1811, his title was not recognised outside the Banda Oriental. There was no hope of receiving military aid from the metropolis, as the intensity and frequency of fighting in various parts of Spain since 1808 prevented the sending of any significant military support. Dona Carlota attempted to intervene in Montevideo, offering support to Elío[25] and even pawning her jewels to help finance him, but she was rejected.[26] No one considered Dona Carlota a viable monarchical option any more. José Artigas' revolution and two Portuguese invasions sealed the fate of the Banda Oriental, which was annexed to Portuguese Brazil in July 1821, renamed Cisplatina Province. Independent Brazil maintained Cisplatina as part of its territory, but the United Provinces of Río de la Prata and Oriental patriots contested its dominance from 1823 onwards. After a three-year war, ended with French and

Open *cabildo* of 22 May 1810, by Pedro Subercaseaux (1880–1956), 1909.
(Museo Histórico Nacional, Buenos Aires, Argentina)

British mediation, the former province became the independent Republic of Uruguay in August 1828.

For some time, Dona Carlota maintained her claim to the Spanish regency, recognised by the Supreme Central *Junta* as a possible successor to Fernando VII in March 1812.[27] However, the defeat of the French and Fernando's return to Spain in March 1814 definitively closed the matter. Dona Carlota no longer had any political involvement in Spain's affairs. Always in conflict with her husband, she engaged in various intrigues and revolts against Dom João VI and his eldest son and successor, Dom Pedro IV, supporting Dom Miguel, her favourite son. Dona Carlota Joaquina ended up imprisoned in the Queluz Palace, where she passed away in 1830.

After returning to Britain, Sir Sidney Smith was promoted to vice-admiral and received a new command in the Mediterranean, where he participated in the blockade of Toulon in 1812. He had an important role in organising the treatment of the wounded of the Battle of Waterloo, received a knighthood[28] and became a prominent anti-slavery campaigner. Regarded as a hero by the people, he was treated with suspicion by the British government, which refused his repeated requests for a new naval command. Sir Sidney Smith died in Paris in 1840.

In February 1810, Lord Strangford achieved his main goal. Dom João signed a new treaty of alliance and commerce with Britain, granting a preferential tariff of 15 per cent on British products in exchange for protection against aggression from other nations.[29] Lord Strangford also kept British trade active in the Río de la Plata region, which underwent numerous changes in a short period. He withdrew to Britain in April 1815 after seven years in Rio de Janeiro.[30]

After the May Revolution, the United Provinces would unsuccessfully attempt to maintain the original territories of the Viceroyalty of Río de la Plata. Besides the Banda Oriental, the new republic would soon lose control of Paraguay (which defeated a military expedition from Buenos Aires in March 1811) and the Audiencia of Charcas, which was incorporated into the former Viceroyalty of Peru and became the Republic of Bolivia in August 1825. After a long and complex history involving military expeditions and political movements, the United Provinces would eventually give rise to the Republic of Argentina, a name officially adopted from 1860 onwards.

Faced with chaos in Europe, caught between Spanish weakness, Portuguese opportunism and French ambition, the citizens of Río de la Plata found themselves compelled to decide their destiny. Thanks to their choices and British protection, always mindful of their mutual commercial interests, there would be no monarch, native or foreign, reigning over the nations that emerged from the former Viceroyalty of Río de la Plata.

Contributors' Biographies

Natacha Abriat is Head of the Cultural Heritage Research Department of the Occitanie region of France. As a curator, she specialises in nineteenth-century architecture, decorative arts and maritime heritage. She conducts a maritime history seminar at the University of Montpellier, France.

Brenden L Bliss holds a PhD in War Studies from King's College London. He has been employed at Hawaii Pacific University since 2005 in a variety of administrative and teaching positions. His main research interests are nineteenth- and twentieth-century naval history with a focus on the Pacific region.

Anthony Bruce, PhD, FRHistS was formerly a director at Universities UK and is now a higher education consultant. His biography of *Anson: Royal Navy Commander and Statesman* was published in 2023. He is currently working on a study of Charles I's Naval Wars, 1625–32.

Samantha A Cavell, PhD is the Associate Professor in Military History at Southeastern Louisiana University. She received her PhD in naval and maritime history from the University of Exeter in the UK. Her research focuses on British naval and maritime subjects of the late eighteenth and early nineteenth centuries.

William S Dudley, PhD is a maritime history consultant, speaker, author and an adviser to the Annapolis Maritime Museum. He was the director of the US Naval Historical Center from 1995 to 2004. In 2024 he received the David A O'Neil Sheet Anchor Award for his service to the National Maritime Historical Society as Trustee, and Trustee Liaison on the Editorial Advisory Board for *Sea History* magazine.

Tom Fremantle believes himself very fortunate to have been born with two great, great, great grandfathers who were naval officers in the late eighteenth century. After a career in the Royal Navy and business he began researching these ancestors and in 2020 self-published a novel *From Norfolk to Trafalgar*. He is now working on a full biography of one of them, Captain Philip Gidley King, who became the third Governor of New South Wales in 1800.

Nicholas James Kaizer is a young Canadian scholar and teacher who studies the cultural history of the Royal Navy during the War of 1812. In particular, he is interested in the Anglo-Canadian responses to single ship losses of that conflict. He has a MA from Dalhousie University and is the author of *Revenge in the Name of Honour* and editor of *Sailors, Ships, and Sea Fights*.

John Easton Law is a graduate of St Andrews (MA) and Oxford (DPhil) and a Fellow of the Royal Historical Society and the Society of Antiquaries of Scotland. He joined University College, Swansea as lecturer in History in 1971, becoming senior lecturer and retiring in 2017. For the National Industrial and Waterfront Museum (Swansea) he organised a conference on Nelson and his legacy.

Captain Steven E Maffeo, USN, Ret served as both an intelligence petty officer and commissioned officer. He holds an MA from the University of Denver and an MS from the US Joint Military Intelligence College. For ten years he was a visiting Age of Sail history consultant and instructor on-board USS *Constitution* ('Old Ironsides') in Charlestown, Massachusetts. He has published six books, all dealing with naval or intelligence history.

Kevin D McCranie, PhD is the Philip A Crowl Professor of Comparative Strategy at the US Naval War College, where he is a member of the Strategy and Policy Department. He is the author of *Admiral Lord Keith and the Naval War against Napoleon*; *Utmost Gallantry: The US and Royal Navies at Sea in the War of 1812*; and *Mahan, Corbett, and the Foundations of Naval Strategic Thought*.

Ricardo Caetano de Moraes is a professor, engineer, writer, independent scholar and member of the Society for Military History. He has published several articles on military history and two history books, about Brazilian independence and the Yom Kippur War. A third book, about the current conflict between Israel and Hamas, is in course of preparation.

David Rothwell, DDS, MA is Department Head of Oral Diagnosis, Sewell's Point Dental Center, Norfolk, Virginia. He graduated from the US Naval War College in 2023 with an MA of Defense and Strategic Studies and a Certificate in Maritime History. He has served in the US Navy since 2014, the year he graduated from the Ohio State College of Dentistry with a Doctorate in Dental Surgery.

Hilary L Rubinstein, PhD, FRHistS lives in Melbourne, Australia. She is a versatile, much-published historian who has returned to her first love, British naval history in the Age of Sail. While researching her book *Catastrophe at Spithead: The Sinking of the Royal George*, she made the original discovery that Admirals Kempenfelt and Rodney were cousins. She was awarded a Medal of the Order of Australia (OAM) in the 2021 Australia Day honours list.

Andrew Venn is a young naval historian from Portsmouth, England. He holds a postgraduate degree in naval history from the University of Portsmouth and has worked as a visitor guide on-board several museum ships, including HMS *Victory*. He is the co-author of the *Trafalgar Times*, a quarterly newsletter presenting little-known facts and under-researched topics to new audiences and enthusiasts alike

Evan Wilson, PhD is an associate professor in the Hattendorf Historical Center at the US Naval War College in Newport, Rhode Island. A recipient of the Sir Julian Corbett Prize in Modern Naval History, he researches the naval history of Britain and other countries from the eighteenth to the twentieth centuries. He is the author or editor of six books, most recently *The Horrible Peace: British Veterans and the End of the Napoleonic Wars*.

Notes

Secret Intelligence in the Age of Nelson
1 Anthony Price, *The Eyes of the Fleet: A Popular History of Frigates and Frigate Captains, 1793–1815* (New York: W W Norton, 1996), p2.
2 N A M Rodger, *The Wooden World: An Anatomy of the Georgian Navy* (Annapolis, Maryland: Naval Institute Press, 1986), p29.
3 Gunther Rothenberg, 'Military Intelligence Gathering in the Second Half of the Eighteenth Century, 1740–1792', in Keith Neilson and B J C McKercher (eds), *Go Spy the Land: Military Intelligence in History* (Westport, Connecticut: Praeger, 1992), p111.
4 Antoine-Henri, Baron Jomini, *The Art of War*. 1838, reprint (Novato, California: Presidio, 1992), pp269–74.
5 Lloyd Hoffman, untitled lecture presented at the US Joint Military Intelligence College (Washington, DC, 15 September 1996).
6 Ernest R May, in Walter T Hitchcock (ed), *The Intelligence Revolution: A Historical Perspective. Proceedings of the 13th Military History Symposium, U.S. Air Force Academy, Colorado Springs, October 12–14, 1988* (Washington: US Government Printing Office, 1991), p72.
7 Mildred G Richings, *Espionage: The Story of the Secret Service of the English Crown* (London: Hutchinson, 1934), pp14–5.
8 Alfred Cobban, *Ambassadors and Secret Agents: The Diplomacy of the First Earl of Malmesbury at the Hague* (London: Jonathan Cape, 1954), p110.
9 Kenneth Ellis, *The Post Office in the Eighteenth Century: A Study in Administrative History* (London: Oxford University Press, 1958), p69.
10 Christopher Andrew, *Secret Service: The Making of the British Intelligence Community* (London: Heinemann, 1985), p3.
11 Geoffrey J. Marcus, *The Age of Nelson: The Royal Navy 1793–1815* (New York: Viking, 1971), pp401–2.
12 Admiral Charles Middleton, Baron Barham, *Letters and Papers of Charles, Lord Barham, Admiral of the Red Squadron, 1758–1813* (London: Navy Records Society, 1907), vol III, pp37–8.
13 Gunther Rothenberg, in Neilson and McKercher, p109.
14 Francis P Renaut, *Le Secret Service de L'Amirauté Britannique au Temps de la Guerre D'Amerique, 1776–1783* (Paris: Editions de Graouli, 1936), pp29–32.
15 Michael I Handel, *Masters of War: Sun Tzu, Clausewitz, and Jomini* (Portland, Oregon: Frank Cass, 1992), p166.
16 Admiral Sir John Jervis, Earl of St Vincent, *Letters of Admiral of the Fleet, the Earl of St. Vincent, whilst the First Lord of the Admiralty, 1801–1804* (London: Navy Records Society, 1922, 1927), vol II, p267.
17 Vice Admiral Horatio Nelson, Viscount, Duke of Bronte, *The Dispatches and Letters of Vice Admiral Lord Viscount Nelson*. Notes by Sir Nicholas H Nicolas (London: Henry Colburn, 1844–46), vol VII, pp2–3.
18 Reverend Alexander John Scott, *Recollections of the Life of the Reverend A. J. Scott* (London: Saunders and Otley, 1842), pp22–3, 33, 64, 73–5, 82, 97, 107, 109, 117–23, 128–33.
19 Geoffrey Bennett, *Nelson the Commander* (New York: Charles Scribner's Sons, 1972), p79.
20 John Masefield, *Sea Life in Nelson's Time* (New York: Macmillan, 1925), p56.
21 Ernest R May, in Hitchcock, p72.
22 Andrew Roberts, Baron Roberts of Belgravia, *Napoleon: A Life* (London: Penguin Books, 2015), p109.
23 Michael I Handel (ed), *Leaders and Intelligence* (Oxfordshire: Routledge, 1989), p42.
24 Claude-François, Baron Méneval, *Memoirs to Serve for the History of Napoleon I from 1802 to 1815* (London: Hutchinson, 1894), vol I, p135.
25 Roberts, p470.
26 Roberts, p472.
27 Will Durant and Ariel Durant, *The Age of*

Napoleon (New York: Simon and Schuster, 1975), p250.
28 Christopher D Hall, *British Strategy in the Napoleonic War, 1803–15* (Manchester: Manchester University Press, 1992), p48.
29 Carola Oman, *Nelson* (Garden City, New York: Doubleday, 1946), p601.
30 Sir James Bland Burges, *Selections from the Letters and Correspondence of Sir James Bland Burges, Bart., Sometime Under-Secretary of State for Foreign Affairs, with Notices of His Life*, James Hutton (ed) (London: John Murray, 1885), pp131–2.
31 James W Thompson and Saul K Padover, *Secret Diplomacy: Espionage and Cryptography, 1500–1815* (New York: Frederick Ungar, 1963), pp197–8.
32 Thompson and Padover, p190.
33 Michael Herman, *Intelligence Power in Peace and War* (Cambridge, Massachusetts: University Press, 1996); Christopher Hibbert, *Nelson: A Personal History* (Reading, Massachusetts: Addison-Wesley, 1994); Martin Van Crevald, *Command in War* (Cambridge, Massachusetts: Harvard University Press, 1985).

A Grand Tour on a Budget
1 The views expressed here are those of the author alone and do not necessarily represent the views, policies, or positions of the US Department of Defense or its components, to include the Department of the Navy or the US Naval War College.
2 Jan Glete, *Navies and Nations: Warships, Navies and State Building in Europe and America, 1500–1860*, 2 vols (Stockholm: Almqvist & Wiksell International, 1993).
3 N A M Rodger, *The Command of the Ocean: A Naval History of Britain, 1649–1815* (London: Allen Lane, 2004), pp413–4.
4 Evan Wilson, *A Social History of British Naval Officers, 1775–1815* (Woodbridge: Boydell Press, 2017).
5 John Jervis, *Journal of Tours by Lord St. Vincent*, British Library, Add MS 31192. Entry for 31 October 1772.
6 Francis Venables Vernon, *Voyages and Travels of a Sea Officer* (London, 1792), pp206–8.
7 James D G Davidson, *Admiral Lord St Vincent—Saint or Tyrant? The Life of Sir John Jervis, Nelson's Patron* (Barnsley: Pen & Sword, 2006), pp22–7.
8 Vernon, p218.
9 Ibid., pp217–8.
10 Jervis, Entry for 31 October 1772.
11 Vernon, p213.
12 Ibid., p212.
13 Jervis. Oliver Hazard Perry did exactly that when he left Erie to fight the British in 1813.
14 *Oxford Dictionary of National Biography*, s.v. 'Jervis, John, Earl of St Vincent'.

Cat and Mouse, Misinformation, Thwarted Plans and the Victory that Never was: Nelson and Villeneuve's Atlantic Chase, 1805
1 N A M Rodger, *The Command of the Ocean: A Naval History of Britain 1649–1815* (London: Penguin Books, 2006), p528.
2 Rodger, p530.
3 Ibid.
4 Sam Willis, *In the Hour of Victory: The Royal Navy at War in the Age of Nelson* (London: Atlantic Books, 2013), pp248–9.
5 Rodger, p532.
6 Roy Adkins, *Trafalgar: The Biography of a Battle* (London: Little, Brown, 2004), p17.
7 Rodger, p528.
8 Ibid., p529.
9 Ibid, p533.
10 Ibid, p533.
11 Iain Ballantyne & Jonathan Eastland, *Victory: From Fighting the Armada to Trafalgar and Beyond* (Barnsley: Pen and Sword, 2013), p102.
12 Martin Robson, *A History of the Royal Navy: The Napoleonic Wars* (London: I B Tauris, 2017), p108.
13 Rodger, p533.
14 Ibid., pp533–4.
15 Ibid., p534.
16 Adkins, p17.
17 Robson, p109.
18 Ibid.
19 Ibid., p110.
20 Julian Corbett, *The Campaign of Trafalgar* (London: Longmans, Green and Co., 1910), p102.
21 Rodger, pp534–5.
22 Ibid., p534.
23 Adkins, p18.
24 Robson, p110.
25 Ibid., p535.
26 Ibid.
27 Corbett, p161.
28 Robson, p111.
29 Ibid., p114.
30 Ibid.
31 Ibid.
32 Adkins, p20.
33 Robson, p115.
34 Ibid., p116.
35 Ibid., p536.

36 Ibid., p116.
37 Ibid., p117.
38 Ibid., p536.
39 Willis, p252.
40 Peter Goodwin, *HMS Victory Pocket Manual 1805: Admiral Nelson's Flagship at Trafalgar* (London: Conway, 2015), p122.
41 Nelson, Vice Adm. Horatio, Viscount, Duke of Bronte, *The Dispatches and Letters of Vice Admiral Lord Viscount Nelson*. Notes by Sir Nicholas H. Nicolas. Vol VI (London: Henry Colburn, 1844–46; republished London: Chatham Publishing, 1997), pp443–445. Nicolas does not name the recipient of the letter. According to Captain Steven Maffeo, USN Ret, Nicholas got Nelson's plan of attack from Clarke, Rev. James S., and John M'Arthur, *The Life and Services of Horatio Viscount Nelson … from His Lordship's Manuscripts*, 3 vols (London: Peter Jackson, Late Fisher, Son, & Company, 1840), vol 2, p427.

'A Great and Signal Service': Admiral Vernon at Porto Bello, November 1739
1 Admiral Edward Vernon (1684–1757), Member of Parliament from 1722; Commander-in-Chief, Jamaica Station, 1739–42; Commander of the Channel Fleet, 1745–46; dismissed from the navy, 1746. See Richard H Harding, 'Edward Vernon (1684–1757)', *Oxford Dictionary of National Biography* (2004). https://doi.org/10.1093/ref:odnb/28237 [accessed 27 November 2023].
2 Order to Captains of the Squadron, 1 August 1739, in Brian McL Ranft (ed), *The Vernon Papers* (London: Navy Records Society, 1958), pp20–1.
3 Third-rate *Burford* (70), Admiral Edward Vernon, Captain Thomas Watson; fourth-rate *Norwich* (50), Captain Richard Herbert; fourth-rate *Worcester* (60), Captain (later Vice-Admiral) Perry Mayne; fourth-rate *Strafford* (60), Captain Thomas Trevor; and fourth-rate *Princess Louisa* (60), Captain Thomas Waterhouse.
4 Richard H Harding, 'Edward Vernon 1684–1757', in Peter Le Fevre and R Harding (eds), *Precursors of Nelson: British Admirals of the Eighteenth Century* (London: Chatham Publishing, 2000), p166.
5 Herbert W Richmond, *The Navy in the War of 1739–48* (Cambridge: Cambridge University Press, 1920), vol I, p41.
6 Order to Captain Herbert of *Norwich*, 2 September 1739, in Ranft, p23.
7 Order to Commodore Brown at Jamaica, 2 September 1739, in Ranft, p23.
8 Richard H Harding, 'The Use of Intelligence in Royal Navy Amphibious Operations, 1739–1783', in Randy Carol Balano and Craig L Symonds, *New Interpretations in Naval History. Selected Papers from the Fourteenth Naval Symposium* (Annapolis, Maryland: Naval Institute Press, 2001), p3.
9 Sir Charles Wager to Edward Vernon, 7 October 1739, in Ranft, p26.
10 Ignacio Rivas Ibáñez, 'Mobilising Resources for War: The British and Spanish Intelligence Systems during the War of Jenkins' Ear (1739–1744)', PhD thesis, University College London, 2008, pp63–6.
11 Order to Lieutenant Francis Perceval, First Lieutenant of *Burford*, 19 October 1739, in Ranft, p28.
12 Allyn C Loosley, 'The Puerto Bello Fairs', *The Hispanic American Historical Review* 13 (1933), p317.
13 Shinsuke Satsuma, 'Severing the Sinews of the Spanish Empire: British Naval Policy and Operations Regarding the Silver Fleets during the War of Jenkins' Ear, 1737–1740', *The Journal of Imperial and Commonwealth History* (2023). https://doi.org/10.1080/03086534.2023.2275330 (p12) [accessed 27 November 2023].
14 Cyril H Hartmann, *The Angry Admiral: The Later Career of Edward Vernon, Admiral of the White* (London: William Heinemann, 1953), pp23–4.
15 Order to Commodore Brown and Captains, 7 November 1739, in Ranft, p32.
16 Ranft, pp32–4.
17 Ibid., p33.
18 Ibid.
19 William Campbell to John Russell, 12 December 1739, in Mary E Matcham (ed.), *A Forgotten John Russell: Being Letters to a Man of Business, 1724–1751* (London: Edward Arnold, 1905), p115.
20 Charles Leslie, *A New History of Jamaica, From the Earliest Accounts to the Taking of Porto Bello by Vice-Admiral Vernon. In Thirteen Letters from a Gentleman to His Friend* (London: J Hodges, 1740), p293.
21 Leslie, p294.
22 Matcham, p116.
23 Ibid.
24 *The Gentleman's Magazine* X (1740), p124.
25 Leslie, p295. Thomas Brodrick (*c*1704–69) rose to the rank of vice-admiral during the Seven Years' War.

26 Arthur Locker, 'Charles Brown (1678/9–1753)', *Oxford Dictionary of National Biography* (2004) https://doi.org/10.1093/ref:odnb/3599 [accessed 27 November 2023].
27 The sword is now in the National Maritime Museum, London (item number: WPN1248).
28 Leslie, p295.
29 Matcham, p117.
30 Hartmann, p29.
31 Governor of Porto Bello's proposed Articles of Capitulation, 22 November 1739, in Ranft, pp35–6.
32 Vernon's draft reply to the Governor's Articles of Capitulation, 22 November 1739, in Ranft, p36.
33 Matcham, p118.
34 Ibid., p119.
35 *The Gentleman's Magazine*, p126.
36 Later Admiral Sir Charles Knowles (c1704–77).
37 Later Admiral the Hon Edward Boscawen (1711–61).
38 Matcham, p120.
39 *The Gentleman's Magazine*, p126.
40 Richmond, p49.
41 Order to Captain Rentone of *Triumph*, 22 December 1739, in Ranft, pp47–8.
42 Craig S Chapman, *Disaster on the Spanish Main: The Tragic British Expedition to the West Indies during the War of Jenkins' Ear* (Lincoln: Potomac Books, 2021), p91.
43 Duke of Newcastle to Edward Vernon, 26 March 1740, in *Original Letters to an Honest Sailor* (London: R Thomas, 1746), p6.
44 Hartmann, p33.
45 Moses Mendez, *A Collection of the Most Esteemed Pieces of Poetry that have Appeared for Several Years* (London: Richardson and Urquhart, 1767), pp154–7.

The Unwanted Coup: James Callander, Spiridon Foresti, and British Espionage in the Ionian Islands during the War of the Second Coalition

1 Most sources, including those consulted here, spell his surname as 'Callender'. In his memoirs, it is spelled 'Callander'.
2 Christopher Lloyd (ed), *The Keith Papers: Selected from the Papers of Admiral Viscount Keith*, vol 2 (London: Navy Records Society, 1950), p159.
3 Colonel Callander to Lord Keith, Zante, 4 March 1801, *Keith Papers*, p188.
4 James Lawrence McKnight, 'Russia and the Ionian Islands, 1798–1807: The Conquest of the Islands and Their Role in Russian Diplomacy', MA Thesis, University of Wisconsin, 1962, pp1–2, pp147–180; Konstantina Zanou, *Transnational Patriotism in the Mediterranean, 1800–1850: Stammering the Nation* (New York: Oxford University Press, 2018), p55; Sakis Gekas, *Xenocracy: State, Class, and Colonialism in the Ionian Islands, 1815–1864* (Oxford: Berghahn Books, 2017), pp23–4.
5 C I Chessell, 'Britain's Ionian Consul: Spiridion Foresti and Intelligence Collection, 1793–1805', *Journal of Mediterranean Studies*, vol 16, no 1 (January 2006), pp1–3.
6 Jim Tildesley, 'Seamen, Safe houses, and Secret Service: A British Consul's Recruiting for the Navy, 1795–1808', in Nicholas James Kaizer (ed), *Sailors, Ships, and Sea Fights: Proceedings of the 2022 from Reason to Revolution 1721–1815, Naval Warfare in the Age of Sail Conference* (Warwick: Helion & Company, 2023), p266.
7 Steven E Maffeo, *Secret and Confidential: Intelligence in the Age of Nelson* (Annapolis, Maryland: Naval Institute Press, 2012), preface (e-book).
8 Chessell, 'Consul', p4.
9 Tildesley, 'Seamen', pp282–7.
10 Chessell, 'Consul', p4.
11 Chessell, 'Consul', pp1–15; Chessell, 'Britain's Ionian Consul: Spiridion Foresti and the return to the islands, 1807–1810', *Journal of Mediterranean Studies*, vol 19, no. 2 (January 2010), pp201–218.
12 Anastasios N Mikalef, 'The local Press in the Ionian Islands during the period of British rule (1849–1864)'. Doctoral Dissertation, University of Birmingham, 2022, pp.30–3; McKnight. 'Russia', p3; Zanou, pp12–3.
13 Chessell, 'Consul', p1.
14 McKnight, 'Russia', pp51–3; Zanou, p13.
15 McKnight, 'Russia', pp13–6.
16 Ibid., p164.
17 Grenville to Elgin, Dowing Street, 13 January 1801, *Keith Papers*, pp87–188.
18 McKnight, 'Russia', pp164–5.
19 'Россия и Европа в 1801–1812 гг'. Россия и Европа. Эпоха Наполеоновских войн. Отв. ред. Т В Черникова (М: Р Валент: Общее научное руководство В И Уколовой, 2012): pp60–2.
20 McKnight, 'Russia', p198.
21 Ibid., p64.
22 Zanou, p70.
23 McKnight, 'Russia', pp70–1; Zanou, p70.
24 Gekas, *Xenocracy*, pp.26–8.
25 Spiridon Foresti to Lord Elgin, Corfu, 26 February 1801, *Keith Papers*, pp189–190.

NOTES

26 McKnight, 'Russia', pp164–5.
27 Ibid., pp51–2.
28 Foresti to Lord Elgin, Corfu, 26 February 1801, *Keith Papers*, pp189–190.
29 Foresti to Lord Keith, Corfu, 1 September 1801, *Keith Papers*, p195.
30 McKnight, 'Russia', pp197–8; Foresti to Lord Keith, Corfu, 1 September 1801, *Keith Papers*, pp195–6.
31 McKnight, 'Russia', pp197–8.
32 Foresti to Sir John Hawkins, 6 June 1801, J/3/5/91. Kresen Kernow.
33 Thomas Henderson, 'Campbell, James (1745–1832)', *Dictionary of National Biography, 1885–1900*: Wikisource, accessed 28 December 2020, https://en.wikisource.org/wiki/Dictionary_of_National_Biography,_1885-1900/Campbell,_James_(1745–1832).
34 Colonel Callander to Lord Keith, Zante, 4 March 1801, *Keith Papers*, p188.
35 James Campbell, *Memoirs of Sir James Campbell, of Ardkinglas*, vols I and II (London: Henry Colburn and Richard Bentley, 1832), pp382–400, pp1–40.
36 Foresti to Lord Keith, Corfu, 1 September 1801, *Keith Papers*, p195.
37 Campbell, *Memoirs* vol II, pp1–20.
38 Henderson, 'Campbell, James'. This source does state that some dispute his claim.
39 Kahraman Sakul, 'An Ottoman Global Moment: War of Second Coalition in the Levant', (Ph.D. dissertation, Georgetown University, 2009), pp422–3.
40 'Coup d'état of Antonios Martinengos (1801)', GoZakynthosgr Online Touristic Guide, accessed January 4, 2024, https://gozakynthos.gr/coup-detat-of-antonios-martinengos-1801/#:~:text=On%20the%20night%20of%207,and%20raised%20the%20British%20flag
41 Sir William Hamilton to Lord Keith, 16 June 1800, *Keith Papers*, p116.
42 Lloyd, *Keith Papers*, p159.
43 Lord Elgin to Admiral Lord Warren, 25 August 1801, *Keith Papers*, p194.
44 Nelson to Nepean (Admiralty), 28 November 1799, in Nicholas Harris Nicolas (ed), *The Dispatches and Letters of Vice Admiral Lord Viscount Nelson*, vol 4 (London: Chatham, 1998), pp114–5.
45 Nelson to Lord Elgin, Palermo, 29 October 1799, *Dispatches*, vol 4, pp75–6.
46 Nelson to Nepean (Admiralty), 28 November 1799, *Dispatches*, vol 4, pp114–5.
47 Nelson to Foresti, Corfu, 28 March 1800, *Dispatches*, vol 4, p213.

48 Nelson to Captain Henry Compton, HM Bomb-Vessel *Perseus*, Palermo, 1 November 1797, *Dispatches*, vol 4, p75–6.
49 The letter consulted was dated 2 May but contained a full copy of an earlier letter that had been sent on 11 April, which did not make it to the Kresen Kernow (Cornwall Archives).
50 Foresti to Sir John Hawkins, 2 May 1801. J/3/5/89. Kresen Kernow.
51 Foresti to Hawkins, 2 May 1801. J/3/5/89. Kresen Kernow.
52 Ibid.
53 Foresti to Hawkins, 6 June 1801. J/3/5/91. Kresen Kernow. Author's emphasis.
54 Ibid.
55 Ibid.
56 McKnight, 'Russia', pp202–5; Lord Elgin to Admiral Lord Warren, 25 August 1801, *Keith Papers*, p194.
57 Campbell, *Memoirs* vol II, p37.
58 McKnight, 'Russia', p204.
59 Campbell, *Memoirs* vol II, p251.
60 Henderson, 'Campbell, James'.
61 Captain Rickets to Captain Rogers, *El Corso*, Bay of Zante, 14 September, *Keith Papers*, pp196–8.
62 Chessell, 'Consul', p3; W D Wrigley, *The Diplomatic Significance of Ionian Neutrality, 1821–31* (Switzerland: Peter Lang, 1988), p43.

Admiral Arthur Phillip, 1738–1814: Naval Officer, Explorer, Spy, Mercenary, Administrator

1 Frost, Alan, *Arthur Phillip, 1738–1816, His Voyaging* (Oxford: Oxford University Press, 1987). Much of the detail for this article has been taken from Professor Frost's detailed and engaging study of Phillip. Individual page references have not therefore been provided.
2 Ibid.
3 Ibid.
4 Historical Records of New South Wales Volume 1 Part 2, Phillip 1783–1792, Alexander Britton (ed), Charles Potter, Government Printer, Sydney, 1892, p22. Lord Howe to Lord Sydney, 3 September 1786.
5 The Journal of Lieutenant Phillip Gidley King RN 1787–1790. Australian Documents Library, Sydney, 1980, Digital Edition, University of Sydney Library.
6 HRNSW, Vol 1 pt 2, p122.
7 HRNSW, p177.
8 Ibid HRNSW, p182 et seq.
9 For further information about Lieutenant, later Captain and Governor, Philip Gidley King, see *Trafalgar Chronicle* New Series vol 2, 2017.

The Fortunes and Misfortunes of Baron d'Imbert, 1760–1844: French Naval Officer and Royalist Agent

1 Olivier Blanc, *La Corruption sous la Terreur (1792–94)* (Robert Laffont, 1992).
2 The genealogy written about this family by Artefeuil in the 1786 supplement to the *Histoire héroïque et universelle de la noblesse de Provence* should be treated with caution, as it is not corroborated by existing civil records. It is most likely a genealogy of convenience commissioned by Jacques-Anne-Magloire d'Imbert.
3 Archives départementales des Bouches-du-Rhône, Marseille, AD13 – 201E 463 – marriages, parish of St Martin. On 20 February 1770, he marries in Marseille Polyxène-Catherine-Félicité de Cambray, granddaughter of Jean-Baptist de Cambray, originating in Picardy, son of a musketeer, captain of the galleys who retired in 1722 in Marseille, where he had already settled by his marriage with the daughter of an alderman of Marseille. He had two sons who were galley officers, and a third, Honoré, married the daughter of a galley captain. They had five sons who were naval officers.
4 Archives Nationales, Paris, F76459. Letter from d'Imbert to Malouet dated 30 March 1808: 'In 1775, I made a trip to Italy and Spain, returning to France via Perpignan.'
5 Service Historique de la Défense, Site de Vincennes, CC7/ALPHA/1212. Copy of a letter from the Minister for the Navy Sartine to the Maréchal de Tonnerre dated 31 July 1775.
6 Valérie Piétri, 'Bonne renommée ou actes authentiques: la noblesse doit faire ses preuves (Provence, XVIIe–XVIIIe siècles)', *Genèses*, 2009/1, no 74, pp5–24.
7 Archives Nationales, Paris, MAR/C7/148, no 72. Certified copy dated 31 March 1819 of the 'Extrait des registres déposés au bureau des Officiers de Marine'.
8 Archives Nationales, Paris, MAR/C7/64, files 36 and 37. The republicans who had retaken Toulon on 22 December 1793 guillotined Marie Gabriel de Chieusses de Combaud de Roquebrune, born in 1760, along with his brother, Victor Justinien, born in 1761, also a naval officer, who had served on Suffren's campaign in India.
9 Archives Nationales, Paris, MAR/B4/226, pp337–352: 'Extrait du journal du vaisseau *Le Northumberland* commandé par M Le Marquis de St Cesaire capitaine des vaisseaux du Roy, brigadier des armées navales, 1782 par D'Imbert, enseigne.'
10 Archives Nationales, Paris, MAR/B4/225, pp188–194. 12 August 1783. 'Interrogation of Mr d'Imbert, ensign on board the *Northumberland*. Council of War composed of Chevalier de Fabry (commander and president of the Council), Monsieur de la Clue, de Coriolis, de Missiessy, de Pontevès-Giens, d'Entrecasteaux appointed rapporteur, Vialis and d'Orsin, ship captains.'
11 He was responsible for ensuring that the Franco–English agreement was applied, as well as determining the capacity of the English to arm their merchant ships in the event of conflict. He was also tasked with securing the cooperation of the Dutch governors and obtaining information on the Spanish forces in the Philippines.
12 Maurice Dupond, *D'Entrecasteaux: rien que la mer, un peu de gloire* (Éditions maritimes et d'outre-mer, 1983).
13 The Lapérouse and d'Entrecasteaux expeditions were complementary. Louis XVI commissioned d'Entrecasteaux to go in search of Lapérouse's expedition in 1791.
14 Michel Vergé Franceschi, 'Les officiers de 1789 et leur devenir', *Neptunia*, no 174, 1989, pp9–24.
15 Michel Vergé Franceschi 'Marine et Révolution. Les officiers de 1789 et leur devenir', *Histoire, économie et société*, 1990, 9e année, no 2. pp259–286. www.persee.fr/doc/hes_0752-5702_1990_num_9_2_2383
16 Martine Acera, Jean Meyer, *Marines et Révolution* (Rennes: Éditions Ouest-France, 1988).
17 The Comte d'Hector was lieutenant general of the naval armies and former commander of the navy in Brest. He emigrated in March 1791. See: Vicomte Grouvel, *Les Corps de troupe de l'émigration française (1789–1815)*, III, Le Corps de la marine, Paris, 1964, p85.
18 He had been promoted to lieutenant of the 3rd class in the organisation of the Marine Corps decided by the King on 1 January 1792.
19 It was intended to remedy the negligence of the executive power, accused of having prolonged 'the state of anarchy and confusion in the navy'. The Minister of the Navy, Bertrand de Molleville, was accused of having encouraged — or at least facilitated — the emigration of officers. Cf. Thibaut Poirot, 'La marine à la tribune. Les députés et la guerre navale pendant la Législative', *La mer, la guerre et les affaires: Enjeux et réalités maritimes de la Révolution française* (Presses Universitaires de Rennes, 2018).

http://books.openedition.org/pur/173577
20 As Michel Vergé Franceschi pointed out, 'Love of country, at least for the nobility, was confused with loyalty to the King: one was an officer on the King's ships: he alone was entitled to obedience.' Those who left to raise troops in countries at war with the Republic never thought of themselves as traitors to their homeland.
21 Gérald Arboit (ed), 'L'invention du contre-espionnage', *Napoléon et le renseignement* (Paris: Perrin, 2022), pp75–109.
22 Franceschi, pp523–4: 'The summary executions of sailors continued in Toulon during the summer of 1792: Lieutenant Désidéry, the Comte de Flotte and the Marquis de Rochemore, ship captains. At La Roquebrussanne, Maxime de Saqui des Tourrès was hanged from a mulberry tree, mutilated with sabre blows, shot twice in the stomach with pistols, decapitated with a knife and his head taken as a trophy to Solliès and then to Toulon.'
23 Jacques de Saint Victor, *La Chute des aristocrates. 1787–1792: naissance de la droite* (Perrin, 1992), pp151–2.
24 Jacqueline Chaumié, *Le Réseau d'Antraigues et la Contre-Révolution 1791–1793* (Paris: Plon, 1965), p47. This conflict would continue throughout the Revolution between the *émigrés* and the fighters in the interior. The *émigrés*, from their safe exile, judged with condescension the extravagances of these young nobles who remained in the heat of the action.
25 This term was meant to humiliate the nobles who tried to defend the King with their swords or pistols, which here become 'daggers', the traitor's weapon. In fact, a group of around three hundred gentlemen secretly broke into the Tuileries and tried to drag the King along, but he refused and asked them to lay down their arms. Among the gentlemen were former soldiers who were brutalised by the national guard. The ringleaders were arrested.
26 Clément Weiss, 'Royalistes de la veille. La défense des derniers gardes de Louis XVI, du 10 août 1792 à la Restauration', *Annales historiques de la Révolution française*, 2021/1, no 403, pp119–134.
27 Service Historique de la Défense, Site de Vincennes – CC7/ALPHA/1212 – dossier d'Imbert de Lebret.
28 A decree of 24 November 1792, based on a report by the Marine Committee, reinstated d'Imbert as a lieutenant at his request.

29 F A Aulard, *Recueil des Actes du Comité de Salut Public avec la correspondance officielle des représentants en mission*, Tome 8 (Paris, 1895), p617. A document preserved in the Archives Nationales in Paris [AF II, 186] in Barras' handwriting, dated 21 November 1793.
30 Hugues Marquis 'L'espionnage britannique et la fin de l'Ancien Régime', *Histoire, économie et société*, 1998, 17e année, no 2, pp261–276, www.persee.fr/doc/hes_0752-5702_1998_num_17_2_1984
31 *Mémoire de M. R. sur les ports de France*, 5 January 1793, The National Archives, Kew, London, PRO, FO95/3, quoted by Marquis: Hugues Marquis, *Agents de l'ennemi - Les espions à la solde de l'Angleterre dans une France en révolution* (Editions Vendémiaire, 2014).
32 4 April 1793. The National Archives, Kew, London, PRO, F095/3. quoted by Marquis, p46. Rey was in London at the time and asked Ponthou, a close friend, to organise the network in Paris.
33 Secretary to Lord Gower, the British ambassador to France, Huskisson followed him to London after the massacres of September 1792. He succeeded Evan Nepean as Under-Secretary of the War Office in 1795 and remained there until May 1801. He was in charge of intelligence services.
34 Above all, as Hugues Marquis pointed out, and this issue will remain constant, Rey belonged to the 'Ultras' party close to the Comte d'Artois, whereas Huskisson, who caused his disgrace, was sympathetic to the constitutional monarchists.
35 Lieutenant François Basterot de la Barrière (1762–93) was put in charge of the Algiers mission. He left with two frigates, *La Minerve* and *La Melpomène,* to return to Algiers to bring two chebecs to the Dey, who was supplying wheat. The sailors initially refused to leave and then accused their commander of treason. The Jacobins brought him before a court martial, sentenced him to death and he was guillotined in front of the whole fleet. See AN Mar/C7/18: His file contains the accusation, signed by the Jacobin Barthélémy.
36 On 26 April he had been given command of a frigate *L'Impérieuse*, which was being refitted. When she was laid up on the 11th, she was given to another captain.
37 For the general context, see: Malcolm Crook, *Toulon in War and Revolution. From the Ancien Régime to the Restoration, 1750–1820* (Manchester University Press, 1991), p270 and Malcolm Crook 'Federalism and the French

Revolution: The Revolt of Toulon in 1793', *History*, vol 65, no 215, 1980, pp383–97.
38 de Brécy, *Mémoire d'un homme de bien*, 1834, pp238–9.
39 Baron d'Imbert, *Précis des événements de Toulon en 1793* (Paris, 1814).
40 William S Cormack, *Revolution and Political conflict in the French Navy, 1789–1794*, (Cambridge, Massachusetts: Cambridge University Press, 1995), 2d edition 2002, p194.
41 Virginie Martin, 'La "trahison de Toulon": une victoire royaliste? Marchands rebelles et commissionnaires infidèles dans la guerre de subsistances de 1793', *La mer, la guerre et les affaires: Enjeux et réalités maritimes de la Révolution française* (Rennes: Presses universitaires de Rennes, 2018), pp145–160. https://doi.org/10.4000/books.pur.173622; See also G Vitse, 'La contre-Révolution à Toulon en 1793: les agents royalistes et le faux problème des subsistances', *Provence historique*, 1970, pp369–374.
42 The National Archives, Kew, London, HO/42/73/22 Folios 332–4.
43 If there was any doubt about d'Imbert's involvement, he was mentioned by Fréron in Toulon on 25 December 1793: 'We have already had 400 villains shot. The prisons are full, and we have set up a military commission that will dispatch hundreds of them. But the majority of the inhabitants have embarked and national justice will not be satisfied as it should be, if we hold the leaders. Trogoff, Puissant, Chaussegros, Imbert and Cazalès [the representative of Monsieur, brother of King Louis XVI, in Toulon] were the first to flee.' Quoted in Edmond Poupé, *Lettres de Barras et de Fréron en mission dans le Midi* (Draguignan, 1910).
44 Son of a naval commissioner, Jean-Baptiste Pasquier (1755–1830) was a commoner. He had only been appointed captain on 8 February 1793. Some 'blue' naval officers were fierce royalists and took part in the Toulon revolt (as did Pierre-Jacques Féraud, Jean-Baptiste Raccord or Henry Van Kempen). Pasquier wrote a *Mémoire* in London on 20 March 1795 for the Duc d'Harcourt, published by Cottin in the *Nouvelle revue rétrospective*, 1899, pp59–72.
45 His 'Journal' and that of another sailor from Rochefort were part of the evidence in the case against the sailors on *L'Apollon*. It was quoted by Edmond Poupé, 'Journal d'un Ponantais de l'Apollon', *Revue Historique de la Révolution française*, vol 2, no 5, 1911, pp34–62.
46 The mayor hoped to obtain permission from Lord Hood to bring some grain-laden vessels into the port. Zénon Pons, *Mémoires pour servir à l'histoire de la ville de Toulon en 1793* (Paris, 1825), p76.
47 D'Imbert's actions are confirmed (and detailed) by Abeille in his *Notice historique des événements*, but it should be noted that he is only mentioned in the second account of the negotiations, in 1815. He probably added it after reading d'Imbert's account (who never mentions Abeille in his supplications in 1814). Jean Abeille, *Notes et pièces officielles relatives aux événements de Marseille et de Toulon, en 1793* (Imprimerie Sétier fils, 1815), pp16–7.
48 Archives Nationales, Paris, MAR/C7/146 Petition from M. d'Imbert to Louis XVIII in 1814. In 1803, d'Imbert had had the idea of sounding the spirits of these officers (at least the survivors) in order to provoke a new uprising in the port of Rochefort.
49 Quoted by R Vallentin du Cheylard, 'Après le siège de Toulon', *Revue Historique de la révolution française*, vol 9, no 26, April–June 1916, pp253–4. The Authorities seized 547 letters and their contents were published in the *Courrier d'Avignon* of 20 September 1793. The mention of Gautier de Brécy as the author of one of the letters lends credence to the information. He himself, in his account published in 1815, admits to having made this error, which put his acquaintances at risk.
50 de Brécy.
51 The British king's declaration of the 29 October 1793 states that England intended to wage a war of principle (against Jacobinism) and not a war of ambition (against France as a state). See Burke 'Our War is not a War of Ambition [...] but a War of Principle'. Quoted in Philip Schofield, 'British Politicians and French Arms: The Ideological War of 1793–1795', *History*, vol 77, no 250, 1992, pp183–201.
52 Jennifer Mori: 'The British Government and the Bourbon Restoration: The Occupation of Toulon, 1793', *The Historical Journal*, vol 40, no 3 (September 1997), pp699–719.
53 Schofield.
54 Ibid.
55 The Antraigues network (whose members had met at the Salon Français) provided reports to British diplomats in Italy, Francis Drake in Genoa, William Hamilton in Naples and John Udny in Livorno (who himself had informers in Toulon).
56 The National Archives, Kew, London, PRO FO-7/36, Private, Grenville to Malmesbury, 27

December, quoted in Jennifer Mori.
57 Paul Cottin, *Toulon et les Anglais en 1793 d'après des documents inédits* (Paris: P Ollendorff, 1898).
58 David Hannay 'The English in Toulon', Review by Paul Cottin, *MacMillian's Magazine* 1899–04: vol 79, issue 474, pp458–486. 'We were to blame for two reasons. The first is that the British Government put a stain on its own good faith by repudiating the engagements of its admiral […] these engagements of Hood's were most inconvenient to Pitt, who had no intention of entering into a war for the restoration of the Bourbons … sending Sir Gilbert Elliot as commissioner to take over the town for King George, served to "convince not only the Toulonese, but our other allies, that we were manoeuvring to keep the town as another Gibraltar." And worse: "… we went into the adventure without in the least understanding the extent of the obligation we had incurred or providing the means to carry it through. The navy did its part, but if Toulon was to be held – and unless it could be held it was sheer cruelty in us to go in – troops were needed, and we had none to reinforce the handful Hood brought with him."'
59 Archives Nationales, Paris, MAR/7/146, no 42 D'Imbert's Petition to the Chamber of Deputies.
60 Mori.
61 Elizabeth Sparrow, 'Secret Service under Pitt's Administrations, 1792–1806', *History*, vol 83, no 70, 1998, pp280–294.
62 The National Archives, Kew, London, HO 42/75/28 folios 99–102. Letter of 5 January 1804 to Howard from Reboul, giving a detailed account of the conduct and supposed services of d'Imbert in Italy.
63 Frédéric d'Agay, tome 2, p196. Born in 1759, son-in-law of Albert de Rioms, the Marquis de Etienne de Colbert-Cannet, a naval officer, had emigrated to Nice at an early age, where he raised a corps of troops from the nobility of Provence known as the 'Colbert Legion', which he placed under the orders of the Comte d'Artois. After *L'Espérance* was disarmed in 1803, he took refuge in Naples, where he lived off a pension paid by the British government. When this pension was withdrawn, he was forced to work in the Neapolitan Navy's shipbuilding yards. Archives Nationales, Paris, MAR/C/7/70, file 42 Colbert du Cannet. Frédéric d'Agay, *La Provence au service du roi (1637-1831). Officiers des vaisseaux et des galères* (Paris:

Honoré Champion, 2011) 2 vols, p703; p776.
64 Compromised with Pichegru during the coup d'état of 18 fructidor an V (4 September 1797), he was deported to French Guiana, whence he escaped. See Jonathan Devlin, 'A problem of royalism: General Amedee Willot and the French Directory', *Renaissance and Modem Studies*, 33, 1990, pp125–143.
65 Maria Sofia Mormile, 'Les Bourbons en exil juges du royalisme. Doutes, nécessité et mesure de la fidélité dynastique (1795–1802)', *Annales historiques de la Révolution française*, vol 403, no 1, 2021, p86.
66 Emmanuel de Waresquiel, 'Joseph Fouché et la question de l'amnistie des émigrés (1799–1802)', *Annales Historiques de la Révolution Française*, 372, April–June 2013.
67 Archives Nationales, Paris, F6459. Note dated 30 March 1808.
68 On 12 October 1815, he sent his manifesto or declaration of rights entitled 'British Faith Violated' to the Minister of Police and Viscount Castlereagh. This document described his actions in England.
69 *Pétition à la Chambre des Députés, sur un acte arbitraire ministériel, suivie de considérations administratives et politiques intéressant l'état, la fortune et l'honneur de tous les militaires français*, Vol in-8°. Paris, 1818. D'Imbert met with Pichegru at a Council of Ministers meeting where his plan was approved. He then described three parallel conspiracies 'each acting separately and without knowing the plans and means of the others' and that each of the three English ministers had his own 'conspiracy': one with Méhée, one with Pichegru and one with him. Addington had hatched the conspiracy with Pichegru; this conspiracy failed, and he was obliged to hand over the portfolio. 'This setback,' said Baron d'Imbert, 'and even more so the conduct of Méhée, forced Mr Addington to leave the Ministry and hand over the government to the famous Pitt.'
70 They were both promoted to rear-admiral in 1814.
71 Chris Coelho, 'The Popham Code', *The Trafalgar Chronicle*, NS5, 2020.
72 The National Archives, Kew, London, HO42/74 folios 14–21 Letter from Rossolin to Baron d'Imbert, 8 November 1803.
73 The National Archives, Kew, London, H42/75 folio 123. 'Mr Stuart lieutenant of the 1ère class commanding *La Poulette* in Toulon, a valuable man destined since 16 August for one of the expeditions proposed by Baron d'Imbert […].' 'Mr de Laa enseigne de vaisseau major de

l'Escadre d'Alger excellent subject fulfilling at this moment in France a secret mission as perilous as it is important […].'
74 The National Archives, Kew, London, HO/42/75/107, folios 272–279. Letter dated 14 April 1804 from Chaussegros, former Commandant of the port of Toulon, Féraud commanding *Le Puissant*, Cazotte commanding *L'Aréthuse*, Poulain commanding the first division of vessels coming from Toulon, and the Comte de Grasse commanding the second division.
75 The National Archives, Kew, London, PRO, W01/923. *Secret instructions to the agents of the French princes.* Quoted by Marquis, pp267–8.
76 The English archives also hold a 'Projet de débarquement sur le point d'Etretat' signed by d'Imbert. The National Archives, Kew, London, FO95/4/4 Folio 275.
77 Born in 1769, du Bouchet emigrated during the Revolution and was in Condé's army, in Toulon, in Spain, in Italy, and was involved in the royalist unrest in the south of France. He returned in France after 18 Brumaire and was recruited by Talleyrand, Minister of Foreign affairs, in 1803 (without Fouché's knowledge, which meant that he was almost arrested on his return from his mission).
78 This report, held in French National Archives, was published in *Correspondence of the Duc d'Enghien (1801–1804) and documents on his abduction and death. La famille, l'Europe, published for the Société d'histoire contemporaine, by Cte Boulay de la Meurthe*, 1904–1913, pp277–282.
79 Ernest d'Hauterive published the bulletins for the period 1804–07 in three volumes between 1909 and 1922 under the title *La Police secrète du Premier Empire. Bulletins quotidiens adressés par Fouché à l'Empereur*. A new series published in 1963 presents the bulletins for the years 1808–09, before the fall of Fouché.
80 Sir Francis Drake, the English ambassador, also had a speciality of making recipes for invisible ink. The recipes varied, but were often made from gallnuts. It was also necessary to find the right developer (which, depending on the composition of the ink, could be water, liqueur, fire or powder).
81 Virgilio Ilari, 'The Dubuc affair (1787–1805). Bonaparte, India and Spies', *Rassegna dell'Arma dei Carabinieri*, 2018, no 1, pp175–195; no 2 pp111–135.
82 Olivier Blanc, 'Les retournés', *Les Espions de la Révolution et de l'Empire* (Paris: Perrin, 1995), pp251–269. Du Bouchet denounced another émigré in the pay of England, Bude de Longchamp, who was also executed.
83 Archives Nationales, Paris, AF1493.
84 The Military Penal Code of 11 November 1796 provided for the death penalty for foreign spies, and this 'crime' was considered to be exclusively military.
85 www.retronews.fr/journal/gazette-nationale-ou-le-moniteur-universel/02-juin-1805/149/1303769/2
86 Hauterive, tome 1, *Bulletin* of Friday 3 May 1805, pp407–8.
87 Arboit, pp75–109.
88 Hauterive, tome 1, *Bulletin* of Friday 5 June 1805, no 1438.
89 Hauterive, tome 1, *Bulletin* of Thursday 6 June 1805, pp462–3.
90 André Laa, aged thirty-four, a native of Arrudy in the Lower Pyrenees, was a former naval officer.
91 The National Archives, Kew, London, HO/42/76/05, folios 21–22. 'Extract [in French] from the report and letters of the Chevalier de l'Aa to Baron D'Imbert describing the assembly of a number of Irishmen at Morlaix [Brittany] to form a demi-brigade in preparation for an expedition to Ireland. He also reports intelligence gained at Rochefort and Bordeaux that Monsieur Lamothe, naval ensign paid by the British as a Toulonnais [refugee], had been living for some while at Blaye.'
92 Hauterive, tome1, *op.cit*, *Bulletin* of Friday 14 June 1805, n°1478, p509.
93 R Dinwiddy, 'The use of the Crown's power of deportation under the Aliens Act, 1793–1826', *Bulletin of the Institute of Historical Research*, vol XLI, no 104, November 1968, pp193–211. 'By the peace-time Aliens Act of July 1814 (54 Geo. Ill, c. 155), aliens ordered out of the country were given the right to appeal to the privy council against the order. (This concession was withdrawn by 55 Geo.III, c. 54, but renewed by 56 Geo. Ill, c. 86.) However, when considering the case of Baron d'Imbert, the privy council decided that the alien was neither entitled to know the charge against him, nor to be defended by counsel; and Mackintosh maintained that this decision rendered the concession worthless (Hansard, *Pari. Deb.*, xxxiv, cols 478, 629–30).'
94 Dinwiddy, 'The possibility of "deporting" suspect aliens was enshrined in the *Alien Bill* of 1793 (and used until 1826): "The aliens who were deported during the war period can be

NOTES

divided into three basic categories: first, those whose political views were considered objectionable; secondly, those who were suspected of being spies or agents of the French government; and thirdly those who were deported not for political or security reasons but simply because they were regarded as undesirable persons.'"
95 *Mémoires de M. de Bourrienne, ministre d'Etat; sur Napoléon, le directoire, le consulat, l'Empire et la restauration*, Paris, 1829, tome 7, pp298–9.
96 Auguste Thévenet dit Danican, was a repentant revolutionary general, sentenced in absentia, who fled to England where he has since been, writes Bourrienne, 'a constant but unskilful agent of the royal cause'.
97 Archives Nationales, Paris, F6459. Laurent Plagne, an officer in the Marine troops, had left Toulon in 1793. In May 1808, his brother-in-law, Mr Blandeau, a lawyer from Montpellier practising in Paris, requested authorisation to return to France as he 'could provide useful information'. On arriving in Paris, he 'frankly gave all the documents he could get his hands on' and as he had no money and life in Paris was difficult for him, he wanted to return to Toulon where his wife and two children were. His expulsion from England must mean that he no longer has the confidence of the agents of the Princes or the British Ministry. His relative vouches for his sincere devotion to his imperial majesty.' Letter from Bourrienne dated 29 March 1808. He 'was in the greatest misery; I gave him money to make his journey.' [to Paris]. He was about fifty years old in 1808.
98 Archives Nationales, Paris, MAR/C7/146, Lebret d'Imbert file.
99 Hauterive, tome 3, Bulletin of Tuesday 13 October 1807: 'Hambourg. Bourrienne sends the notes which Butler and d'Imbert gave him on 3 emigrants employed: Du Bouchet (had relations with Rumbold, was in England), Robert (amnestied emigrant, lives near Toulon), Lamothe (returned sailor; domiciled at Blaye, already arrested (I. 1508. 1523), was sent to Poitiers for surveillance). Details on them.'
100 Archives Nationales, Paris, F76459. From Imbert to Fouché, 25 April 1808.
101 Archives Nationales, Paris, F76459. From Imbert to Fouché, 12 May 1809.
102 Bernard Lutun, '1814–1817 ou l'épuration dans la marine', *Revue historique*, 1992, 583/3, pp63–86.
103 *Colloque obligé de M. Xavier Lebret,*

Baron d'Imbert avec Mulder, le Brabançon; précédé de quelques détails sur trente ans de révolution ... et suivi d'explications nécessaires sur le pamphlet intitulé: 'Procès de l'Ermite en province', et d'observations sur l'action intentée aux citoyens rédacteurs du Courrier soi-disant français. (Paris: Imprimerie Lefebvre, 1822), p38.

The Evolution of British Naval Leadership and Decision-Making in the Face of Sickness

1 J R McNeill, *Mosquito Empires: Ecology and War in the Greater Caribbean, 1620–1914* (New York: Cambridge University Press, 2010), p80, p168; Michael Duffy, *Soldiers, Sugar, and Seapower: The British Expeditions to the West Indies and the War Against Revolutionary France* (Oxford: Clarendon Press, 1987), pp339–47, p362.
2 Edward Vernon: Lt 1702; Captain 1706; Vice-Admiral 1739; failed invasion as CoC against Cartagena March—May 1741; Admiral 1745; died 1757. Inventor of grog.
3 George Rodney: Lt 1739; Captain 1742; Vice-Admiral 1763; Admiral 1778; died 1792.
4 John Jervis: Lt 1755; Captain 1760; Rear-Admiral 1787; Vice-Admiral 1793; Admiral 1795; died 1823.
5 Thomas Wentworth: Colonel 1737; Lieutenant General ?; Major General ?; died 1747.
6 Charles Cathcart: Captain 1704; Major 1709; Colonel 1717; Brigadier-General 1735; Major-General 1739; CoC in America 1740; died 1740.
7 McNeill, *Mosquito Empires*, pp159–64; N A M Rodger. *The Command of the Ocean: a Naval History of Britain, 1649–1815*. First American edition. (New York: W W Norton, 2005), p237.
8 Kenneth Breen, 'Rodney, George Bridges, First Baron Rodney (bap. 1718, d. 1792), naval officer and politician', *Oxford Dictionary of National Biography*, 23 September 2004; Rodger, *Command of the Ocean*, p348.
9 Charles Grey: Ensign 1744; Lt 1752; Captain 1755; Lt Colonel 1761; Colonel 1772; Major General 1777; Lieutenant General 1782; CoC West Indian Expedition 1793; Died 1807.
10 Duffy, *Soldiers, Sugar, and Seapower*, pp95–118; Rodger, *Command of the Ocean*, pp476–9.
11 Erica Charters, *Disease, War, and the Imperial State: The Welfare of the British Armed Forces During the Seven Years' War* (Chicago: University of Chicago Press, 2014), p20, p51.

213

12 Cori Convertito, 'The Health of British Seamen in the West Indies, 1770–1806' (University of Exeter PhD Thesis, 2011), p140.
13 William Parker: Lt 1766; Captain 1773; Rear-Admiral 1794; Duckworth's Commander-in-Chief at Jamaica 1795–1796; died 1802.
14 N A M Rodger, 'Honour and Duty at Sea, 1660–1815', *Historical Research* 75, vol 190, 2002, p447.
15 Henry Dundas: Lord Advocate 1775; Home Secretary 1791; President of the Board of Control 1793; Secretary of State for War 1794; First Lord of the Admiralty 1804; died 1811.
16 Rodger, *Command of the Ocean*, p426.
17 Hugh Christian: Lt 1771; Captain 1778; Rear-Admiral 1795; CoC Leeward Islands 1795; died 1798.
18 Ralph Abercromby: Cornet 1756; Lt Colonel 1773; Colonel 1781; CoC West Indies Expedition 1795; Lt General 1797; died 1801.
19 Victor Hughes: French Governor of Guadeloupe 1794–98; died 1826.
20 Rodger, *Command of the Ocean*, p426, pp434–6.
21 Alexander Lindsay: Ensign 1769; Captain 1771; Major 1775; Colonel 1780; Major General 1793; Governor of Jamaica 1794–1801; Lt General 1798; General 1803; died 1825.
22 John Thomas Duckworth, *Papers and Correspondence of Admiral Sir John Thomas Duckworth, Vol. 1: The French Revolutionary War, 1793–1802,* ed. J D Grainger (London: Navy Records Society, 2022), p115.
23 Duckworth, *Papers and Correspondence*, p118.
24 Duckworth, *Papers and Correspondence*, p72; A B Sainsbury, 'Duckworth, Sir John Thomas, First Baronet', *Oxford Dictionary of National Biography*, 23 September 2004.
25 Duckworth, *Papers and Correspondence*, p72.
26 Master of Brig HMS *L'Espiegle* in 1796.
27 Thomas Drury: Lt 1773; Captain 1782; Rear-Admiral 1804; Admiral 1814; died 1832.
28 Hugh Pigo. Lt 1790; Captain 1794; murdered 1797.
29 George Tripp: Lt 1776; Captain 1786; dismissed 1800.
30 Robert Winthrop: Lt 1780; Captain 1796; Rear-Admiral 1819; died 1832.
31 James Bennett: Lt 1794; killed in action 1808.
32 Duckworth, *Papers and Correspondence*, p100, 101, 106, 108, and 125.
33 George Spencer: 1783 2nd Earl; 1st Lord of the Admiralty 1794–1801; Home Secretary 1806–07; died 1834.
34 Duckworth, *Papers and Correspondence*, p135.
35 Ibid., pp90–1.
36 Ibid., pp75–6, 91, 95–6.
37 Rodger, *The Command of the Ocean*, pp467–72.
38 Toussaint L'Ouventure: Haitian political and military leader 1791 through Haitian Revolution and independence; promulgated the Haitian constitution 1801; freed former slave; imprisoned in France and died through despicable deception, 1803.
39 Duckworth, *Papers and Correspondence*, p333.
40 Hugh Seymour: Lt 1776; Captain 1779; Rear-Admiral 1795; died 1801.
41 Duckworth, *Papers and Correspondence*, p208, 333–6.
42 Ibid., p337.
43 Ibid., pp338–9.
44 Ibid, p338.
45 Ibid.
46 Ibid., p368, 371.
47 Thomas Trigge: Ensign 1759; Lieutenant-General and CoC of the West Indies 1799 (?); General (date?); died 1814.
48 Duckworth, *Papers and Correspondence*, p403.
49 Ibid., pp407–9.
50 Horatio Nelson: Lt 1777; Captain 1779; Rear-Admiral 1797; Vice-Admiral 1801; died 1805 at Trafalgar.
51 George Keith Elphinstone: Lt 1770; Captain 1775; Rear-Admiral 1794; Admiral 1801; died 1823.
52 Emma Hamilton: English actress and model married Sir William Hamilton (British Ambassador to the Kingdom of Naples 1764–1800) 1791; mistress of Horatio Nelson.
53 Duckworth, *Papers and Correspondence*, p226, 388, 434, 441.
54 Charters, *Disease, War, and the Imperial State*, pp1–5, 62; Duffy, *Soldiers, Sugar, and Seapower*, p197; Duckworth, *Papers and Correspondence*, p71.
55 Duckworth, *Papers and Correspondence*, p159.
56 James Alexander Miller, *Milestones in Medicine* (Freeport, New York: Books for Libraries Press, 1971), p84.

The Seafaring Saga of Joshua Penny, 1788–1815
1 Christopher P Magra, 'Thralls in Nelson's

NOTES

Navy: Impressment and American Mariners', in *From Across the Sea: North Americans in Nelson's Navy*, ed. Sean M Heuvel and John A Rodgaard (Wickham, UK: Helion & Co. Ltd, 2020), pp81–97.
2 For example, see the Vagabonds Act, 1597, Navigation Act 1703, Recruitment Act, 1703 and the Trade to America Act, 1707. See en.wikipedia.org/wiki/impressment#cite_note-RNM-5.
3 The issue of American citizens versus British subjects is discussed thoroughly in A Roger Kirch, *American Sanctuary: Mutiny, Martyrdom, and National Identity in the Age of Revolution* (New York: Pantheon (Bertelsmann), 2017); and Nathan Perl-Rosenthal, *Citizen Sailors: Becoming American in the Age of Revolution* (Cambridge, Massachusetts: Belknap (Harvard University) Press, 2015).
4 Joshua Penny, *The Life and Adventures of Joshua Penny, a native of Southold, Long Island, Suffolk County, NY* (New York: Spooner Publishing, 1815) is an 'as told to' autobiography, not uncommon in an age when many seamen did not have the writing skills essential for a successful publication. This account was printed and published by Alden Spooner in Brooklyn, New York. Spooner did not claim to be Penny's amanuensis, though he may have been. Occasionally, however, the copyist or editor speaks silently, inserting a patriotic or moralist comment that seems high flown or unnatural to the seaman's voice. Penny's narrative is one of the more unusual, impressed sailors' stories. See also, Spooner Family Papers. findingaids.library.NYU.edu/cbh/arc_098_spooner
5 Penny, *Life and Adventures*, p27.
6 Ibid., p31.
7 Ibid., pp39–40.
8 Peace of Amiens, 1802–03, a peace treaty negotiated by Britain, France, Spain and the Batavian Republic (Netherlands). They agreed to exchange some territories seized in the previous years of war. The cessation of hostilities ended the Wars of the French Revolution but lasted only fourteen months. The Peace did not last because the British realistically suspected Napoleon's warlike ambitions would interfere. In fact, the collapse of the Peace heralded the beginning of the Napoleonic Wars that would end with his defeat and banishment to St Helena in 1815.
9 https:/tracks4africa.co.za; www.vacorps.com/2014/08/extraordinary-tale-jpshua-penny-table-mountain
10 Penny, *Life and Adventures*, p43.
11 Decatur to Jones, in Dudley and Crawford, *Naval War of 1812: A Documentary History*, Vol. II, (Washington, DC: Naval Historical Center, 1992), pp135–6, nos 1 and 2.
12 This location, still called the Fire Place, was a high bluff facing Gardiner's Island where fires were set in to notify Lion Gardner that he had visitors or shipments of food waiting for pick up in his boats. In the early twentieth century, an elaborate girls' campground was built there called the Fire Place Lodge.
13 Major Benjamin Case to Captain Sir Thomas M Hardy, RN, in Dudley and Crawford, eds, *Naval War* II, pp245–6.
14 Hardy to Case, 24 August 1813, Dudley and Crawford, eds, *Naval War*, II, pp246–7.
15 Penny, *Life and Adventures*, pp56–7; Among this number was Ned Myers, of whom James Fenimore Cooper wrote *Ned Myers, A Life Before the Mast*, see Dudley, ed. *Classics of Naval Literature* (Annapolis, Maryland: Naval Institute Press, 1989).
16 Secretary Jones to President Madison, August 1813; and Madison to Jones, 6 September 1813, in Dudley and Crawford, eds, *Naval War*, II, p247.
17 James Madison to John Mason, 23 September 1813, in Dudley and Crawford (eds), *Naval War*, II, p248.

Trafalgar's Last Survivors
1 *United Service Journal*, 1839, part 1, p340.
2 *Oxford University and City Herald*, 29 September 1866.
3 *North British Agriculturist*, 28 October 1874.
4 *Worcestershire Chronicle*, 4 September 1880.
5 *The Graphic*, 16 November 1889.
6 *St James's Gazette*, 26 March 1892; *Sheffield Telegraph*, 4 January 1893.
7 *Globe*, 21 September 1891.
8 Royal Commission for the Chicago Exhibition. *Official Catalogue of the British Section*, 2nd ed. (London: William Clowes and Sons, 1893), p279, where his name is given as 'Emmanuel Cartigny'.
9 *Hereford Times*, 2 August 1856.
10 *Tribuno* (Seville), 9 April 1892, quoted in Edward Fraser, *The Enemy at Trafalgar* (London: Hodder and Stoughton, 1906), 1906, pp259–60.
11 *Yorkshire Herald*, 1 April 1892; *Northern Ensign*, 3 May 1892; *The Times*, 21 October 1915;

www.tapatalk.com/groups/aboutnelson/lastveteran-1612.html citing Mark Adkin, *The Trafalgar Companion* (London: Aurum Press, 2005); Jiří Kovařík, *Trafalgar: Anatomie námo ní bitvy* (Prague: Elka Press, 2008), p489, gives Zia Martinez's death date as 1 February 1898 and his age as 109.
12 *Yorkshire Herald*, 4 April 1892; *Army and Navy Gazette*, 5 March 1892.
13 W Laird Clowes, 'The Trafalgar Captains', *The Nineteenth Century*, vol 38, October 1895, pp576–99, at p594.
14 *Cheltenham Examiner*, 21 July 1858.
15 *Liverpool Mercury*, 22 April 1867; *Staffordshire Sentinel*, 27 April 1867; www.1805club.org/ayshford-trafalgar-roll/q/saunders/page/2; www.ancestry.com
16 *Buchan Observer*, 26 November 1869; www.ancestry.com
17 *Edinburgh Evening News*, 14 November 1876; Fraser, *Enemy*, p259.
18 *Shields Daily Gazette*, 23 October 1862; *Perth Constitutional Journal*, same date.
19 *The Anglo-American Times*, 7 February 1879; www.nationalarchives.gov.uk/trafalgarancestors/details.asp?id=12278; *Aberdeen Evening Post*, 17 June 1879. John Groombridge (born at Yalding, Kent, in 1754) was reputedly the Battle of Copenhagen's last survivor, and according to some reports, Trafalgar's too. But he was evidently confused with a much younger Kent-born namesake. *Reynolds's News*, 7 May 1854; *Bradford Observer*, 11 May 1854; ancestry.com; www.1805club.org/ayshford-trafalgar-roll/q/groombridge
20 www.1805club.org/ayshford-trafalgar-roll/q/haswell; *Edinburgh Evening News*, 28 September 1877; Bryan MacMahon, *The Story of Ballyheigue* (West Kerry: Oidhreacht, 1994), p88.
21 *Advocate*, 25 September 1880.
22 *Liverpool Weekly Courier*, 9 March 1872, citing the *Family Herald* n.d.
23 *Leeds Times*, 9 September 1882; *Stonehaven Journal*, 11 September 1882.
24 See such online sources as www.nationalarchives.gov.uk/trafalgarancestors; www.1805club.org/research-database/area/all; www.1805club.org/ayshford-trafalgar-roll
25 *St James's Gazette*, 2 November 1901. Similarly, a claim that a seaman from New York named Wade, who reputedly witnessed Captain Cook's death in Hawaii, served at Trafalgar seems far-fetched: *North London News*, 21 June 1879.
26 *Christian News*, 16 August 1856 (surname misspelled Brown); R H Mackenzie, *The Trafalgar Roll* (London: George Allen & Co., 1913), p14, 214; www.ancestry.com
27 *Exeter and Plymouth Gazette*, 29 July 1870; Mackenzie, *Trafalgar Roll*, pp106–7, 140; *Belfast News-Letter*, 21 March 1876; *South Wales Daily News*, 27 March 1877; www.ancestry.com
28 *Edinburgh Evening News*, 25 January 1879. A contemporaneous John Mills seems to have resided near Southampton Water, so it is possible that he could have made his way to Portsmouth or Gosport to attend those events.
29 www.nationalarchives.gov.uk/trafalgarancestors. For the *Africa* at Trafalgar and its towing by *Conqueror* see *Logs of the Great Sea Fights*, vol 2, T Sturges Jackson (ed), (London: Navy Records Society, 1905), pp297–9.
30 *Sydney Morning Herald*, 19 October 1923.
31 *Sydney Morning Herald*, 20 August 1929; *Daily Telegraph*, 26 August 1929.
32 www.1805club.org/ayshford-trafalgar-roll; Mackenzie, *The Trafalgar Roll*, p157, describes him as a 'midshipman' at the battle.
33 *East Anglian Daily Times*, 18 October 1905, citing research by London vicar and antiquarian Reverend Noel Kynaston Gaskell. The Royal Navy Club of 1765 is sometimes referred to as the Royal Naval Club, but the former appears to have been its original and correct title.
34 *Belfast News-Letter*, 23 March 1880.
35 *Hampshire Advertiser*, 1 March 1884.
36 *Daily Telegraph*, 22 December 1904; *The Sphere*, 7 April 1906.
37 *Naval and Military Gazette*, 8 March 1882. In 1950 someone, unnamed in the brief report in the *Montrose Standard*, 14 September 1950, which notes in passing the fuller report in an unnamed Sunday newspaper, recalled that as a boy more than seventy years earlier he had been taken to see Sir George Sartorius in Lymington, Hampshire, on the assumption that the latter was the last survivor, so that he could later boast of having done so (see also *Montrose Review*, 22 September 1950).
38 *Yorkshire Telegraph*, 26 March 1907.
39 www.ancestry.com; *Weekly Argus*, 30 March 1907.
40 *The World News*, 11 May 1907.
41 www.1805club.org/ayshford-trafalgar-roll; www.1805club.org/research-database; www.nationalarchives.gov.uk/trafalgarancestors
42 https://en.wikipedia.org/wiki/List_of_the

NOTES

_verified_oldest_
43 *Bromley Journal*, 12 April 1889; *Morning Post*, 10 March 1890; *Folkestone Chronicle*, 15 March 1890. A comparable hero's funeral was accorded at Montrose, Scotland, to local able seaman James Coull (born 7 January 1786, died 1 October 1880), a pressed deep-sea fisherman who had reputedly steered *Shannon* into her ferocious duel with *Chesapeake* in Boston Harbour in 1813. A troublesome wound acquired while boarding the American frigate resulted in Quartermaster Coull's discharge from the Navy in 1814 and in the amputation of his left forearm in 1816. Afterwards he spent many years as a cook on a whaler, stirring 'pease soup' with a fork that had replaced a hook at the end of a wooden block fitted to his upper arm (see his photo in *The Strand Magazine*, vol 10, 1895, p38). That he had served on *Centaur* at Trafalgar, as widely reported, was untrue: *Centaur* was not at the battle, nor is Coull listed in any of the Trafalgar databases. It was also widely reported that he served aboard *Centaur* at Copenhagen; if this was true, it must have been at the bombardment of Copenhagen in 1807. But not, contrary to reports, under Captain W R Broughton, who never commanded *Centaur*. *Montrose Standard*, 8 October 1880; *Montrose Review*, 22 September 1950.

The War of 1812 in Parliament: Britain's Naval Operations and the Political Discourse, 1812–15
1 Log of *Julia*, 29 July 1812, Admiralty Papers [hereafter ADM] 51/2506, The National Archives of the United Kingdom, Kew, Surrey, England [hereafter TNA]; John Bennett (Lloyds' of London) to Croker, 20 July 1812, ADM 1/3993, TNA. The positions expressed are mine alone and do not represent the Naval War College, the US Navy, the Department of Defense, or the US Government, and my views are not necessarily shared by them.
2 Prince Regent's Speech at the Close of the Session, 30 July 1812, *The Parliamentary Debates from the Year 1803 to the Present Time* [hereafter *Parliamentary Debates*] (London: T C Hansard, 1812), vol 23, p1286.
3 *London Gazette*, 23–27 June 1812; Jon Latimer, *1812: War with America* (Cambridge: Yale University Press, 2007), pp33–4. It should be noted that the suspension of the Orders in Council would become permanent only if several conditions were met to include the US Government ending its restrictions on British shipping, see Castlereagh to Foster, 17, 23 June 1812 (and Attached Memorandum), *Instructions to British Ministers of the United States*, (ed) Bernard Mayo (New York: DeCapo Press, 1971), pp381–3.
4 *Parliamentary Debates* (1812), vol 23, p1288, (1812–13) vol 24, p1; William A Hay, *Lord Liverpool, A Political Life* (Woodbridge: Boydell, 2018), p149.
5 Prince Regent's Opening Speech 30 November 1812, *Parliamentary Debates* (1812–13), vol 24, p14. See Kevin D McCranie, *Utmost Gallantry: The U.S. and Royal Navies at Sea in the War of 1812* (Annapolis, Maryland: Naval Institute, 2011), xiii, p22.
6 Canning (House of Commons) Response to Prince Regent's Speech on the Opening Session, 30 November 1812, *Parliamentary Debates* (1812–13), vol 24 (1812–13), p72.
7 Samuel Whitbread (House of Commons) Response to Prince Regent's Speech on the Opening Session, Monday, 30 November 1812, *Parliamentary Debates* (1812–13), vol 24 (1812–13), p93.
8 *Morning Chronicle* (London), 28 December 1812.
9 Lord Castlereagh (Commons), 3 February 1813, *Parliamentary Debates* (1812–13), vol 24, p363.
10 Lansdowne (Lords), Address Concerning the War with America, 18 February 1813, *Parliamentary Debates* (1812–13), vol 24, p582.
11 Ships in Sea Service, 1 July 1812, ADM 8/100, TNA; Hamilton to Cheves, 3 December 1811, *The New American State Papers, Naval Affairs, Vol 1 General Naval Policy*, (ed) Jack K Bauer (Wilmington, Delaware: Scholarly Resources, Inc., 1981), vol 1, p72; Jan Glete, *Navies and Nations: Warships, Navies and State Building in Europe and America, 1500–1860* (Stockholm: Almqvist & Wiksell, 1993), vol 2, p376.
12 Kevin D McCranie, 'The War of 1812 in the Ongoing Napoleonic Wars: The Response of Britain's Royal Navy', *Journal of Military History*, 76 (October 2012), pp1067-1094; McCranie, 'Britain's Royal Navy and the Defeat of Napoleon,' in Michael V Leggiere (ed), *Napoleon and the Operational Art of War: Essays in Honor of Donald D Horward* (Brill: Leiden, 2016), pp476–99.
13 Melville (Lords), Address Concerning the War with America, 18 February 1813, *Parliamentary Debates* (1812–13), vol 24, p584.
14 Wellesley (Lords), Address Concerning the

War with America, 18 February 1813, *Parliamentary Debates* (1812–13), vol 24, p584.
15 Liverpool (Lords), Address Concerning the War with America, 18 February 1813, *Parliamentary Debates* (1812–13), vol 24, pp584–5.
16 Castlereagh (Commons), Address Concerning the War with America, 18 February 1813, *Parliamentary Debates* (1812–13), vol 24, p599.
17 George Ponsonby (Commons), Address Concerning the War with America, 18 February 1813, *Parliamentary Debates* (1812–13), vol 24, p618.
18 Baring (Commons), Address Concerning the War with America, 18 February 1813, *Parliamentary Debates* (1812–13), vol 24, p622.
19 Canning (Commons), Address Concerning the War with America, 18 February 1813, *Parliamentary Debates* (1812–13), vol 24, p642.
20 John Severn, *Architects of Empire: The Duke of Wellington and His Brothers* (Norman: University of Oklahoma Press, 2007), pp360–1, p364; Hay, *Liverpool*, p149.
21 William Dundas (Commons), Navy Estimates, 12 March 1813, *Parliamentary Debates* (1813), vol 25, p89.
22 Croker (Commons), Navy Estimates, 12 March 1813, *Parliamentary Debates* (1813), vol 25, p93.
23 Darnley (Lords), Naval Administration, 18 March 1813, *Parliamentary Debates* (1813), vol 25, p203.
24 *Examiner* (London), 21 March 1813.
25 Darnley (Lords), Naval Administration, 23 March 1812, *Parliamentary Debates* (1813), vol 25, p256.
26 Melville (Lords), Naval Administration, 6 April 1813, *Parliamentary Debates* (1813), vol 25, p595.
27 Darnley (Lords), Naval Administration, 14 May 1813, *Parliamentary Debates* (1813), vol 26, 174.
28 Darnley (Lords), Naval Administration, 14 May 1813, *Parliamentary Debates* (1813), vol 26, p179.
29 Darnley (Lords), Naval Administration, 14 May 1813, *Parliamentary Debates* (1813), vol 26, p182.
30 Melville (Lords), Naval Administration, 14 May 1813, *Parliamentary Debates* (1813), vol 26, pp183–7.
31 Bathurst (Lords), Naval Administration, 14 May 1813, *Parliamentary Debates* (1813), vol 26, p198.
32 George Stewart, eighth Earl of Galloway (Lords), Naval Administration, 14 May 1813, *Parliamentary Debates* (1813), vol 26, p191.
33 Vote total (Lords), 14 May 1813, *Parliamentary Debates* (1813), vol 26, p202.
34 McCranie, *Utmost Gallantry*, pp210–3.
35 Croker to Warren, 4 November 184, ADM 2/1378/146-51, TNA; Melville to Warren, 24 November 1813, Warren Papers, WAR/82/96-8 and Warren to Melville, 3 February 1814, LBK/2, National Maritime Museum, London; McCranie, *Utmost Gallantry*, pp212–3, 218.
36 Croker to Several Commanders in Chief …, 10 July 1813, ADM 2/1377/154-56, TNA.
37 Christopher Lloyd, *Lord Cochrane: Seaman, Radical, Liberator* (reprint, New York: Henry Holt, 1998), p99; 'Cochrane, Thomas,' *Oxford Dictionary of National Biography*, new edition.
38 Cochrane (Commons), State of the Navy, 5 July 1813, *Parliamentary Debates* (1813), vol 26, pp1102–3.
39 Cochrane (Commons), State of the Navy, 5 July 1813, *Parliamentary Debates* (1813), vol 26, p1103.
40 *Liverpool Mercury*, 16 July 1813.
41 Cochrane (Commons), 5 July 1813, State of the Navy, *Parliamentary Debates*, vol 26 (1813), p1115.
42 Croker (Commons), 5 July 1813, State of the Navy, *Parliamentary Debates*, vol 26 (1813), pp1106–7.
43 Croker (Commons), 8 July 1813, Motion Respecting Seamen's Wages and Prize Money, *Parliamentary Debates*, vol 26 (1813), p1159.
44 *Edinburgh Advertiser*, 13 July 1813.
45 *Parliamentary Debates* (1813–14 and 1814), vols 27 and 28.
46 Darnley (Lords), Naval Administration, 21 February 1815, *Parliamentary Debates* (1814–15), vol 29, p905. For an assessment of the Royal Navy at the end of the War of 1812, see Evan Wilson, *The Horrible Peace: British Veterans and the End of the Napoleonic Wars* (Amherst: University of Massachusetts Press, 2023).
47 Darnley (Lords), Naval Administration, 21 February 1815, *Parliamentary Debates* (1814–15), vol 29, p908.
48 Darnley (Lords), Naval Administration, 12 June 1815, *Parliamentary Debates* (1815), vol 31, p732.
49 John Rolle, first Baron Rolle, Naval Administration, 12 June 1815, *Parliamentary Debates* (1815), vol 31, p737.

Facts and Firsts for The United States Navy: Remembering the Cruise of the USS *Essex*,

NOTES

1812–14

1 Frances Diane Robotti and James Vescovi, *The USS Essex and the Birth of the American Navy* (Holbrook, Massachusetts: Adams Media Corp., 1999), pp41–2.
2 Robotti and Vescovi, p42.
3 David F Long, *Gold Braid and Foreign Relations: Diplomatic Activities of U.S. Naval Officers, 1798–1883* (Annapolis, Maryland: Naval Institute Press, 1988), pp72–3.
4 C S Forester, *The Age of Fighting Sail: The Story of The Naval War of 1812* (Garden City, New York: Doubleday & Co. Inc., 1956), p206.
5 Ralph D Paine, *The Fight for a Free Sea: A Chronicle of the War of 1812* (New Haven, Connecticut: Yale University Press, 1920), p157.
6 B Shepard (ed), *Bound for Battle: The Cruise of the U.S. Frigate Essex in the War of 1812 as told by Captain David Porter* (New York: Harcourt, Brace World, 1967), p121.
7 Forester, p207.
8 David Porter, *Journal of a Cruise made to the Pacific Ocean by Captain David Porter in the United States Frigate Essex in the years 1812, 1813, and 1814* (New York: Wiley & Halsted, 1822), vol 2, p143.
9 Harry L Coles, *The War of 1812* (Chicago: University of Chicago Press, 1965), p87.
10 William James, *A full and correct account of the Chief Naval Occurrences of the Late War between Great Britain and the United Stated of America* (London: T Egerton, 1817), p306.
11 Robotti and Vescovi, p189.
12 Coles, p88.
13 Alexander Begg, *History of British Columbia from its earliest discovery to the present time.* (Toronto: William Briggs, 1894), pp105–6.
14 Paine, p158.
15 Francis F Bierne, *The War of 1812* (New York: E P Dutton & Co. Inc., 1949), p195.
16 Forester, p209.
17 Ibid.
18 Robotti and Vescovi, p214.
19 Robotti and Vescovi, p222. See also The National Archives of the United Kingdom, Kew, ADM 1/1950: Francisco de la Lastra to James Hillyar, 11 April 1814.
20 Bierne, p195.
21 Ibid.
22 Forester, p210.
23 Donald R Hickey, *Don't Give up the Ship! Myths of the War of 1812* (Urbana: University of Illinois Press, 2006), p114.
24 The National Archives of the United Kingdom, Kew, Surrey, ADM 1/1950: George Cood et. al. to James Hillyar, 25 February 1814.
25 Eugenio Pereira Salas and A S Merrill (tr.), 'First Contacts – The Glorious Cruise of the Frigate Essex', *Proceedings*, vol 2, February 1940.
26 Paine, p159.
27 Robotti and Vescovi, p157.
28 Bierne, p196.
29 Ibid.
30 Forester, p211.
31 Hickey, p233.
32 Paine, p156.
33 Bierne, p193.
34 Hickey, p114.
35 Paine, p151.
36 Ibid.
37 Forester, p206.
38 Ibid.
39 Ibid.
40 Ibid., p211.
41 Ibid., p212.
42 James Ripley Jacobs and Glenn Tucker, *The War of 1812: A Compact History* (New York: Hawthorn Books, 1969), p164.

The Cost of Wartime Innovation: Copper Bottoms and British Naval Operations during the American Revolutionary Wars, 1779–83

1 N A M Rodger, *The Command of the Ocean: A Naval History of Britain, 1649–1815* (New York: W W Norton, 2005), pp340–1.
2 For details on the disruptions of the Keppel-Palliser Affair see N A M Rodger, *The Insatiable Earl: A Life of John Montagu, 4th Earl of Sandwich* (New York: W W Norton, 1993), pp345–51; 'Keppel, the Hon. Augustus', History of Parliament Online, www.historyofparliamentonline.org/volume/17 54-1790/member/keppel-hon-augustus-1725-86; Nicholas Rogers, 'The Trial of Admiral Keppel', *Crowds, Culture, and Politics in Georgian Britain*, Online ed. (Oxford: Oxford Academic, 1998), https://doi.org/10.1093/acprof:oso/9780198201 724.003.0005,
3 Rodger, *Command*, pp339–42; Rodger, *Insatiable Earl*, pp238–263.
4 Rodger, *Insatiable Earl*, pp230–7.
5 Rodger, *Command*, p332.
6 Rodger, *Insatiable Earl*, p237.
7 Sheathing the hulls of ships with various materials including lead was an ancient practice dating back to the fourth century BCE. Lionel Casson, 'More Evidence for Lead

Sheathing on Roman Craft', *The Mariner's Mirror*, 64, no 2 (1978), pp139–142; Mark Stainforth, 'The Introduction and Use of Copper Sheathing – A History', *Bulletin of the Australian Institute of Maritime Archaeology*, 9 (1985), pp21–48.
8 Stainforth, 'Introduction and Use', p21.
9 Randolph Cock, '"The Finest Invention in the World": The Royal Navy's Early Trials of Copper Sheathing, 1708–1770', *The Mariner's Mirror*, 87, no 4 (2001), p447.
10 R J B Knight, 'The Introduction of Copper Sheathing into the Royal Navy, 1779–1786', *The Mariner's Mirror*, 59, no 3 (1973), pp299–309; Cock, 'The Finest Invention', pp446–459; J R Harris, 'Copper and Shipping in the Eighteenth Century', *The Economic History Review*, vol 19, no 3 (1966), pp550–568.
11 'The average ship of the line was docked 0.87 times a year from 1770–1777, but only 0.52 times a year from 1778–1782,' Rodger, *Insatiable Earl*, p296. Captain Sir Peter Parker noted that in wartime, uncoppered frigates in the West Indies needed careening every six months, Parker to Sandwich, 25 April, in G R Barnes and J H Owen, *The Private Papers of John, Earl of Sandwich,* (hereafter *Sandwich Papers*), vol 1, p69 (London: Navy Records Society (NRS), 1932), p410.
12 Rodger, *Insatiable Earl*, p296.
13 Middleton probably to Sandwich, undated in G R Barnes and J H Owen, *Sandwich Papers*, vol III, 75 (London: NRS, 1934), p175. In 1803 Middleton revised his estimate to a one third increase, see 'On the State of the Navy,' April 1803, in J K Laughton, *The Letters and Papers of Charles, Lord Barham, 1758–1813* (hereafter *Barham Papers*), vol III, p39 (London: NRS, 1911), pp15–6.
14 Knight, 'Introduction', pp301–2.
15 Mulgrave to Sandwich, 2 Jul. 1779, *Sandwich Papers,* III, p35.
16 Kempenfelt to Middleton, 5 Sep. 1779, in J K Laughton, *Barham Papers*, vol I, p32 (London: NRS, 1908), pp296–7.
17 Kempenfelt to Sandwich, 3 Jan. 1782, G R Barnes and J H Owen, *Sandwich Papers*, vol IV, p87 (London, NRS, 1938), p82.
18 Rodney to Philip Stephens, 11 Feb. 1780, in David Syrett, *The Rodney Papers*, vol II, p151 (London: NRS, 2007), p362.
19 Rodney quoted in Rodger, *Command*, p345.
20 Young to Middleton, 28 Apr. 1780, *Barham Papers*, I, p55.
21 Report from 1779 quoted in Harris, 'Copper and Shipping', no 1, p555.

22 An experiment with all-copper fastenings was conducted in 1770 on the sloop *Swallow*. The vessel served seven years in the East Indies and was re-coppered in Bombay in 1776, although she sank in a storm before returning to the London dockyards for a full assessment of her hull, see Cock, 'The Finest Invention', p456.
23 *Barham Papers*, I, p252.
24 Knight, 'Introduction', p306.
25 Manners to his brother, the Duke of Rutland, 27 September 1781, Historical Manuscripts Commission (HMC), *The Manuscripts of the Duke of Rutland (Rutland)*, III (London: Eyer and Spottiswoode, 1894), pp37–8. For details of her flooding see Donald Schomette, *Shipwrecks, Sea Raiders, and Maritime Disasters along the Delmarva Coast, 1632–2004* (Baltimore: Johns Hopkins University Press, 2007), pp91–3.
26 Manners to Rutland, 27 September 1781, HMC, *Rutland*, III, p38.
27 Manners to Rutland, 10 March 1782, HMC, *Rutland*, III, p50; also quoted in Rodger, *Insatiable Earl*, p297.
28 Court Martial records for the loss of HMS *Ramillies* and HMS *Centaur*, TNA, ADM 1/5322.
29 Line of battle ships, HMS *Ardent* (64), HMS *Canton*, and the frigate HMS *Pallas* (36) all returned to port due to leaks. K Breen, 'The Foundering of HMS *Ramillies*', in The *Mariner's Mirror*, 56, no 2 (1970), pp190–2; Harris, 'Copper and Shipping', p554.
30 Various sources give the number of casualties between 500 and 1000 including about 200–300 women and children who were aboard. Hilary L Rubinstein, *Catastrophe at Spithead: The Sinking of the Royal George* (Barnsley, UK: Seaforth, 2020), pp81–2, p111.
31 Court martial verdict quoted in Rubinstein, *Catastrophe*, p143. Other recent analysis agrees with this verdict and the role of copper sheathing and its attendant problems as the cause of the *Royal George*'s rotten state and subsequent sinking. David Syrett, *The Royal Navy in European Waters during the American Revolutionary War* (Columbia, South Carolina: University of South Carolina Press, 1998), p161.
32 Gunner's Mate Smart, court martial testimony quoted in Rubinstein, *Catastrophe*, pp131–2.
33 Harris, 'Copper and Shipping', p554 For Barrington's politics see Rodger, *Command*, p355; for his opposition to coppering see Harris, 'Shipping and Copper', p554.

NOTES

34 Officers presiding: Vice-Admirals Barrington, John Evans, Mark Milbanke; Rear-Admirals Alexander Hood, Richard Hughes; Commodores William Hotham, John Levenson Gower; Captains John Carter Allen, John Dalrymple, John Moutray, Jonathan Faulknor, John Jervis, Adam Duncan, in Rubenstein, *Catastrophe*, p124.
35 According to Isaac Schomberg's estimates from 1802, a total of 217 ships and vessels of all sizes *were in commission* during the American War of Independence, cited in Rodger, *Command*, Appendix III, p615. Losses are taken from *A Collection of Papers on Naval Architecture*, LIV, (London: James Aspern, 1805), Appendix 1, p6, cited in Harris, 'Shipping and Copper', pp554–5.
36 Hood to Middleton, 28 February 1783, *Barham Papers*, I, pp253–4.
37 Navy Board to Secretary Stephens, 5 November 1783, in John Hattendorf et al., *British Naval Documents, 1204–1960*, 131 (London: NRS, 1993), pp499–503.
38 For criticism of reckless adoption see Harris: 'should anything go wrong with a technical process adopted at this headlong pace, the results could be disastrous,' Harris, 'Shipping and Copper', p554; Robert Albion, *Forests and Sea Power: The Timber Problem of the Royal Navy, 1652–1862* (Cambridge, Massachusetts: Harvard University Press, 1926). For a critique of Sandwich's slow adoption of the technology, see Maurer, 'Coppered Bottoms for the Royal Navy: A Factor in the Maritime War 1778–1783', in *Military Affairs*, 14, no 2 (1950): pp57–61.
39 Rodger, *Insatiable Earl*, p299. Also see Paul Kennedy, *The Rise and Fall of British Naval Mastery* (London: Ashfield Press, 1990), pp107–10.
40 Middleton 'On the State of the Navy', April 1803, in *Barham Papers* III, pp15–6; also see Harris, 'Shipping and Copper', pp553–4.
41 The solution was 'a copper and zinc bolt hardened by mechanical means,' now known as marine brass. The alloy was developed independently by William 'Copperbottom' Forbes, and 'Westwood and Collins, under the direction of Thomas Williams,' which led to heated competition for naval contracts. See Knight, 'Introduction', p306.
42 Although Admiral Richard Howe became First Lord in December 1783, Middleton was responsible for seeing the project through to completion. He remained at the Navy Board until 1790.

43 Rodger, *Insatiable Earl*, p298. In 1781 Middleton voiced fears that the enemy were reaping the rewards of copper sheathing and suggested that the Royal Navy had squandered its chance when the 'advantages of copper were, in a manner, confined to our own fleet' – although his concerns were unfounded. Middleton to Sandwich, 25 December 1781, J K Laughton, *Barham Papers*, vol II, 38 (London: NRS, 1910), p40.
44 Sandwich defended his decision in a Naval Enquiry in the House of Commons in 1781–82 in which he expressed the achievements of the coppered fleet. *Sandwich Papers*, IV, pp285–7.

The Historical Significance Behind the Name of Villeneuve's Flagship *Bucentaure*
1 Captured in 1800, the ship was renamed HMS *Malta*.
2 Gareth Glover, *The Forgotten War against Napoleon. Conflict in the Mediterranean* (Barnsley: Seaforth Publishing, 2017). Norman Davies' *Vanished Kingdoms* (London: Allen Lane, Penguin, 2011) brings out Napoleon's personal interests in ch 10, 'Etruria'. For the narrative of events leading up to the fall of the Venetian Republic I have largely followed John Julius Norwich, *A History of Venice* (Harmondsworth: Penguin, 1982), 'The Fall', for the detail of his narrative and his understanding of the European and diplomatic context. Also of value is Christopher Hibbert, *Venice* (London: Grafton Books, 1988), ch 12; Elizabeth Horodowich, *Venice* (London: Constable and Robinson, 2009), pp181–190. To mark the anniversary of the fall of the Republic, two valuable, wide-ranging exhibition catalogues covering this period of transition in Venetian history were published by the Commune of Venice, *Dai Dogi agli Imperatori. La Fine della Repubblica fra Storia e Mito* (Milan: Electra, 1997), and the Regione del Veneto and the Fondazione Giorgio Cini, *Venezia da Stato a Mito* (Venice: Marsilio, 1997).
2 An effective, much-read, critic of Venice and its constitution was Amelot de le Houssaye (1634–1706), who had served as secretary to the French embassy in the city. His *Histoire du Gouvernment de Venise* was published in 1676 and sought to expose the closed and vindictive nature of its government. Venetian protests caused the author to spend time in the Bastille.
3 Caroline Webb, *Visitors to Verona* (London/New York: Tauris, 2017), pp78–9.
4 Webb. Napoleon used intimidation and the threat of plunder against the Knights of St John

221

on Malta in 1798. Brian N Tarpey (ed), Peter Clayton, 'Nelson at Malta', *The Nelson Dispatch* (2021), vol 14, nos 1 and 2. For these tactics used earlier in Tuscany, see Davies.
5 Cynthia Saltzman, *Napoleon's Plunder and the Theft of the Veronese's Feast* (London: Thames and Hudson, 2021). The work is still in the Louvre. Saltzman's study gives a clear account of the fall of the Republic.
6 The Arsenale may have been a model for the French dockyards at Toulon. Philippe de Commynes, ambassador for Charles VIII in Venice in 1494–95, was impressed by the Republic's sea power: George Bull, *Venice: The Most Triumphant City* (London: Folio Society, 1980), pp25–8. For a detailed account associated with the court of Louis XII read Philippe Braunstein and Rheinhold C Mueller, *Descripcion ou Traicte du Gouvernement et Regime de la Cite et Seigneurie de Venise* (Venice/Paris: The Sorbonne, 2015).
7 Deborah Howard, *Venice Disputed* (New Haven, Connecticut: Yale University Press, 2011), p146. A good summary of the building history of the Arsenale can be found in Richard J Goy, *Venice* (New Haven, Connecticut: Yale University Press, 2010), pp43–50.
8 For the *Bucintoro*, I accessed Wikipedia on 21 March 2023, where *that* entry was detailed and well referenced.
9 The closest she came to battle was in what has become known as the War of Chioggia. This was a 'close-run thing' for Venice, and its narrative is as dramatic as those surrounding the Royal Navy's engagements with France and its allies. See for example, Frederic C Lane, *Venice: A Maritime Republic* (Baltimore: Johns Hopkins, 1973), pp189–201.
10 Both descriptions derive from the anthology edited by John Julius Norwich, *Venice: A Traveller's Reader* (London: Robinson, 2017), pp209–11. This valuable collection contains several accounts of the ceremonies associated with the *Bucintoro*.
11 Johann Wolfgang von Goethe, *Italian Journey* (London: Penguin 1970), pp87–8. Goethe recalled inspecting an 84-gun vessel being built in the Arsenale. Invited visitors, who needed to be impressed, noted the 'conveyor belt' efficiency of the dockyard, as recorded from the late Middle Ages.
12 A Wikipedia entry describes her as 'the mighty Venetian ship Bucentaur'. The vessel was not a ship, but a galley powered by oars. The Republic's banner flew on the mast, which could be lowered. In Venetian it was the *Bucintoro*. The ceremony has been much described and discussed, more recently by Lina P Urban, 'La Festa della Sensa nelle Arti e nella Iconografia', *Studi Veneziani*, vol 10, 1969, especially pp217–9; Edward Muir, *Civic Ritual in Renaissance Venice* (Princeton, New Jersey: Princeton University Press, 1978), ch 3; Asa Boholm, *The Doge of Venice. The Symbolism of State Power in the Renaissance* (Gothenburg, Sweden: Gothenburg University Press, 1990), ch 14; Braunstein and Mueller, p411.
13 An important exhibition was held in the Royal Academy of Arts in London, 1983. The catalogue, *The Genius of Venice,* edited by Jane Martineau and Charles Hope, has entries on the 'Bird's Eye of Venice', pp392–3 and an engraved map of *c*1563 showing the 'Golfo di Venezia', pp398–9. The catalogue's introduction records Venice's claim to lordship over most of the east coast of the Adriatic. The Republic's claims to 'territorial waters' was discussed by Alberto Tenenti, *Storia di Venezia: Il Mare* (Rome: Treccani,1 990), 'Il Senso del Mare', especially pp37–47.
14 Early pilgrim accounts note the presence of Venetian war galleys in the Adriatic and beyond. For a perceptive account of early pilgrimages through Venice with accounts of La Sensa, read Rosamund J Mitchell, *The Spring Voyage* (London: Murray, 1965) and *The Pylgrymage in 1506 of Sir Richard Guylforde*, edited by Henry Ellis for the Camden Society (London: 1851).
15 An excellent analysis of the De' Barbari view is Emiliano Balistreri and others, *Venezia Citta Mirabile* (Verona, 2009) under 'Arsenale' and 'Bucintoro'. The original 'blocks' for the engraving are held in the Museo Correr in Venice.
16 E T Cook and Alexander Wedderburn (eds), *The Complete Works of John Ruskin*, vol 28 (London: Allen and Unwin, 1970), pp90–3.
17 Rawdon Lubbock Brown, *Four Years at the Court of Henry VIII. Selections from the Despatches of the Venetian Sebastiano Giustiniani* (Cambridge: Cambridge University Press, 2013), vol I, p85.
18 For the Thames, Robert Crouch and Beryl Pendley, *Royal Bargemasters* (Cheltenham: History Press, 2019). On 14 January, the river receives an Anglican 'blessing', no ring but a wooden cross is offered to the river.
19 Beatrice Mezzogori, *Splendour displayed: state barges, embroideries and power in Renaissance Ferrara* (PhD thesis, Manchester University, 2014). For an insight into how Venice used La Sensa and other ceremonies to

impress ruling families and nobles from the mainland in 1493, see Julia Cartwright, *Beatrice d'Este Duchess of Milan* (London: Dent, 1899), p174 and pp185–194.
Who Will Rule? The Struggle for Power in Río de la Plata, 1808–10
1 David Gates, *The Spanish Ulcer: A History of the Pensular War* (Cambridge, Massachusetts: Da Capo Press, 2001), pp5–12.
2 John Barrow, *The Life and Correspondence of Admiral Sir William Sidney Smith, G C B* (London: Richard Bentley, 1848), ii, pp260–76.
3 António Ventura and Maria de Lourdes Viana Lyra, *Carlota Joaquina [e] Leopoldina de Habsburgo: rainhas de Portugal no Novo Mundo* (Lisboa: Temas e Debates, 2019), pp78–9.
4 Kenneth H Light, 'British Naval Involvement in Brazil, 1807–1815', *British Historical Society of Portugal*, newsletter 17, 2022, pp4–5.
5 Barrow, ii, pp280–4.
6 Adam Zamoyski, *Napoleon: The Man behind the Myth* (London: William Collins, 2018), pp434–40.
7 J Holland Rose, 'Canning and the Spanish Patriots in 1808', *The American Historical Review*, 12:1, 1906, pp39–52.
8 Barrow, ii, pp286–304.
9 João Paulo Garrido Pimenta, 'O Brasil e a América espanhola (1808–1822)' (Ph.D. diss., Universidade de São Paulo, 2003), pp53–54, www.teses.usp.br/teses/disponiveis/8/8138/tde -02082022-190637 [accessed 8 July 2023].
10 Francisca L Nogueira de Azevedo, 'Carlota Joaquina, a herdeira do império espanhol na América', *Revista Estudos Históricos*, 10:20, 1997, p260.
11 William W Kaufmann, *British Policy and the Independence of Latin America, 1804–1828* (Hamden, Connecticut: Archon Books, 1967), p58.
12 Kaufmann, p55.
13 Marcela Ternavasio, 'Diplomacia, linaje y política durante la crisis de las monarquías ibéricas. Disputas en torno a la candidatura de Carlota Joaquina de Borbón entre 1808 y 1810', *Historia y Política: Ideas, Procesos y Movimientos Sociales*, 38, 2017, p177, https://recyt.fecyt.es/index.php/Hyp/article/vie w/51541 [accessed 18 November 2023].

14 José M Olivero Orecchia, 'La Junta de Montevideo en 1808, una situación interna con repercuciones internacionales: algunos aspectos de los intereses y acciones portuguesas', *Revista Digital Estudios Historicos*, 3, 2009, https://fortalezasmultimidia.ufsc.br/midias/arq uivos/1742.pdf [accessed 18 November 2023].
15 José Presas, *Memórias secretas de D. Carlota Joaquina* (Brasília: Senado Federal, 2010), pp44–8.
16 Ternavasio, 'Diplomacia, linaje y política', p178.
17 Marcus Cheke, *Carlota Joaquina, Queen of Portugal* (Freeport, New York: Books for Libraries Press, 1969), p43.
18 Barrow, ii, pp304–10.
19 John Street, 'Lord Strangford and Río de La Plata, 1808–1815', *Hispanic American Historical Review*, 23/4 (1953), pp480–2.
20 Barrow, ii, pp317–22.
21 Azevedo, p260.
22 Deborah Besseghini, 'Imperialismo informal e independencia: Los británicos y la apertura del comercio en el Río de La Plata (1808–1810)', *Illes i Imperis*, 23, 2021, pp52–8.
23 Gates, pp206–10.
24 Marcela Ternavasio, *Historia de la Argentina: 1806–1852* (Buenos Aires: Siglo Veintiuno Editores, 2009), pp67–73.
25 Presas, pp202–3.
26 Azevedo, pp265–7.
27 Cheke, pp48–9.
28 His first knighthood had been granted by King Gustav III of Sweden and formally invested by King George III in 1792. See Kenneth H. Light, 'Sidney Smith, um marinheiro herói', *Revista Marítima Brasileira*, 3o. trimestre, 2006, p112.
29 Kaufmann, p55.
30 John Street, 'Lord Strangford and Río de La Plata, 1808–1815', *Hispanic American Historical Review*, 23:4, 1953, pp477–510.

The 1805 Club

President: Admiral Sir Jonathon Band GCB DL
Chairman: Captain John A Rodgaard USN

The 1805 Club is a registered charity no. 1201272

The 1805 Club was established in 1990, and as of 2024, celebrates its thirty-fourth year of dedication toward commemorating and conserving the history and heritage of the Georgian Era sailing navies, with emphasis toward the Royal Navy of the period.

No other organisation is so dedicated in its programmes of commemorative and conservation initiatives, education, publications and support to scholastic research of the Georgian era throughout the world, as exhibited in such a publication as the *Trafalgar Chronicle*.

For thirty-four years, the members of the club have demonstrated their enthusiasm for all aspects of the sailing world of the Georgian era, and through the partnership of Seaforth Publishing, the *Trafalgar Chronicle* represents such a singular endeavour.

To join The 1805 Club go to www.1805club.org
and complete the membership application form.